AF371983

WILLIAM KLEIN

CELEBRATION

WILLIAM KLEIN

CELEBRATION

LA FABRICA

PUBLISHER
La Fábrica

TEXT, IMAGES AND LAYOUT
William Klein

GRAPHIC DESIGNER
Feriche Black

EDITORIAL COORDINATION
Miriam Querol

TRANSLATIONS
Philip Sutton

PRE-PRESS
Museoteca

PRINTING
Brizzolis

BINDING
Encuadernación Ramos

WILLIAM KLEIN ACKNOWLEDGMENTS
Pierre-Louis Denis, Tiffanie Pascal, Raphaëlle
Stopin, Pierre Klein, Nathalie Martel, Bruno
Ryterband, Christine Renaud, Remedios Intal.
La Fábrica: César Martínez-Useros, Miriam Querol,
Camino Brasa, Álvaro Matías, Gonzalo Golpe.
Fundación Telefónica: Maria Brancos-Barti,
Elena Peña Riquelme, Marta Banach Gorina.
Museoteca, Brizzolis, Encuadernación Ramos.

ISBN: 978-84-17048-79-2
Legal Deposit: M-7233-2019

COVER IMAGE
Club Allegro Fortissimo, Paris, 1990 (painted 2001)

BACK COVER IMAGE
Gun 1, Broadway & 103rd Street, New York, 1954
(painted 2003)

| LA FABRICA |

CHAIRMAN
Alberto Anaut

VICE-CHAIRMAN
Alberto Fesser

MANAGING DIRECTOR
Álvaro Matías

EDITORIAL CONTENT MANAGER
Camino Brasa

PUBLISHING DEVELOPMENT MANAGER
César Martínez-Useros

DISTRIBUTION MANAGER
Raúl Muñoz

La Fábrica
Verónica, 13
28014 Madrid
T. +34 91 360 13 20
edicion@lafabrica.com
www.lafabrica.com

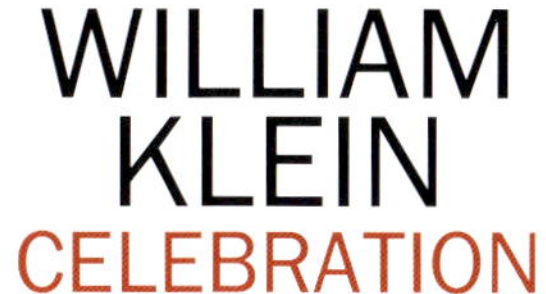

WILLIAM KLEIN
CELEBRATION

Here is my preface for Celebration, with photos rather like Proust's madeleine. Is that a good idea?

La Fábrica have proposed *Celebration* for the title of this book. I agree but perhaps it ought to be put in the plural, adding an "s", as every photo is without doubt a celebration.

Celebration, affirmation, discovery, confirmation, revelation. All that every time I release. And if all goes well, I celebrate millions of surprises.

And why not celebrate a small miracle?

I didn't expect it but there it is.

Why not *Celebration New York, Rome, Moscow, Tokyo*? What I know, what I discover, what I affirm, what I show you, what I love. It comes from nowhere, from everywhere, but it's there and I celebrate it. That's the photography I love.

I affirm that I can surprise myself. What I discover here, what I love and lcarn, is now assembled, and I affirm to you that nearly a century is being celebrated.

Is it possible to live without photography? No doubt, like everyone I did it for a time… and I didn't die from it. But today it's no longer worth it.

DELAY MAY BE SERIOUS NOW

FOR ONLY

FREE

FREE   THIS WAY TO HEAVEN   FREE

S-A-A-Y these are good GOOD
pure and better, my new medical
discovery you my tangy goodness
you with the secret KLEEN-
KLEER-VU my blended you my
heaping HOT my MILK FED
my MIGHTY mound so FLAVOR
so REALLY oh S-A-A-Y my
GIANT HOT THRILL you you're
my GOODNESS my HOTNESS
you oh YOU MY GOLDEN

REMEMBER THERE IS ONLY ONE

NEW YORK

ow wonder life designed to

AVOID GRIEF

REPLACEMENT OR REFUND OF MONEY
Guaranteed by
Good Housekeeping
IF NOT AS ADVERTISED THEREIN

FOR ONLY

CONTAINS FLUOROMYCIN TYROTHRICYN THE NEW

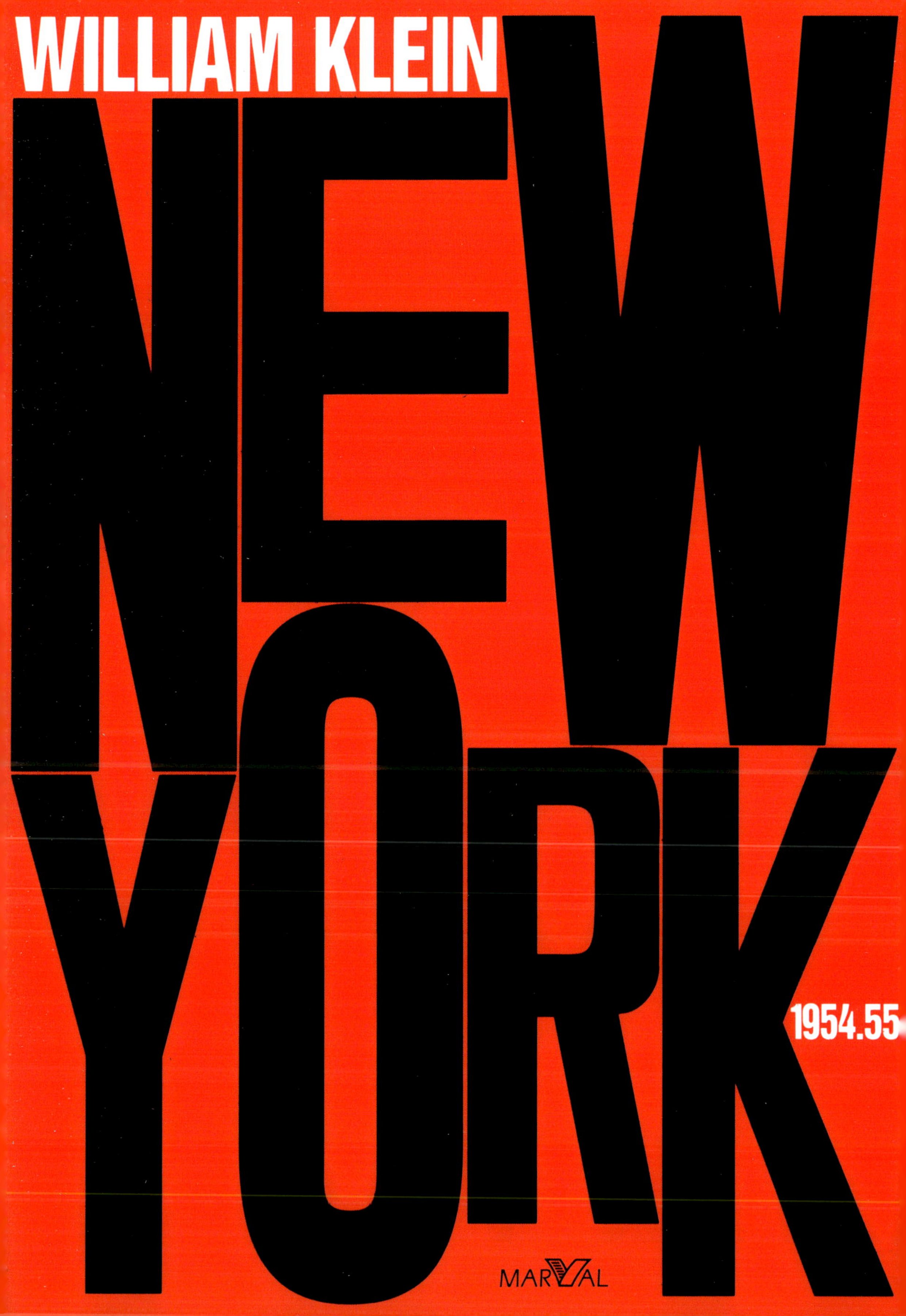

WILLIAM KLEIN
NEW
YORK
1954.55
MARVAL

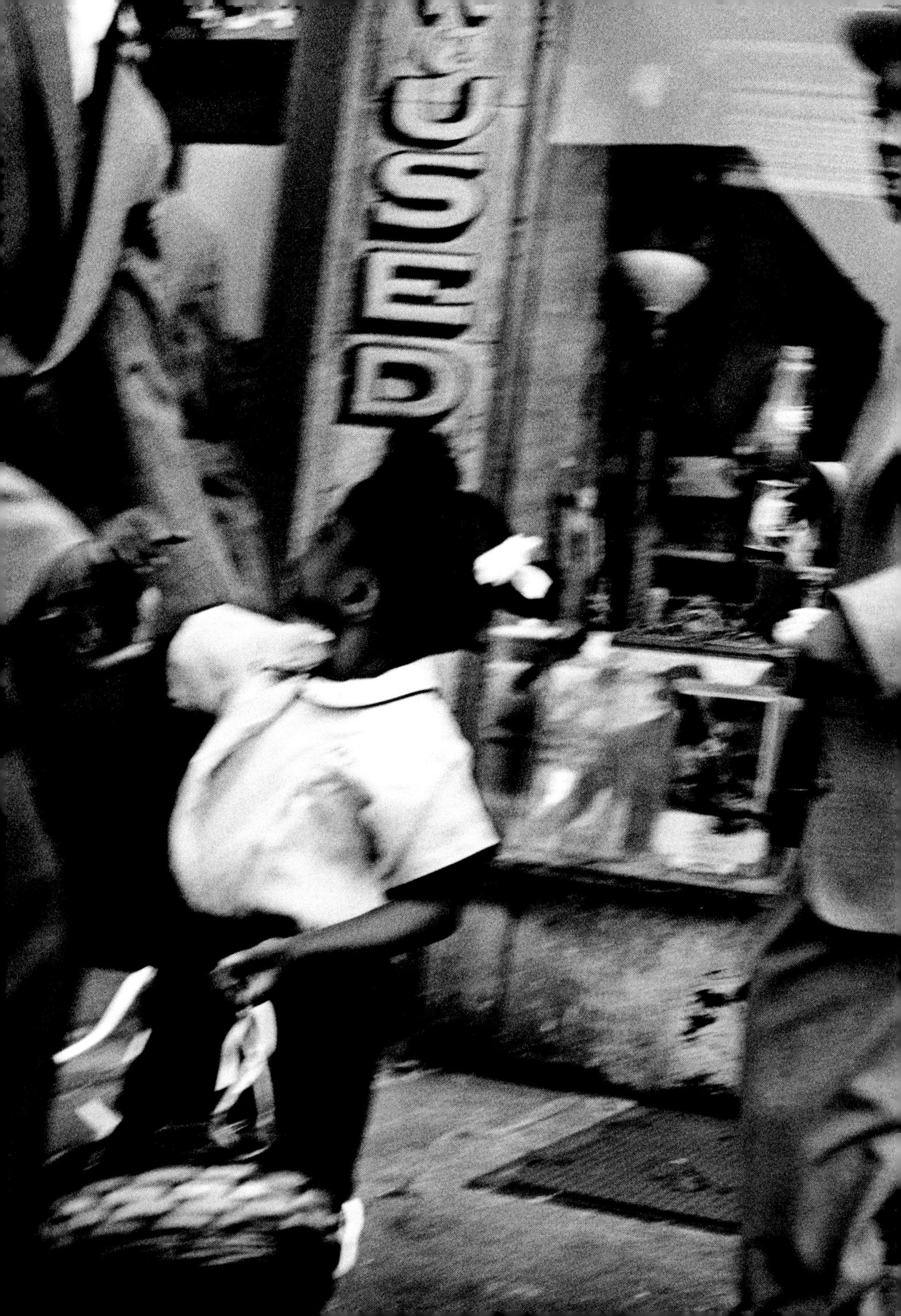
CLOSED

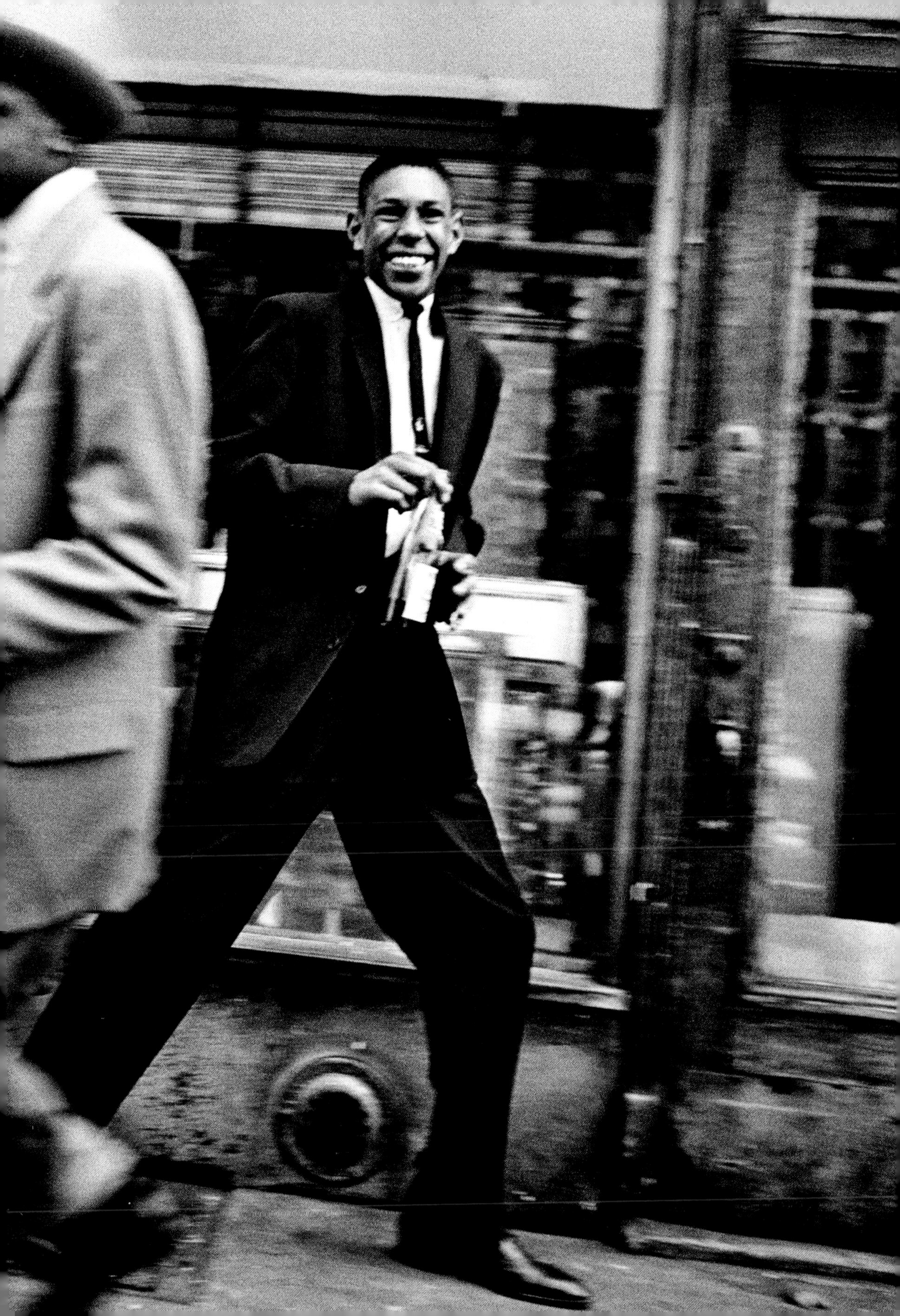

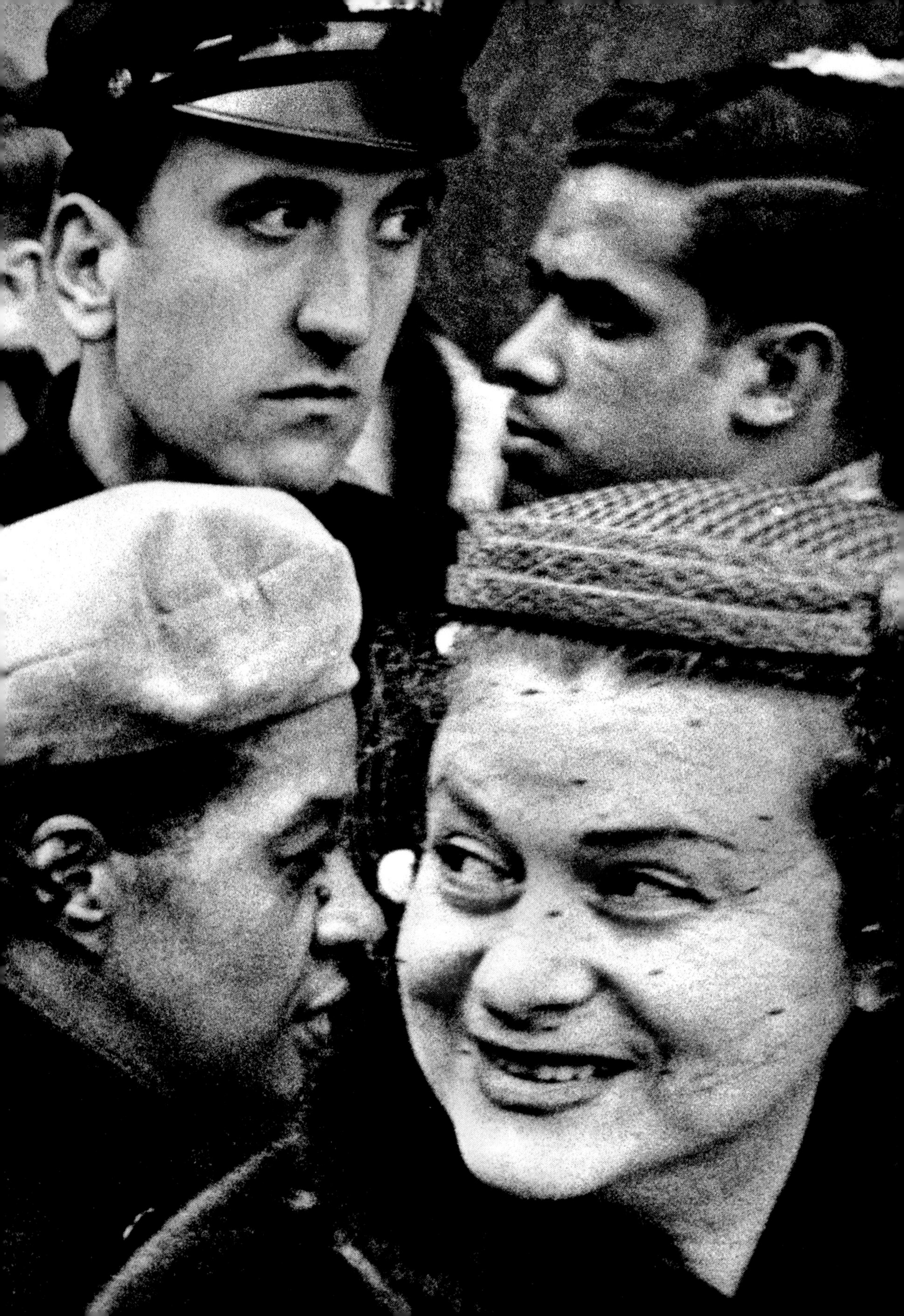

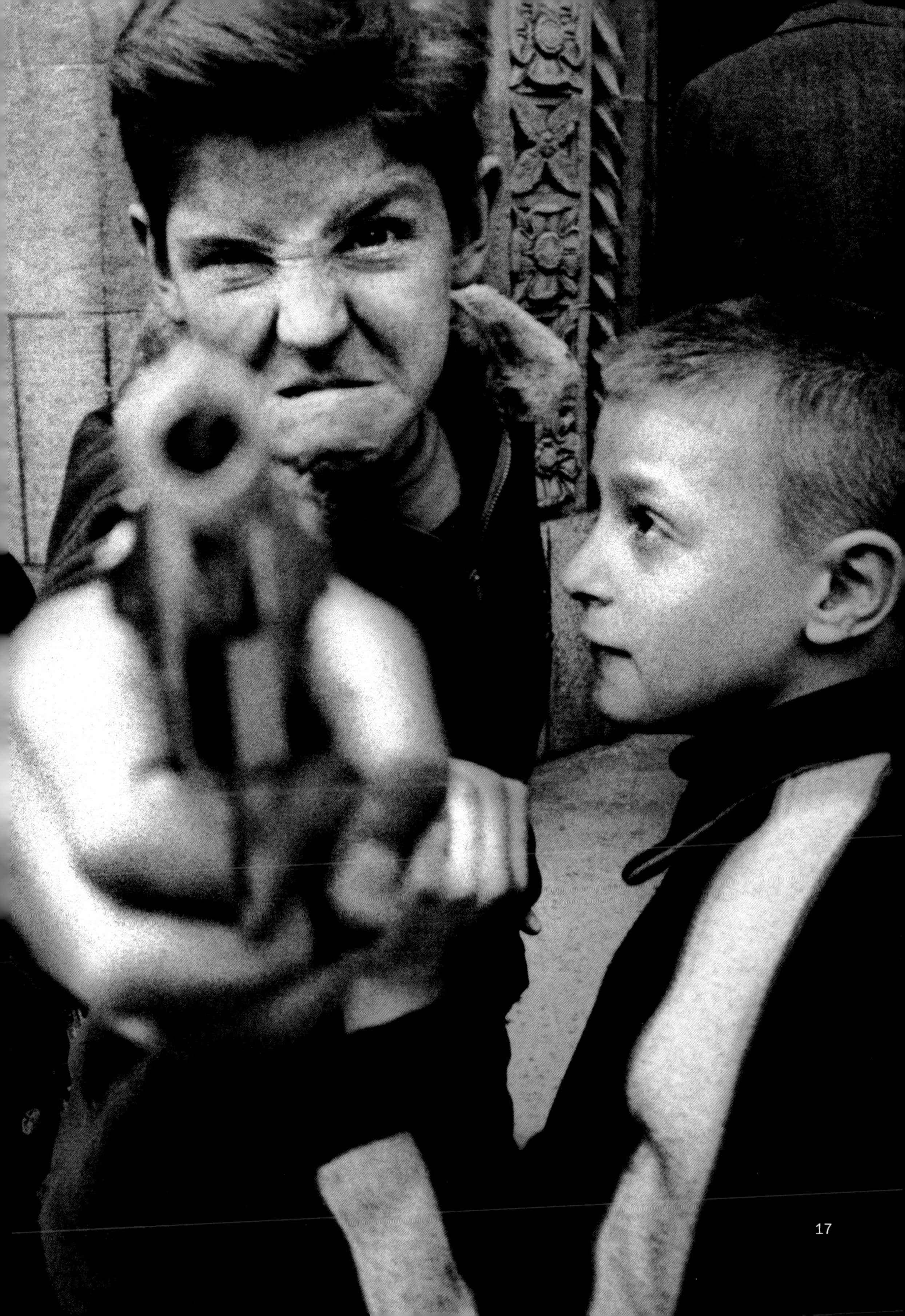

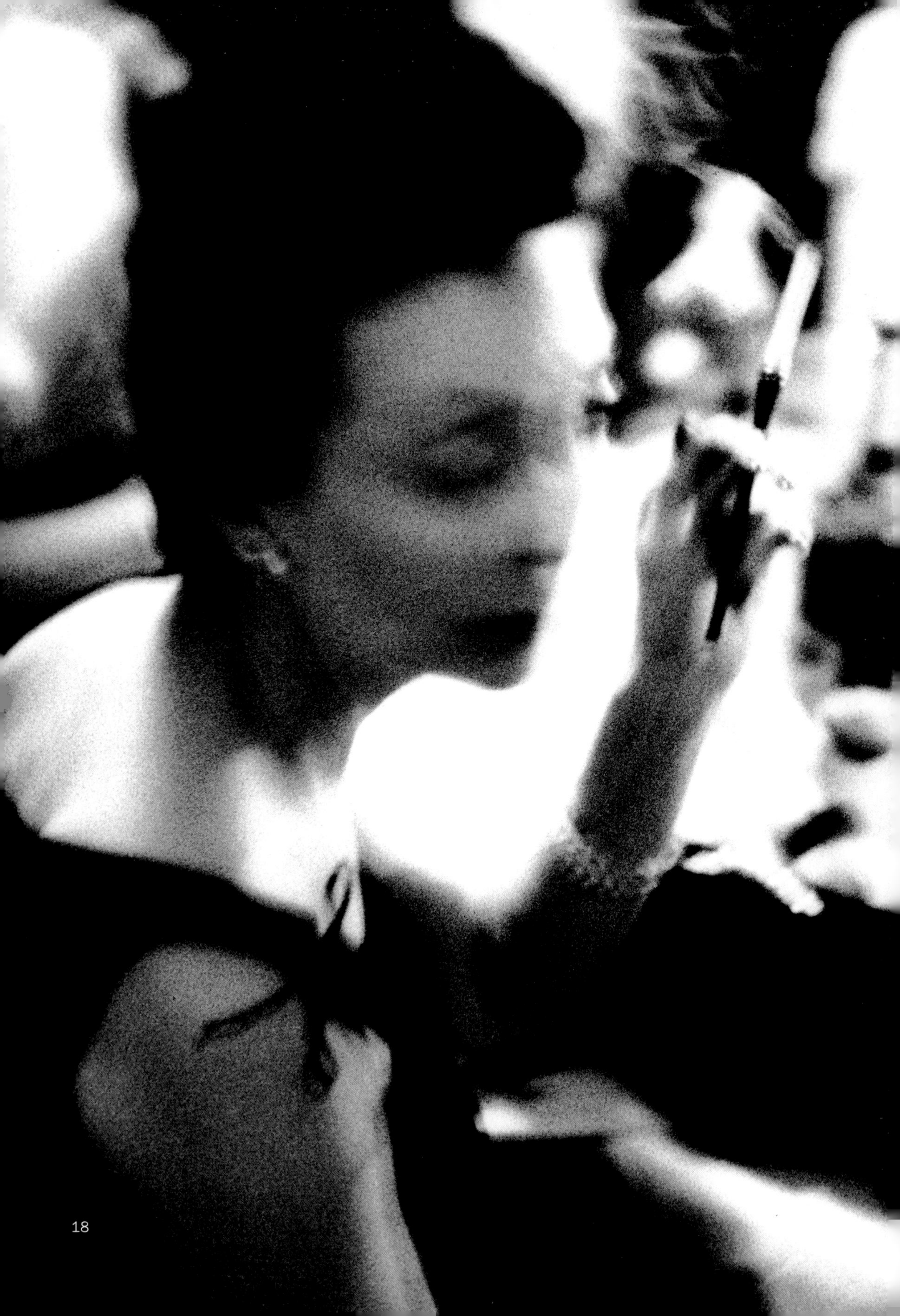

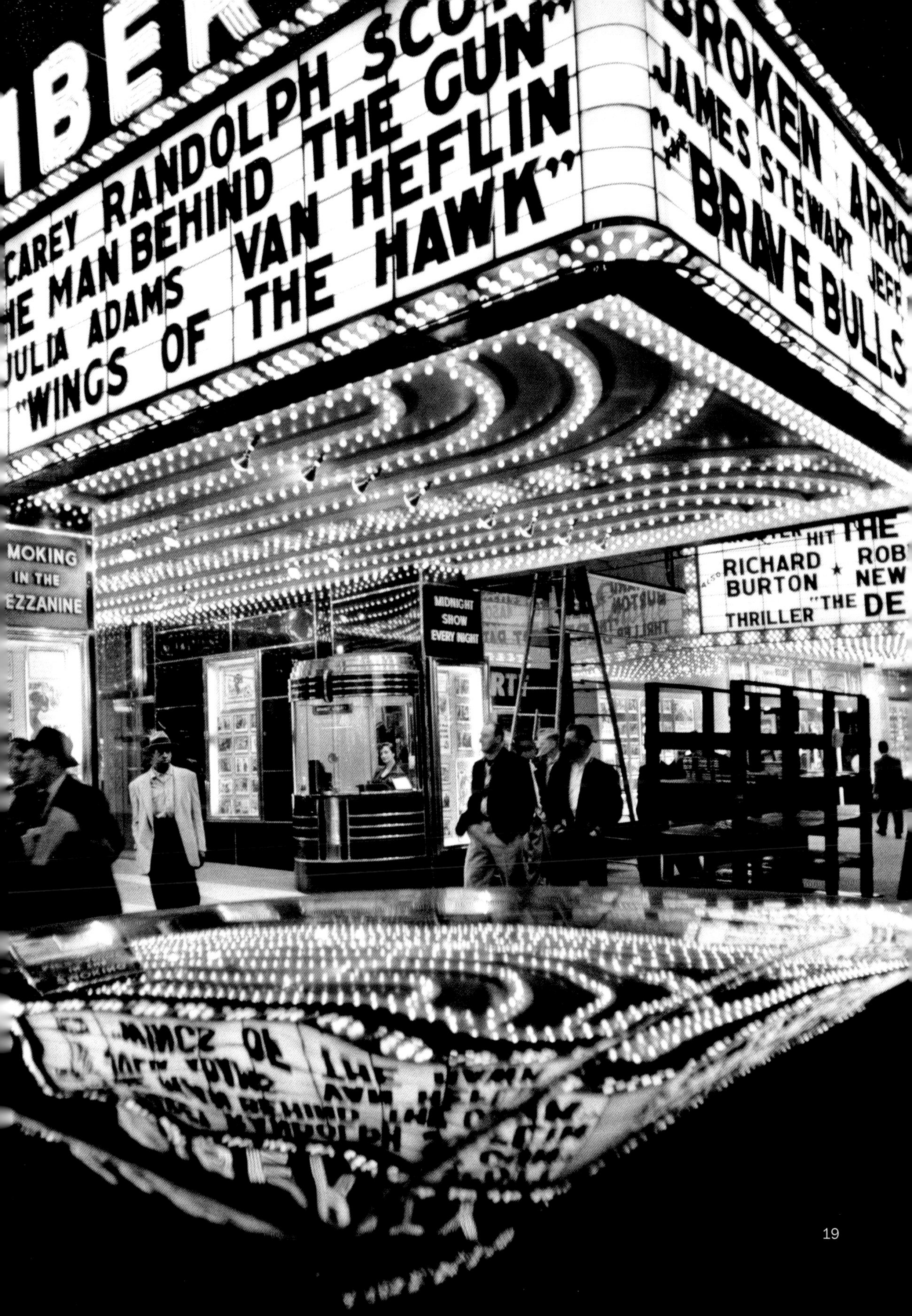
IBER
CAREY RANDOLPH SCO
HE MAN BEHIND THE GUN
JULIA ADAMS VAN HEFLIN
"WINGS OF THE HAWK"
BROKEN ARRO
JAMES STEWART JEFF
"BRAVE BULLS
MOKING IN THE EZZANINE
MIDNIGHT SHOW EVERY NIGHT
HIT THE
RICHARD ROB
BURTON NEW
THRILLER "THE DE

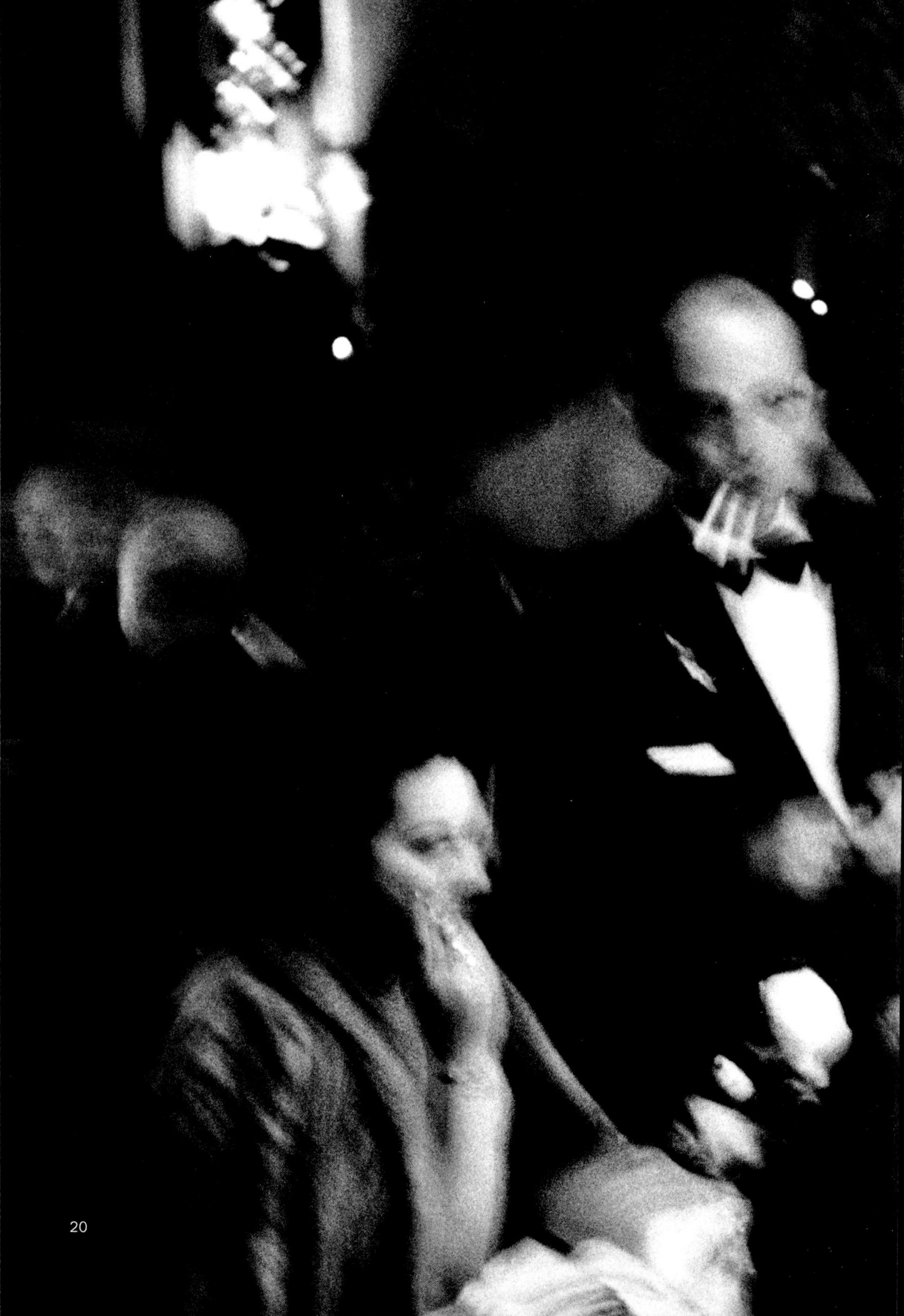

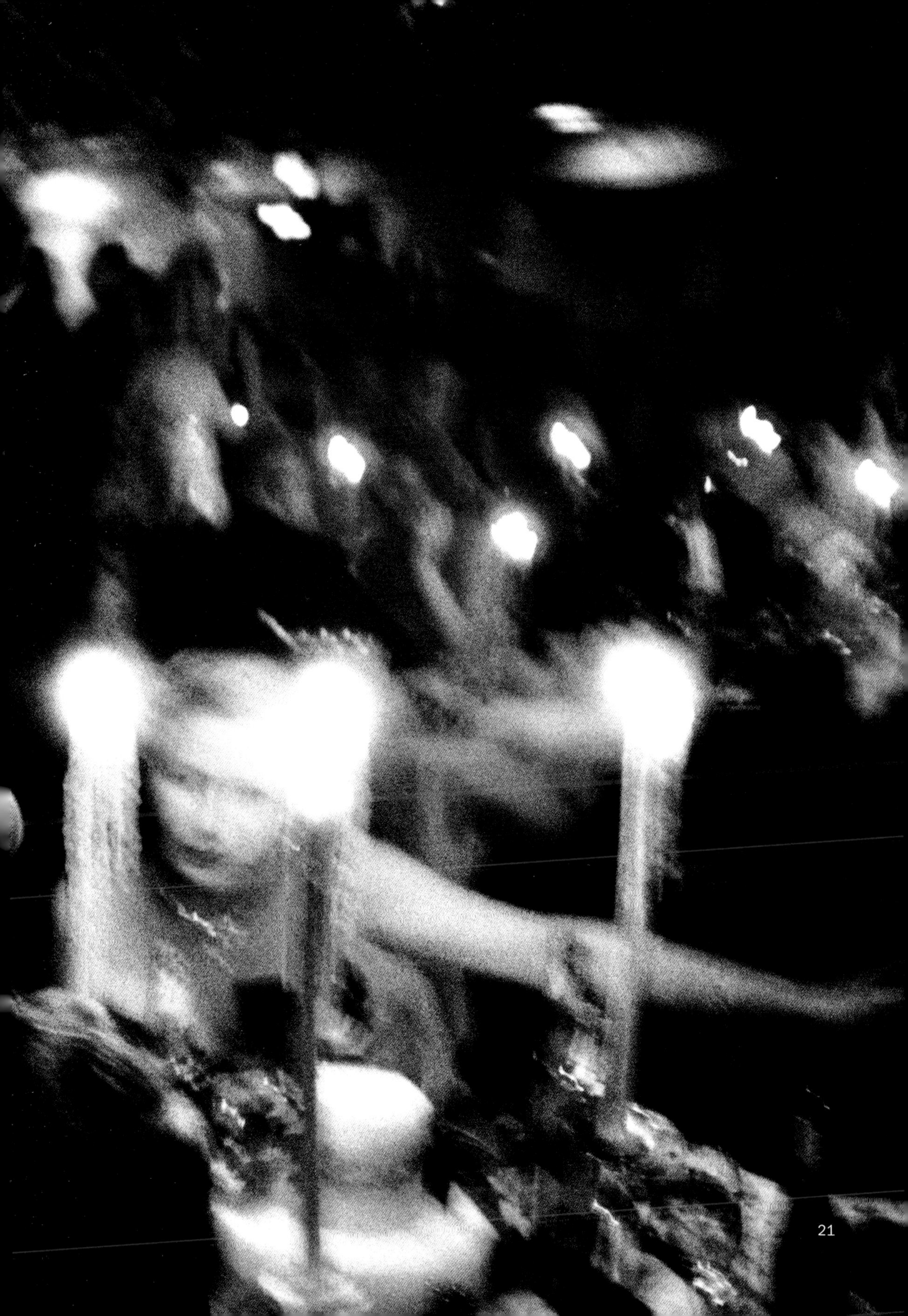

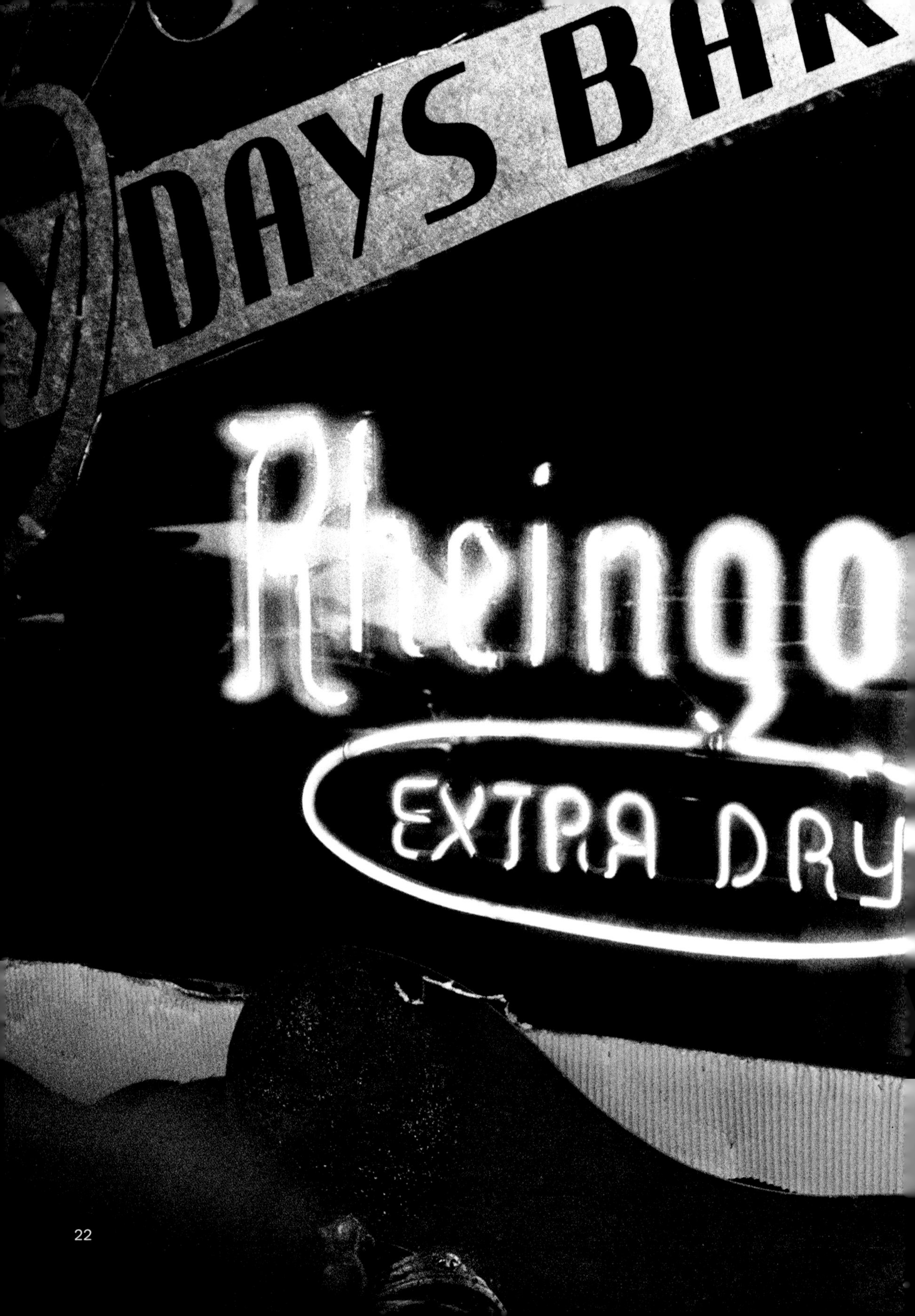

DAYS BAR
Rheingo
EXTRA DRY

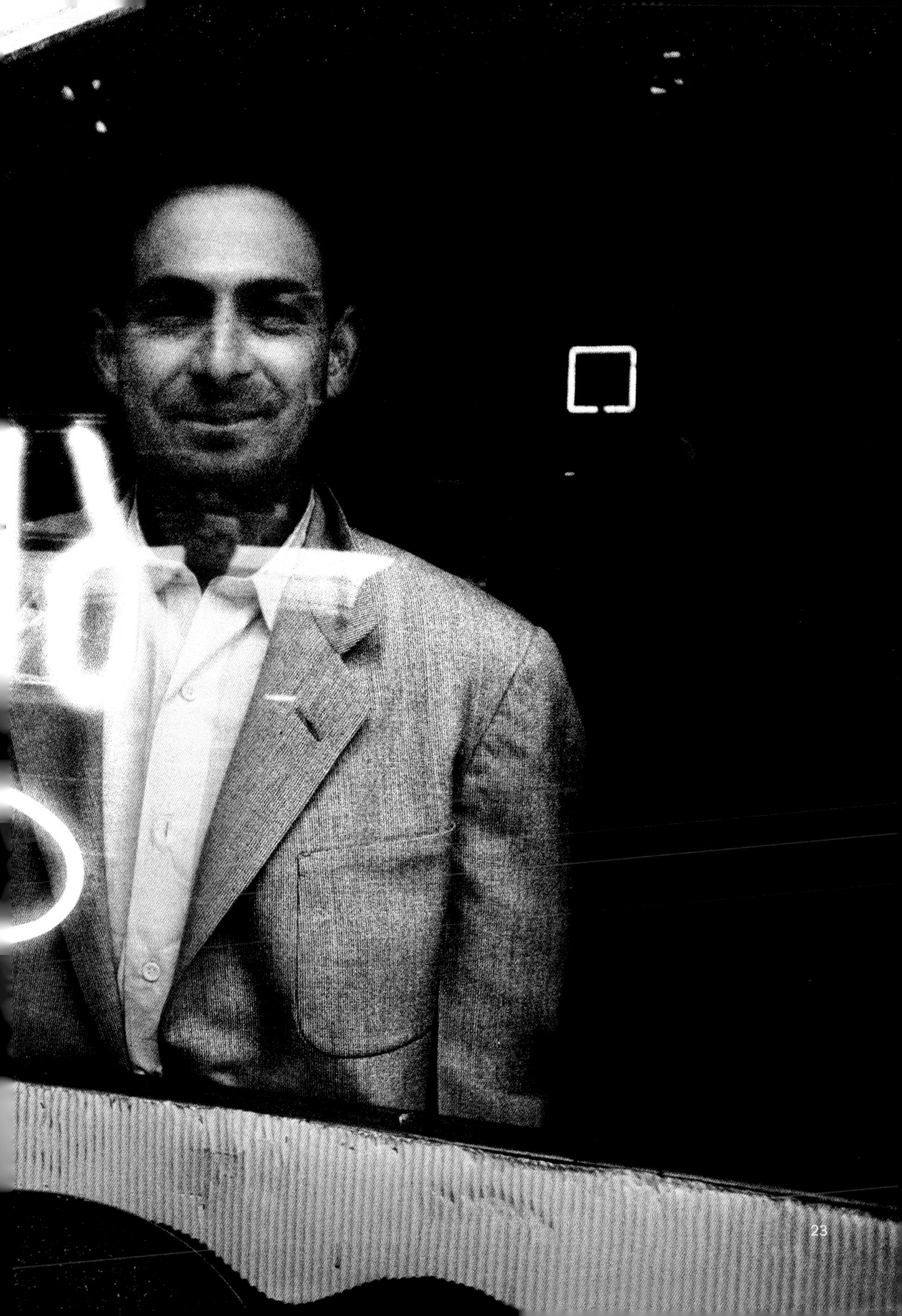

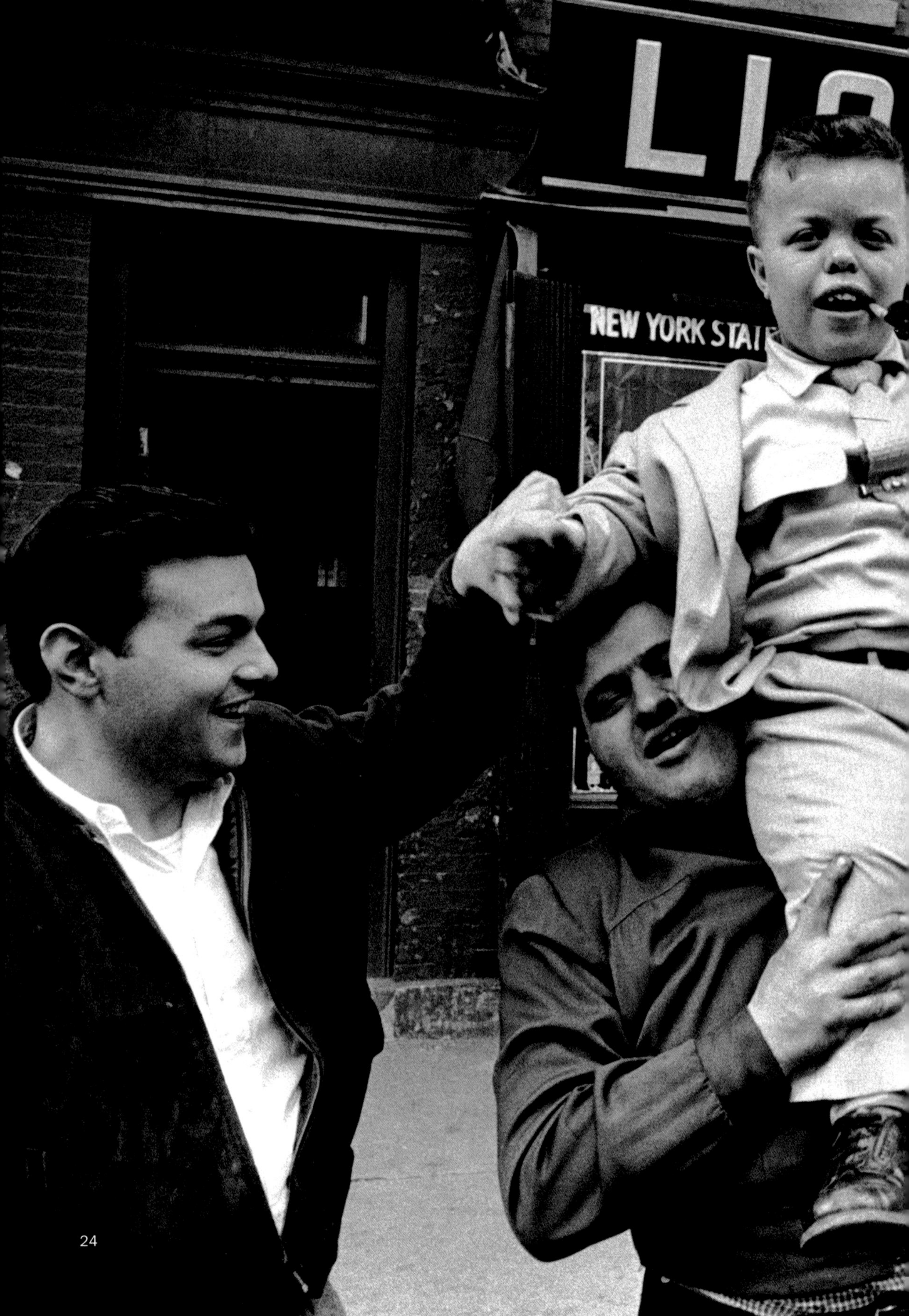

LIQ
NEW YORK STAT

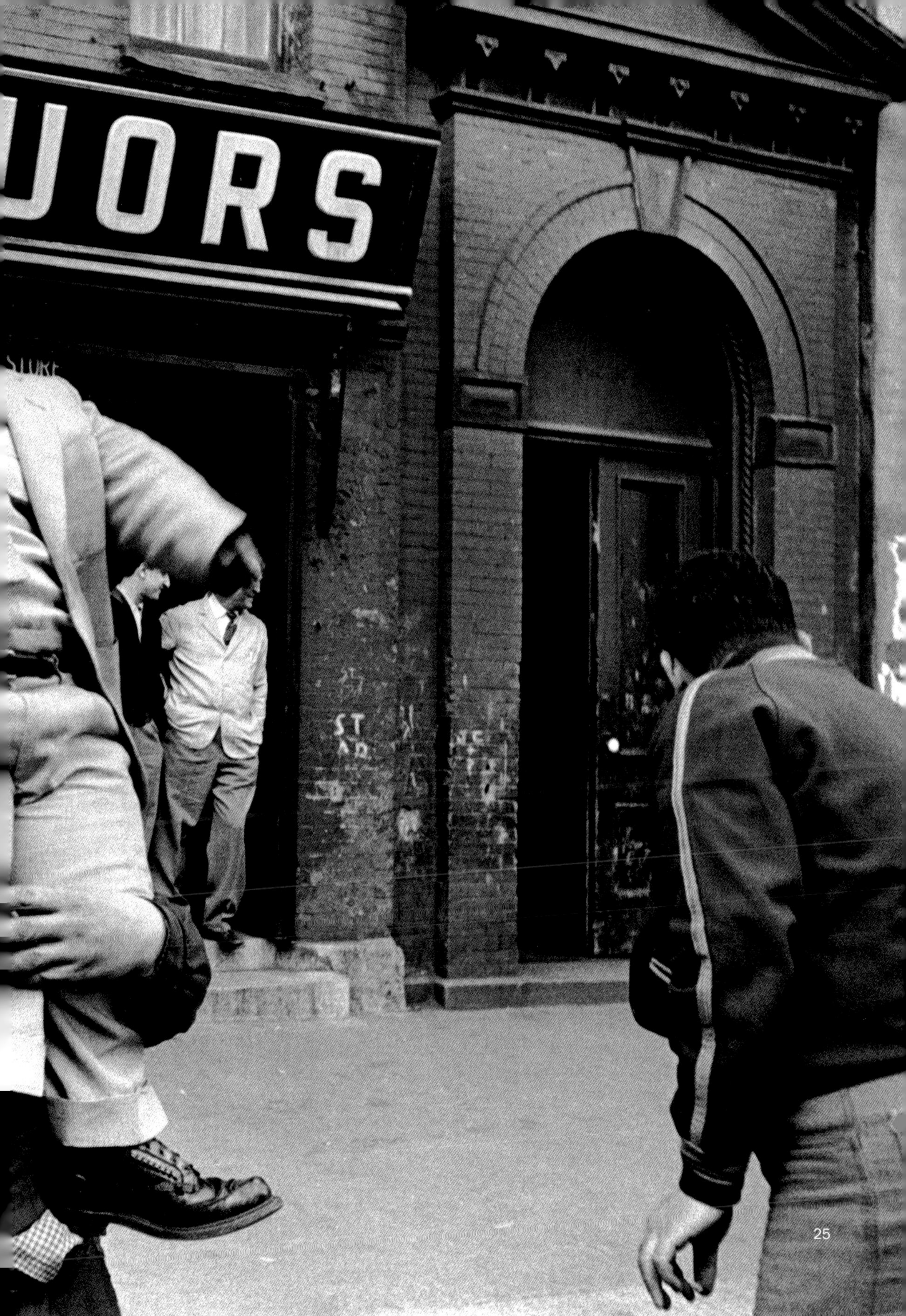
UORS
STORE

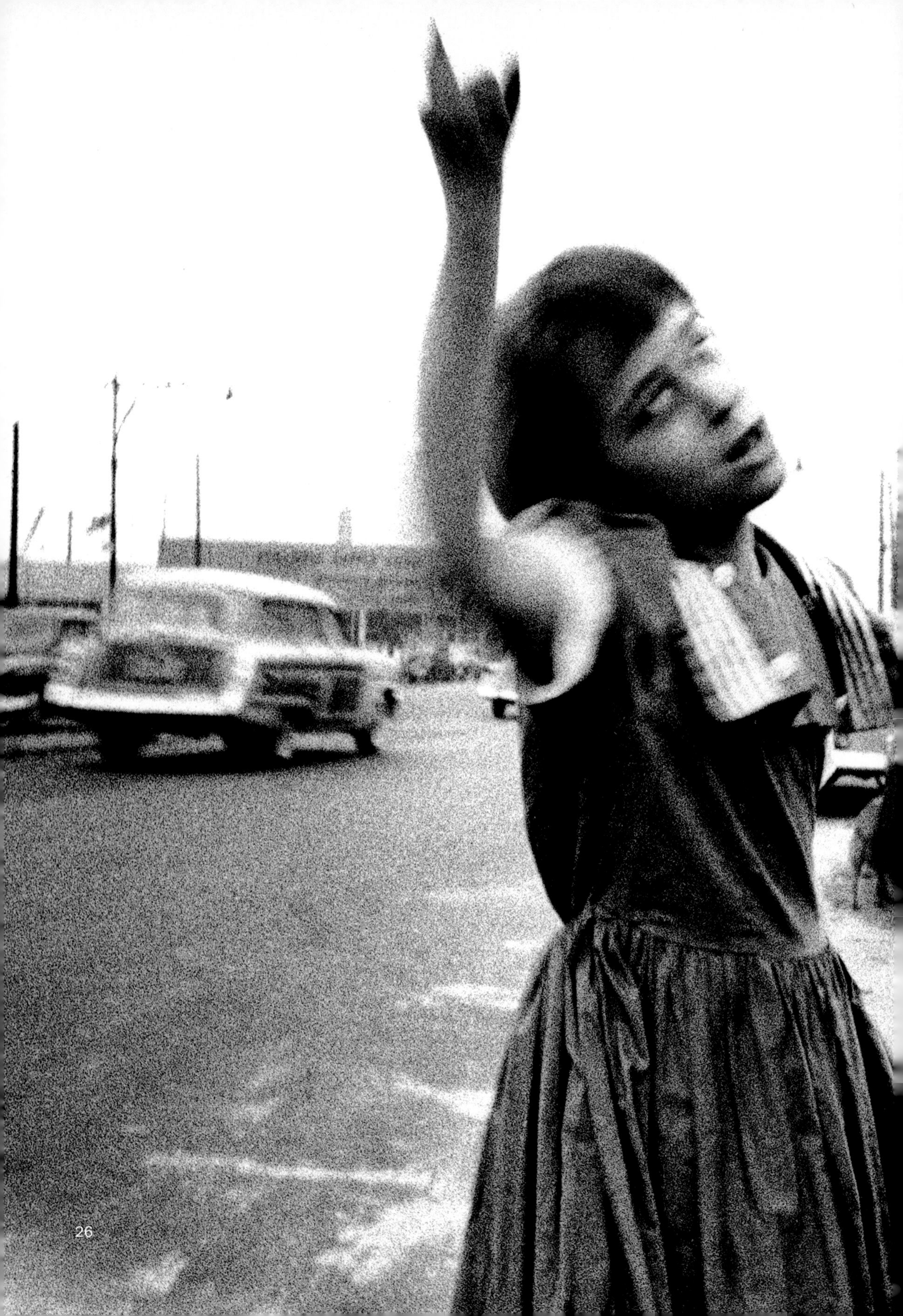

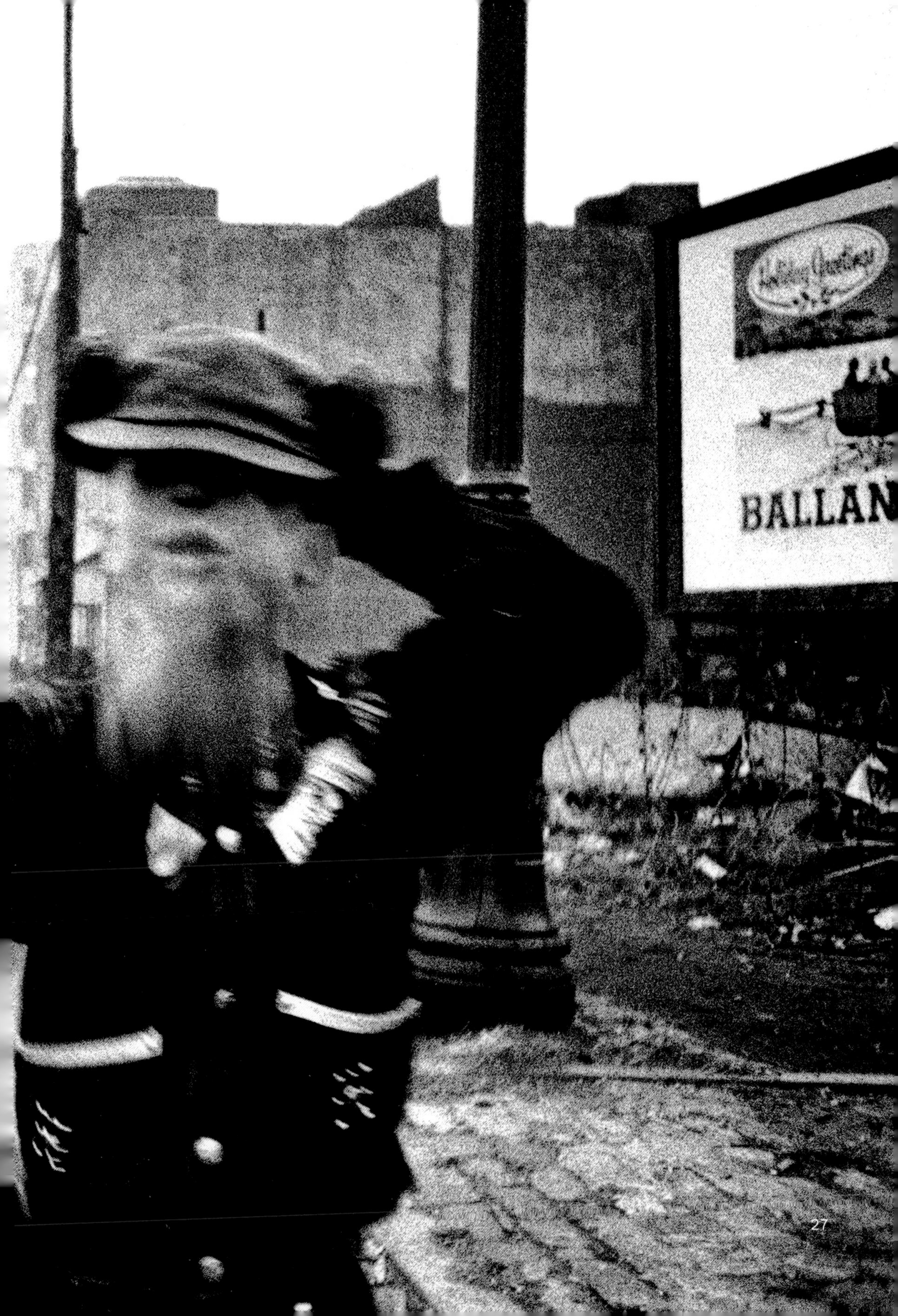
BALLAN

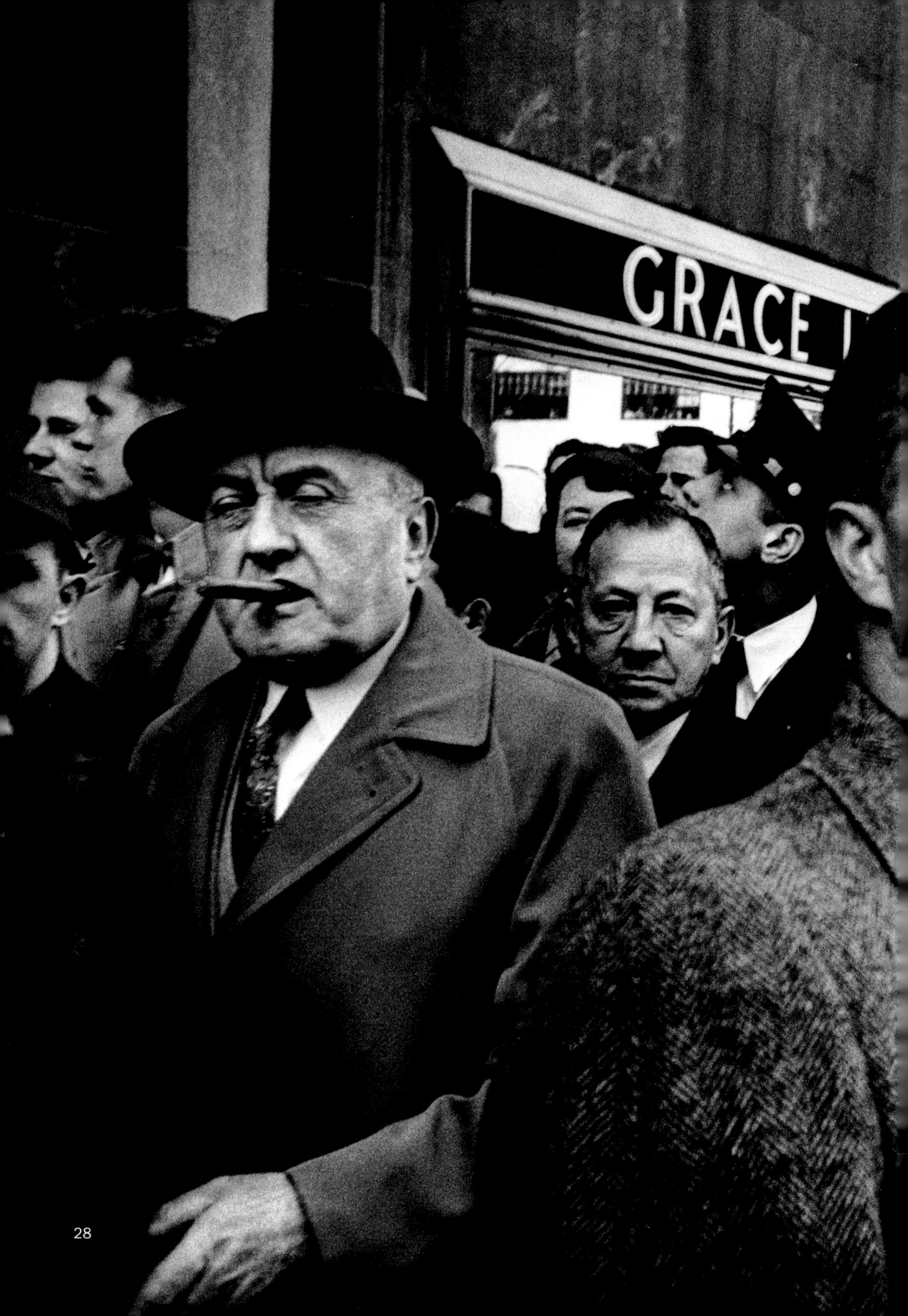
GRACE

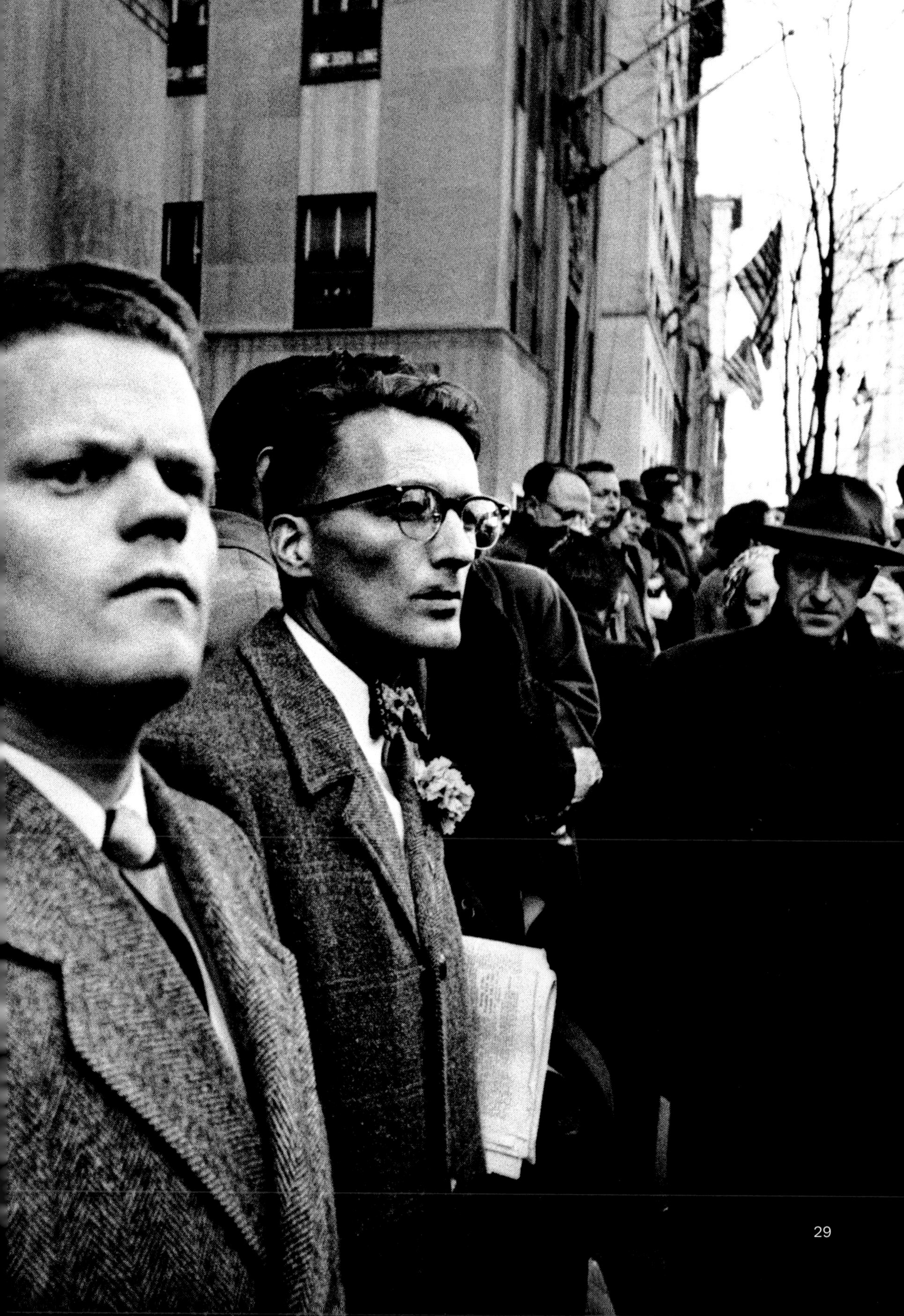

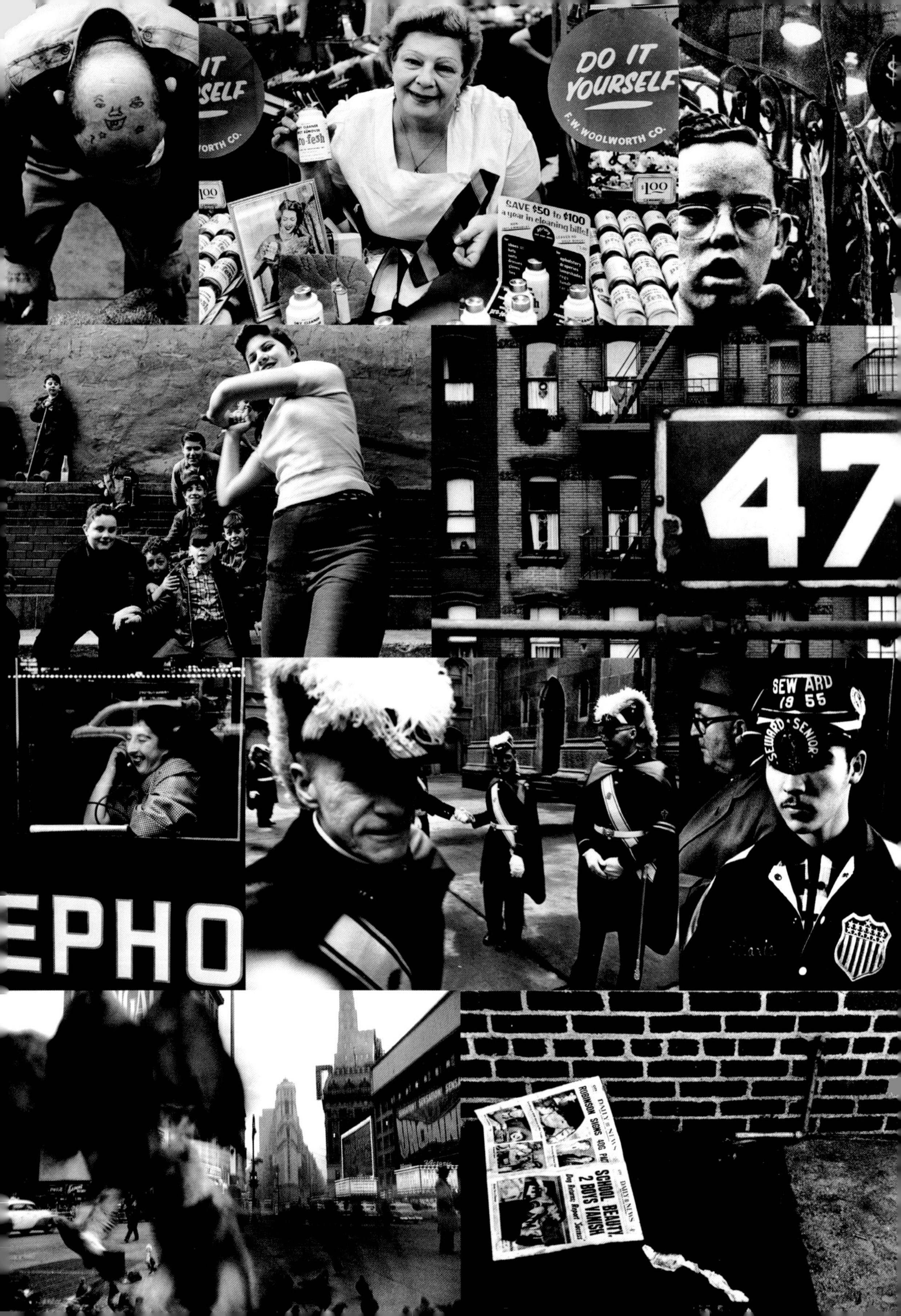

SELF
ORTH CO.
DO IT
YOURSELF
F.W. WOOLWORTH CO.
pro-fesh
SAVE $50 to $100
a year in cleaning bills!
47
SEWARD 18 55
SEWARD SENIOR
EPHO
SCHOOL BEAUTY.
2 BOYS VANISH
ROBINSON SIGNS 40G

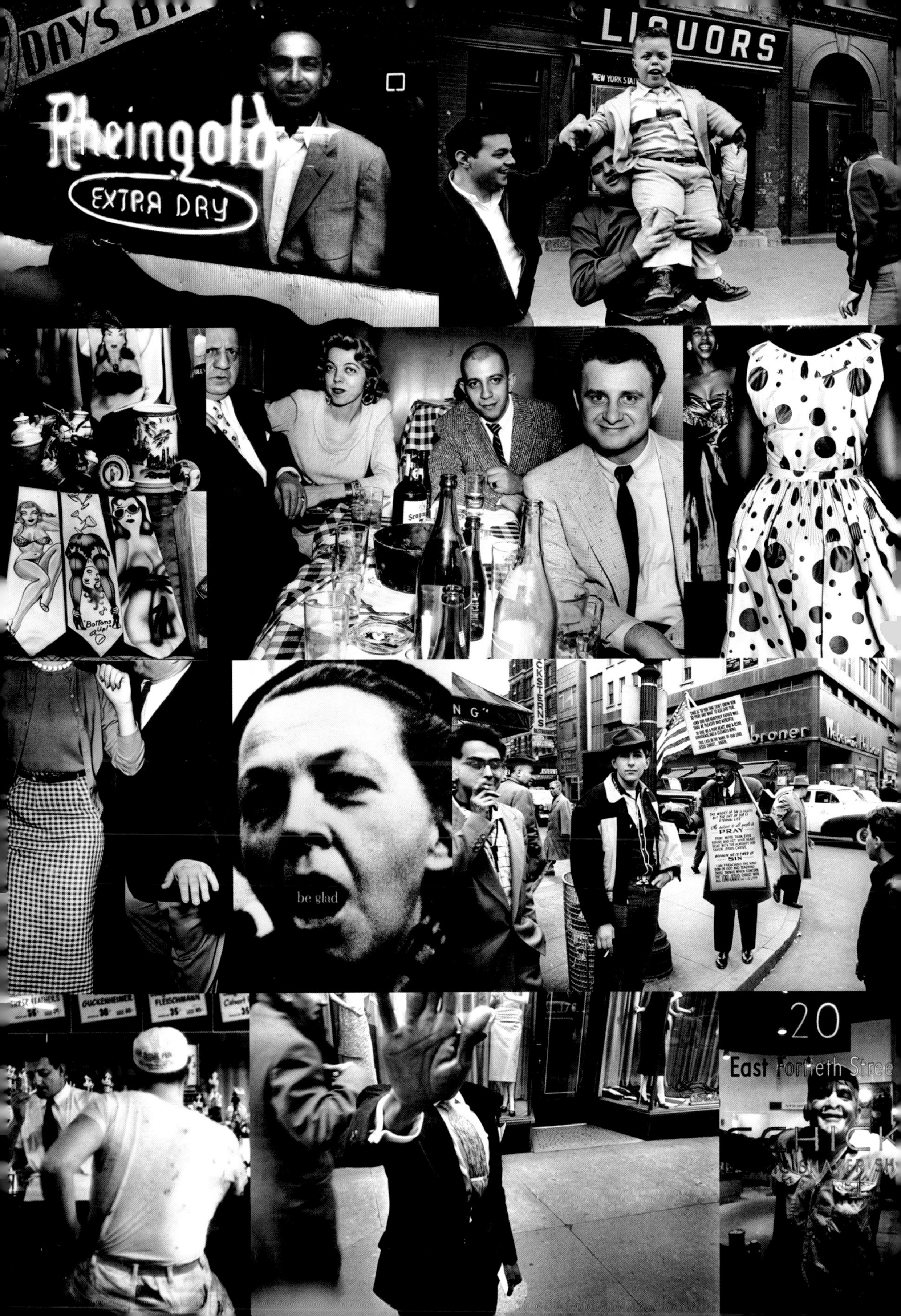

DAYS B
Rheingold
EXTRA DRY
LIQUORS
NEW YORK STATE
Bottoms Up!
be glad
PRAY
SIN
.20
East Fortieth Street

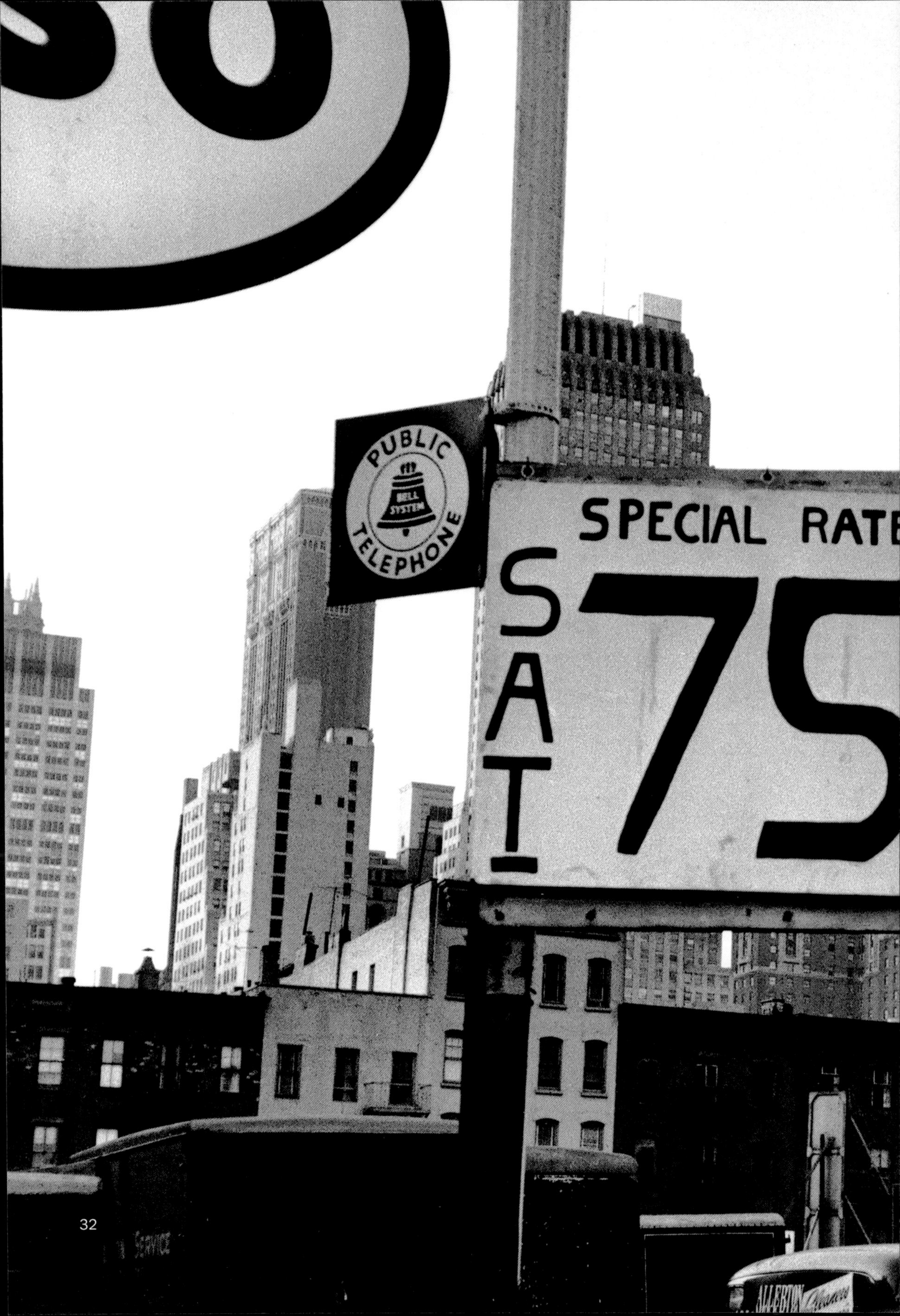

SO
PUBLIC
BELL SYSTEM
TELEPHONE
SPECIAL RATE
SAT
75
SERVICE
ALLERTON

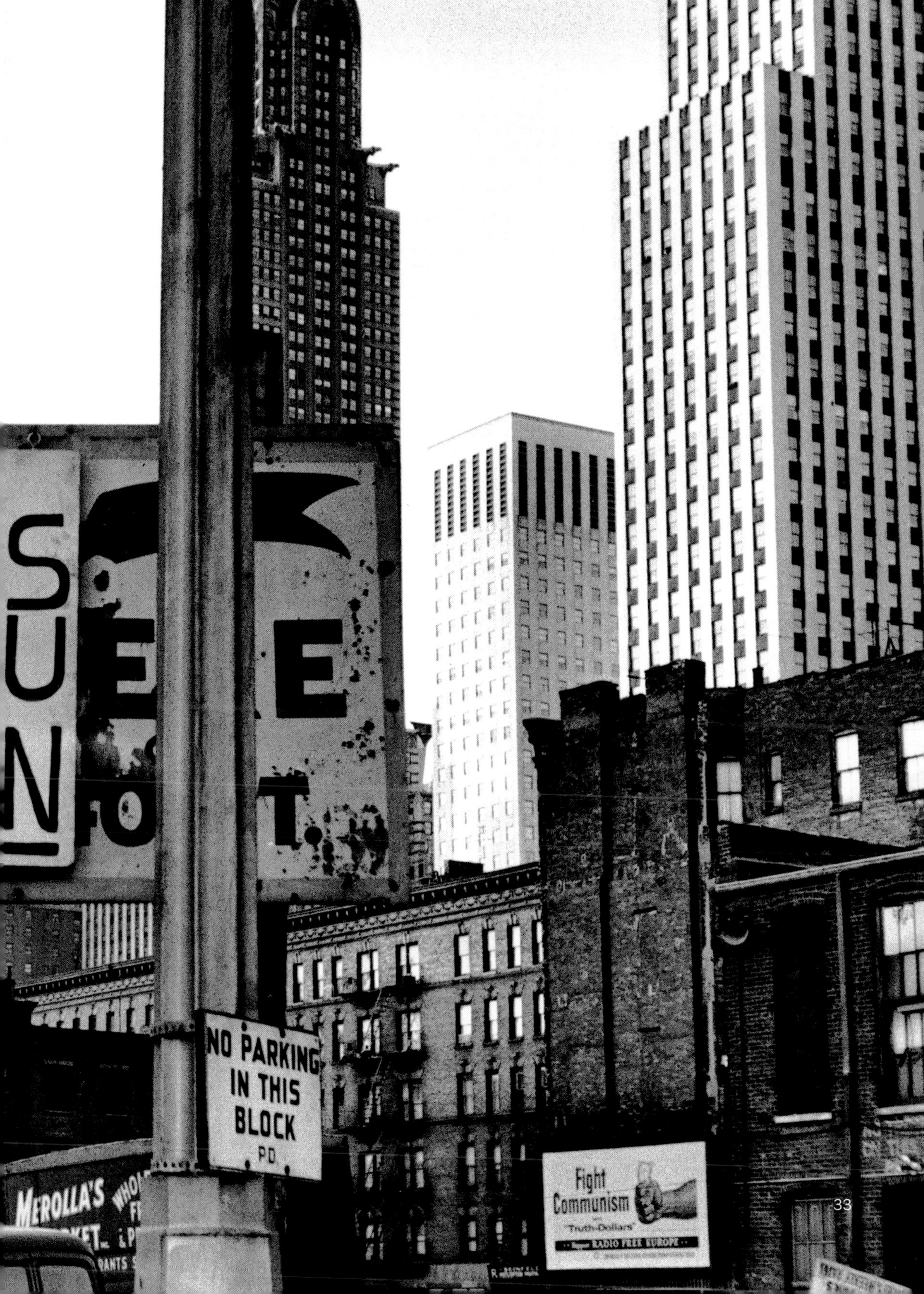
SUN
KET
S E
E
T
fo
NO PARKING
IN THIS
BLOCK
P.D.
MEROLLA'S
WHOL
F
KET
& P
PANTS S
Fight
Communism
with
Truth-Dollars
Bring RADIO FREE EUROPE
33

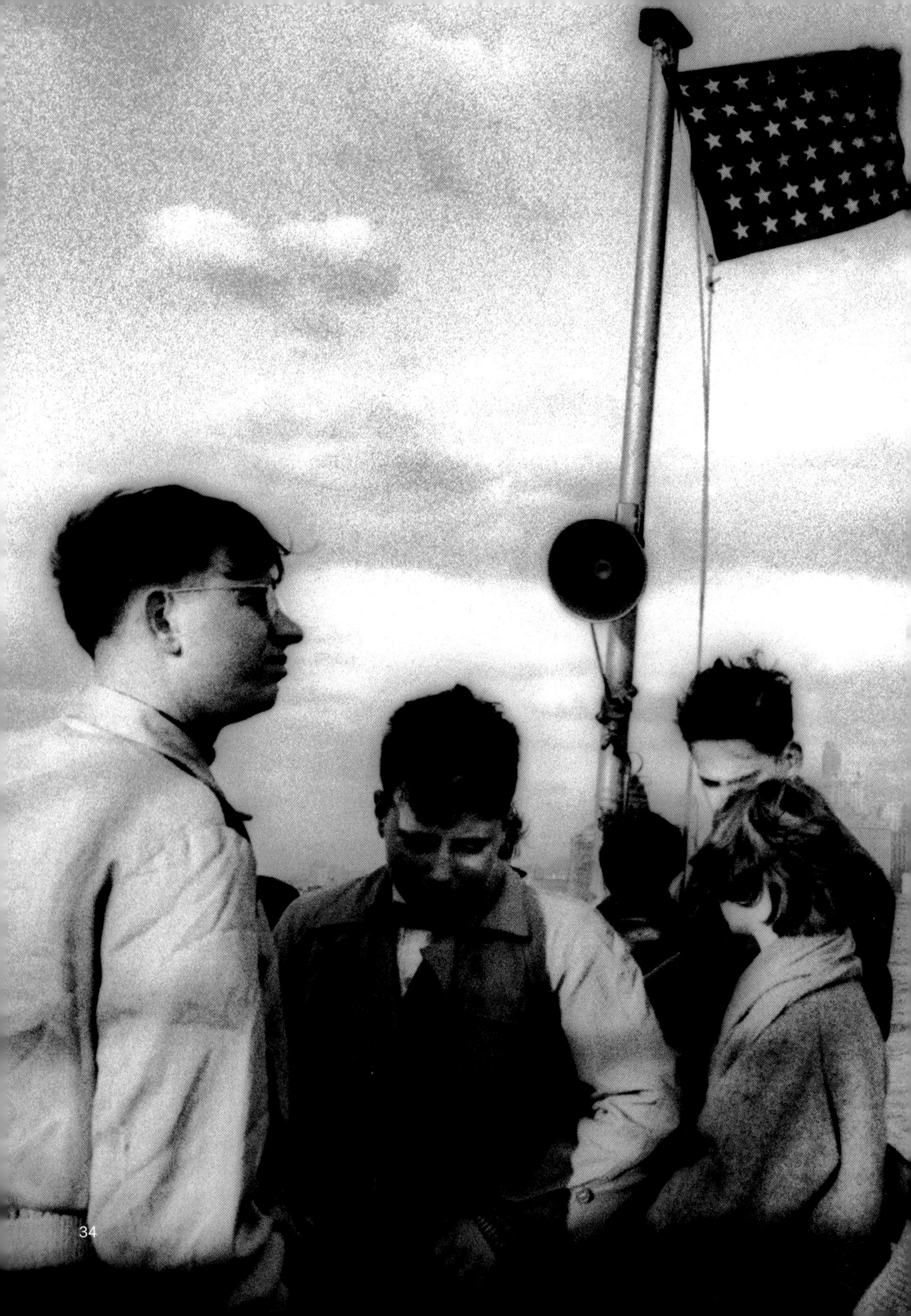

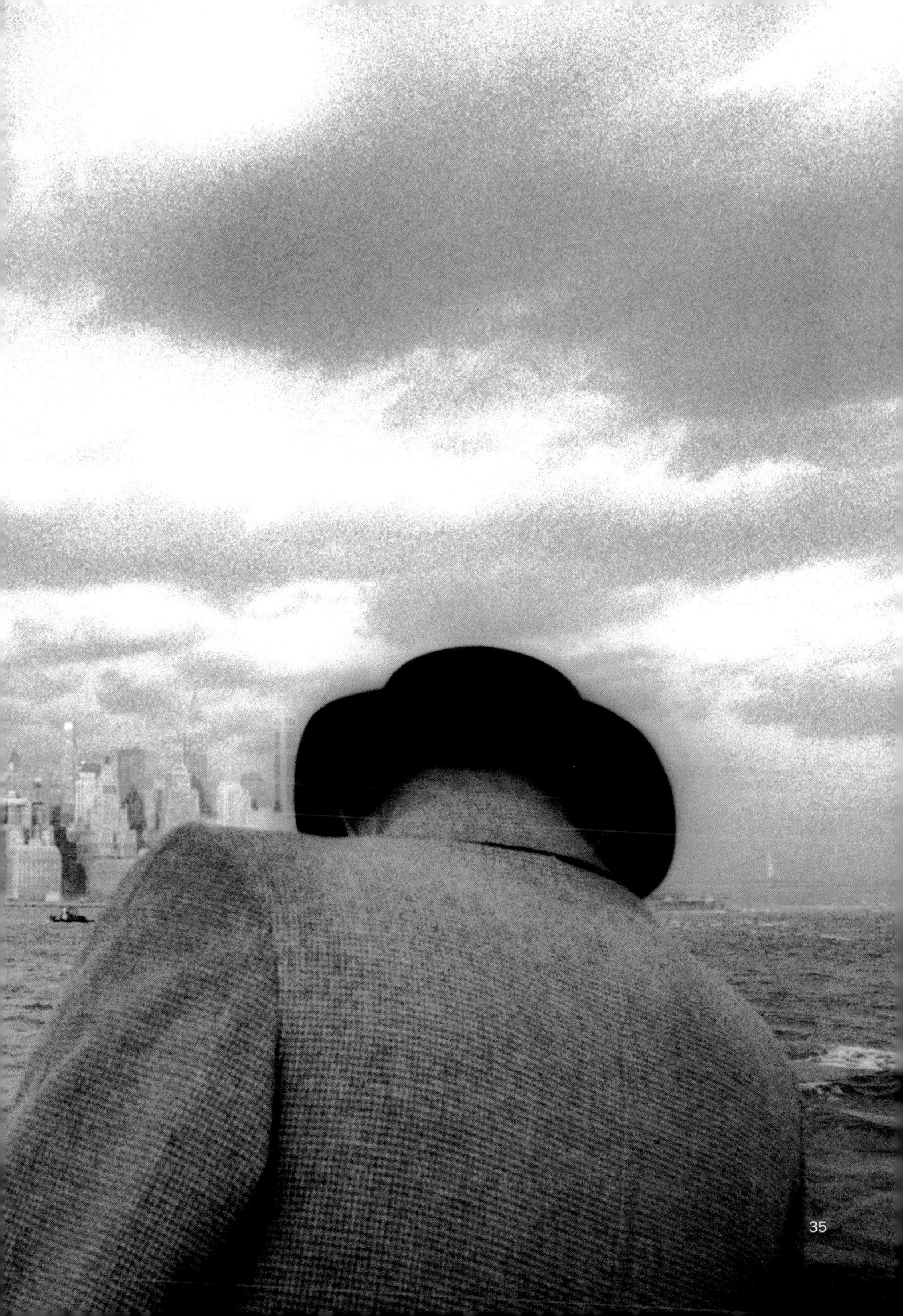

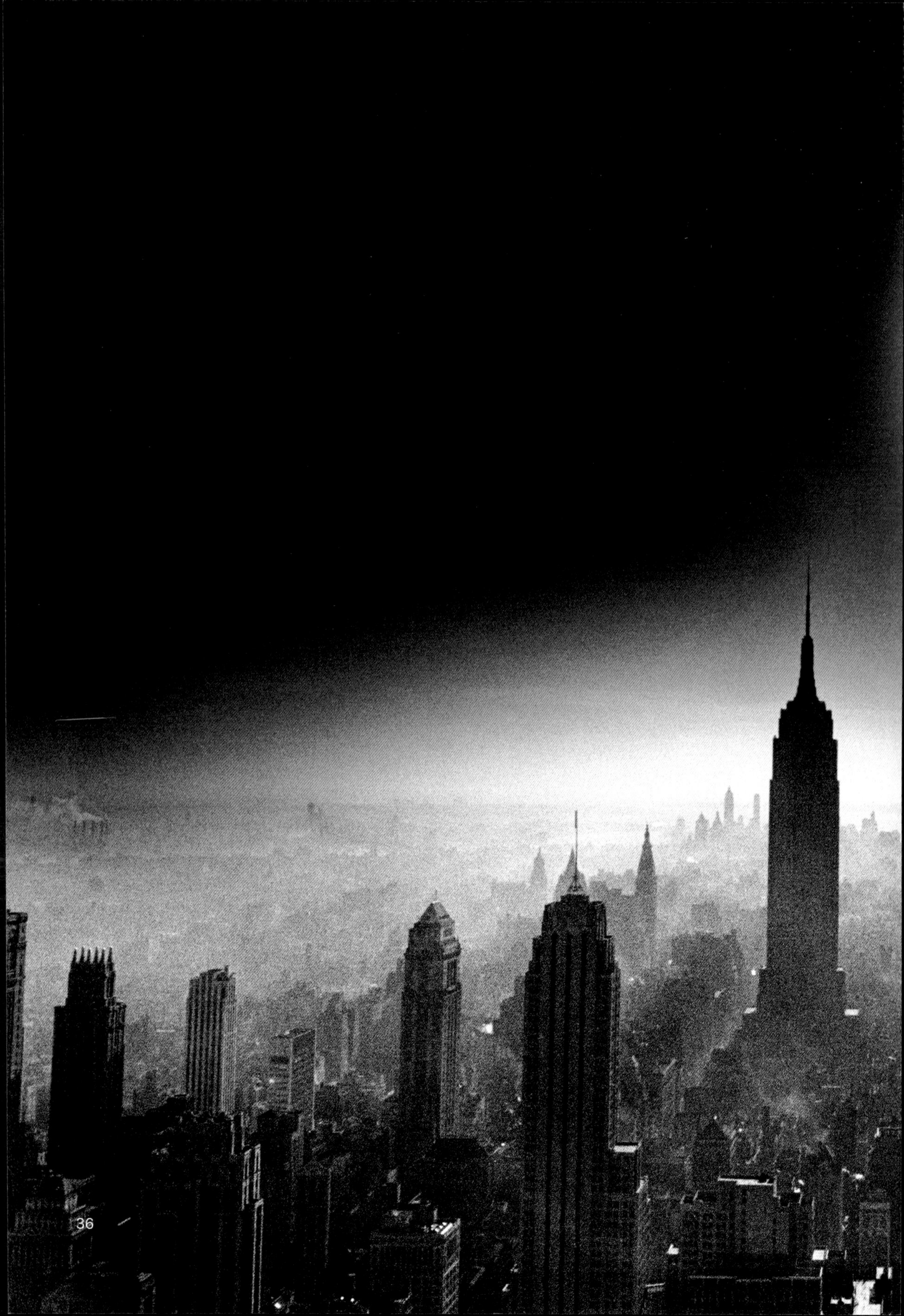

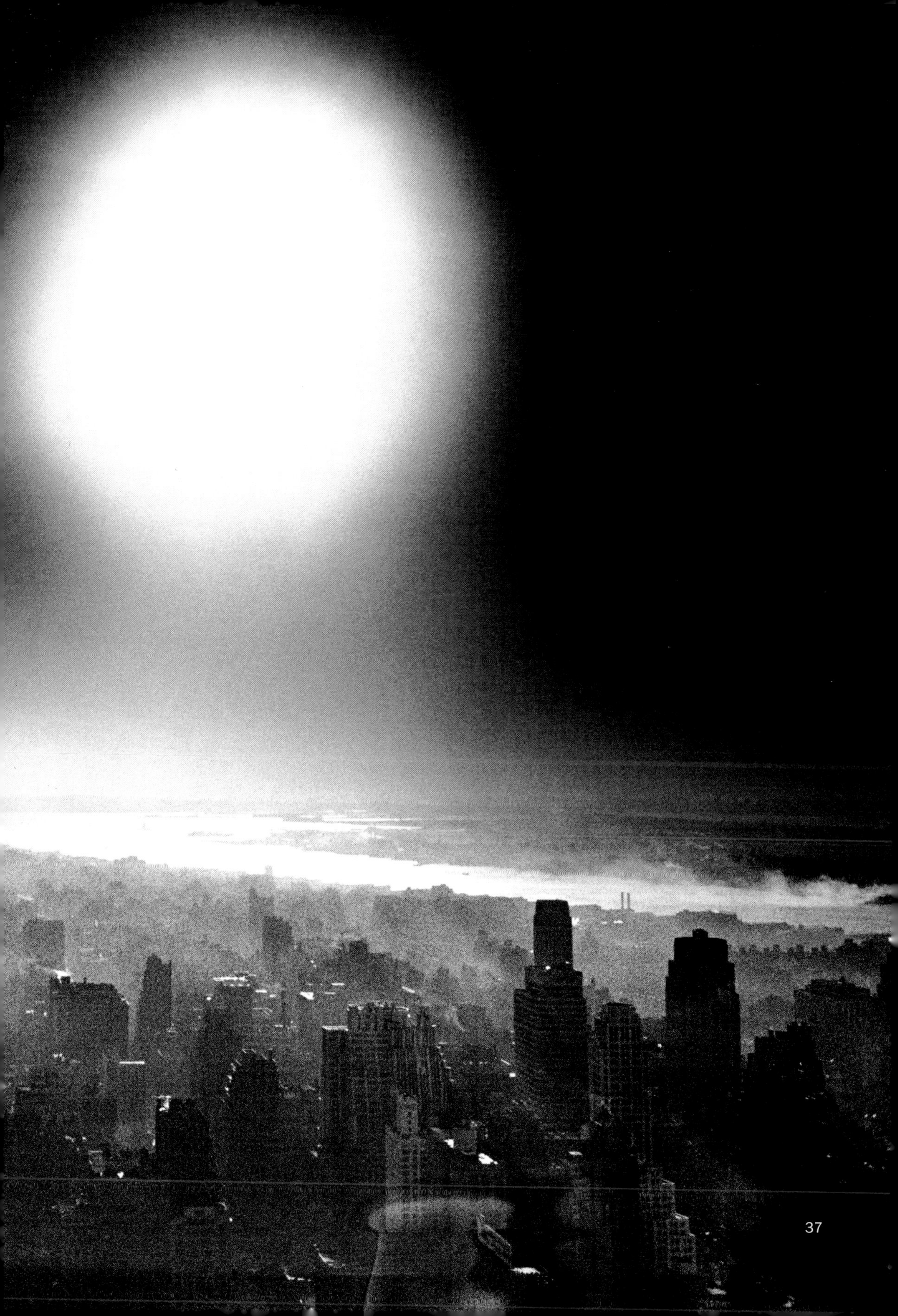

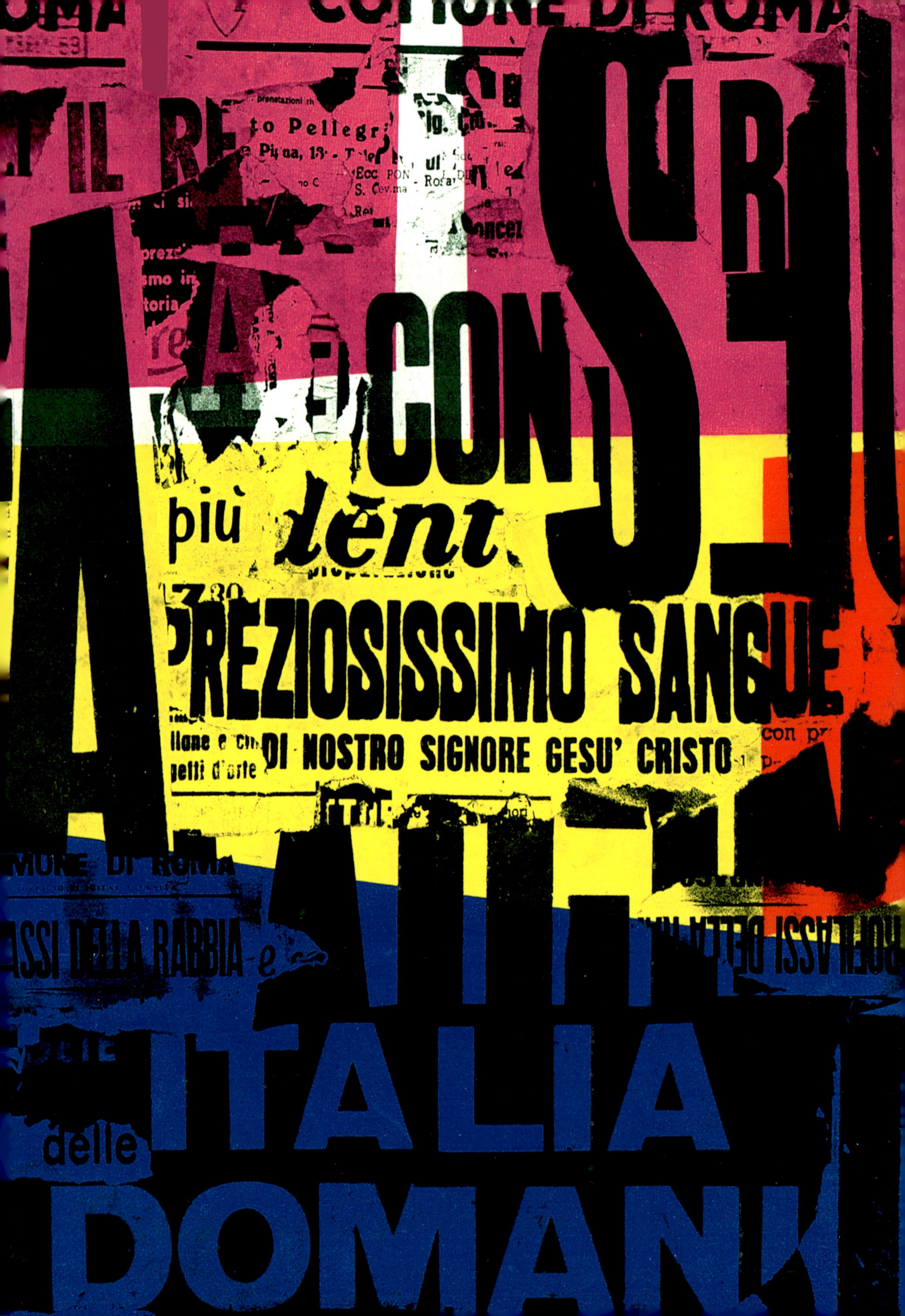
COTONE DI ROMA
IL RE
CON
più lent.
PREZIOSISSIMO SANGUE
DI NOSTRO SIGNORE GESU' CRISTO
MUNE DI ROMA
DELLA RABBIA e
ITALIA
delle
DOMANI

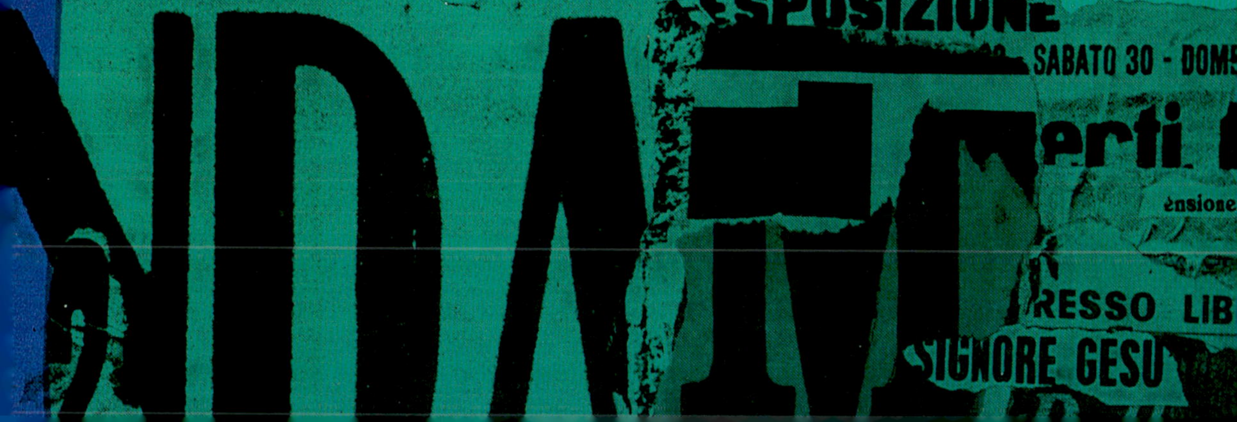
WILLIAM KLEIN
ROME

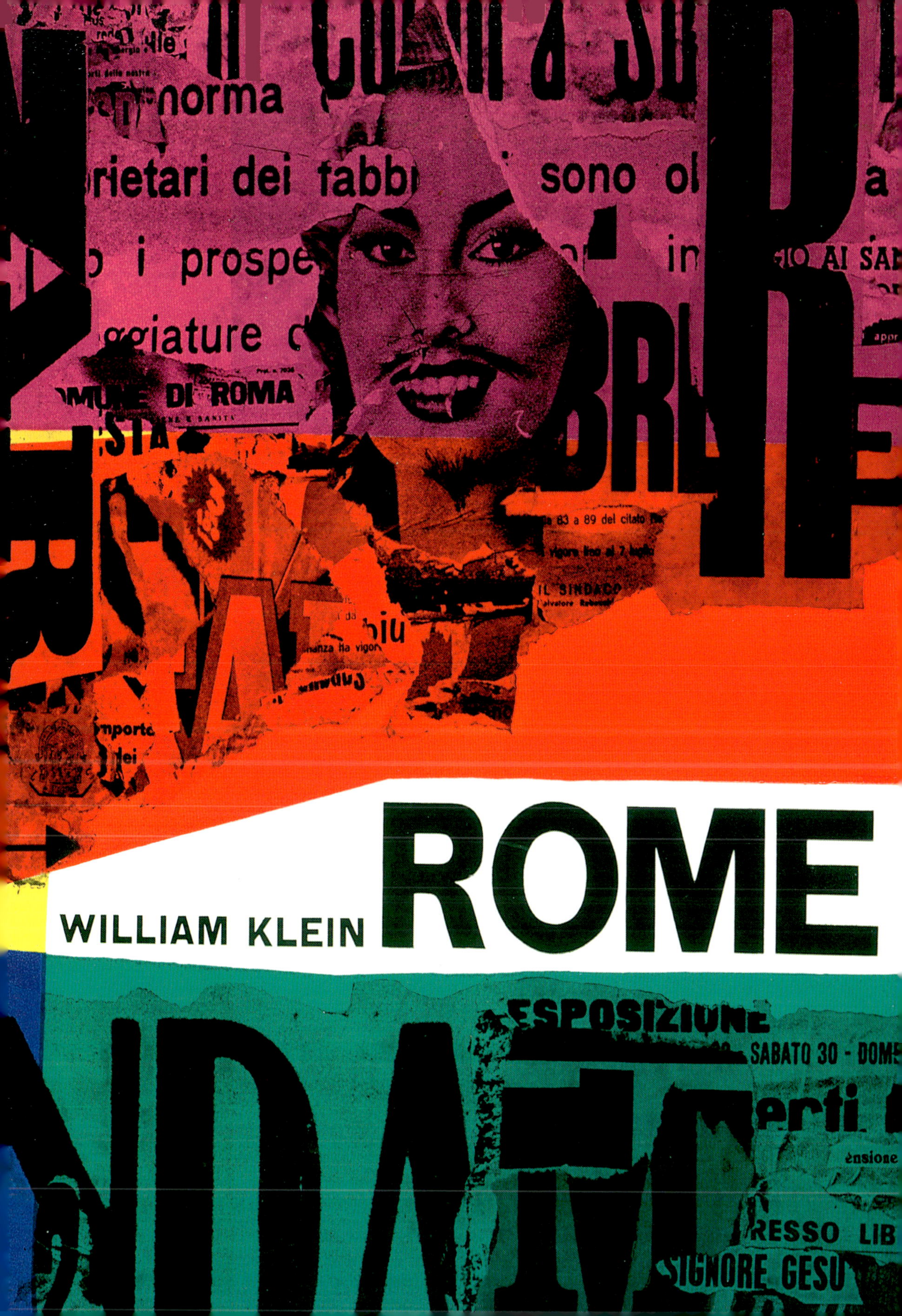

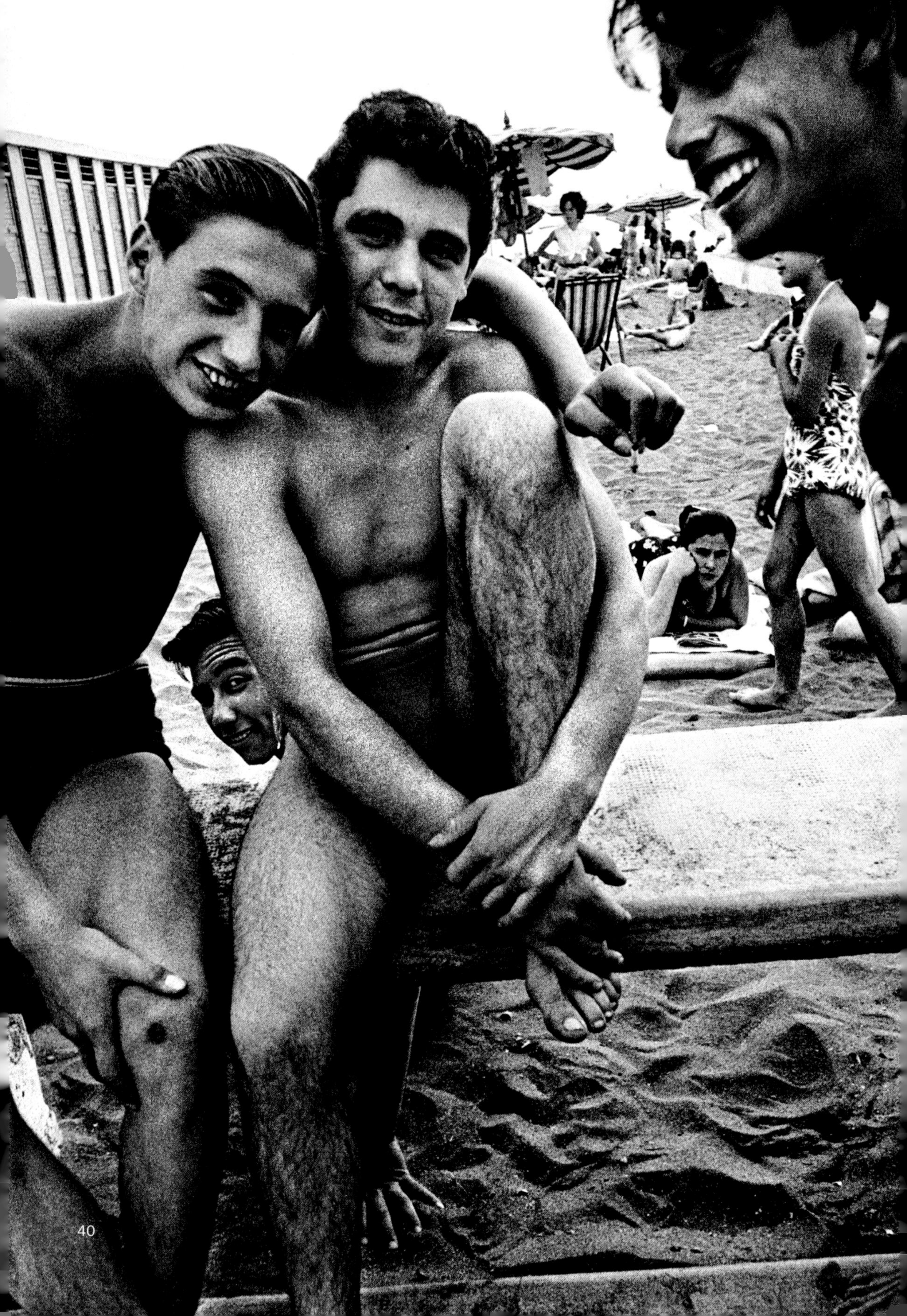

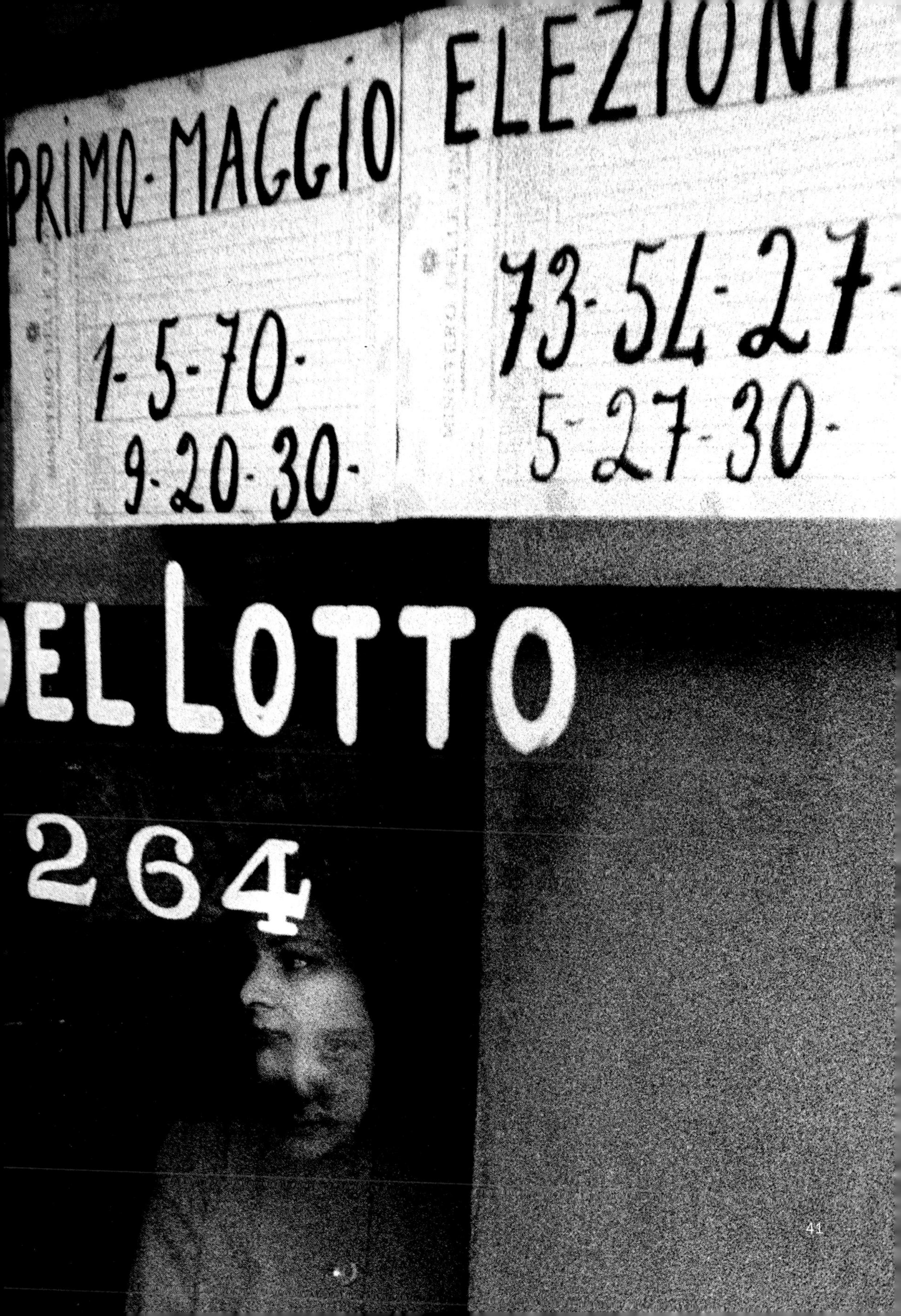

PRIMO·MAGGIO ELEZIONI
1-5-70·
9-20-30·
73-54-27·
5-27-30·
DEL LOTTO
264

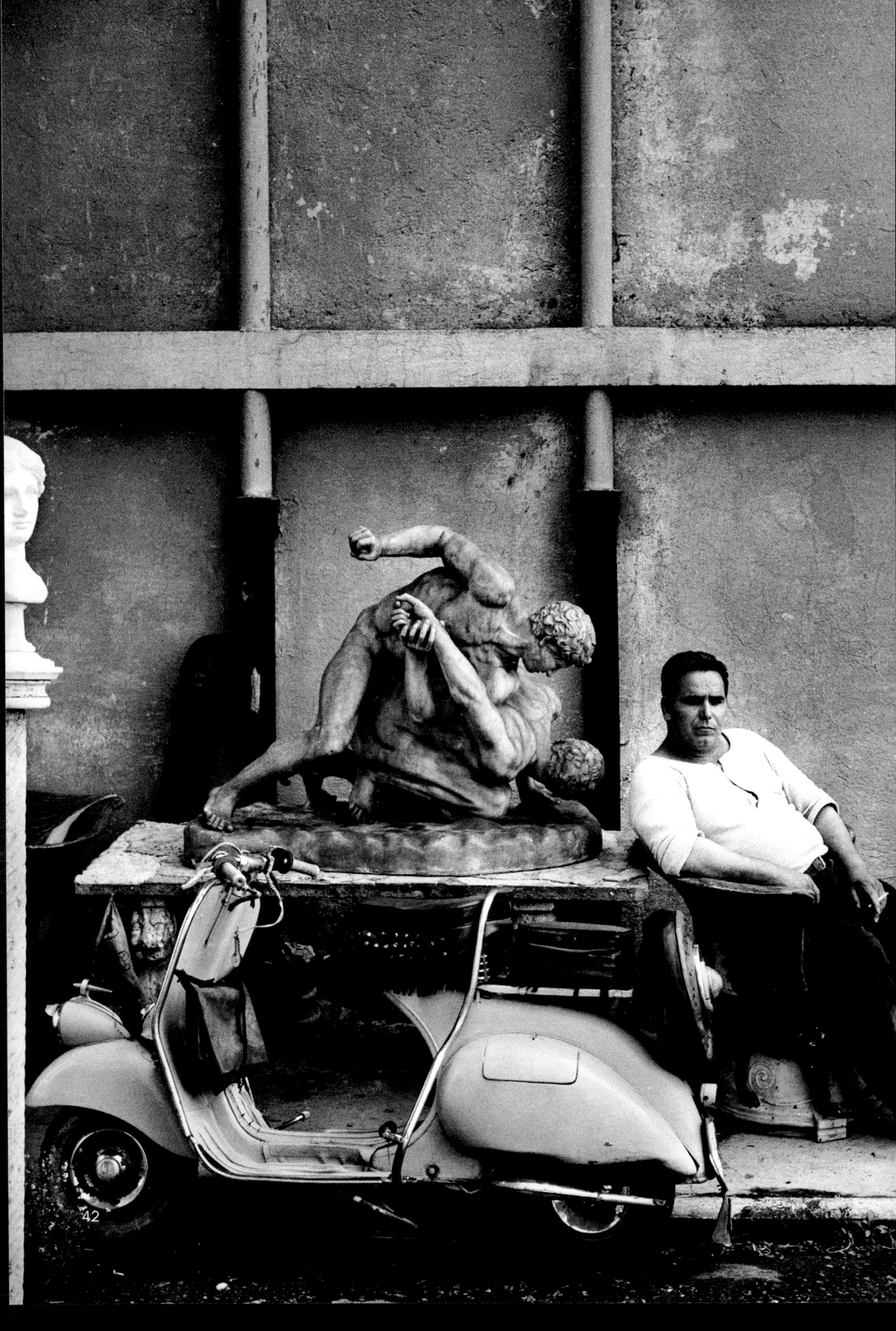

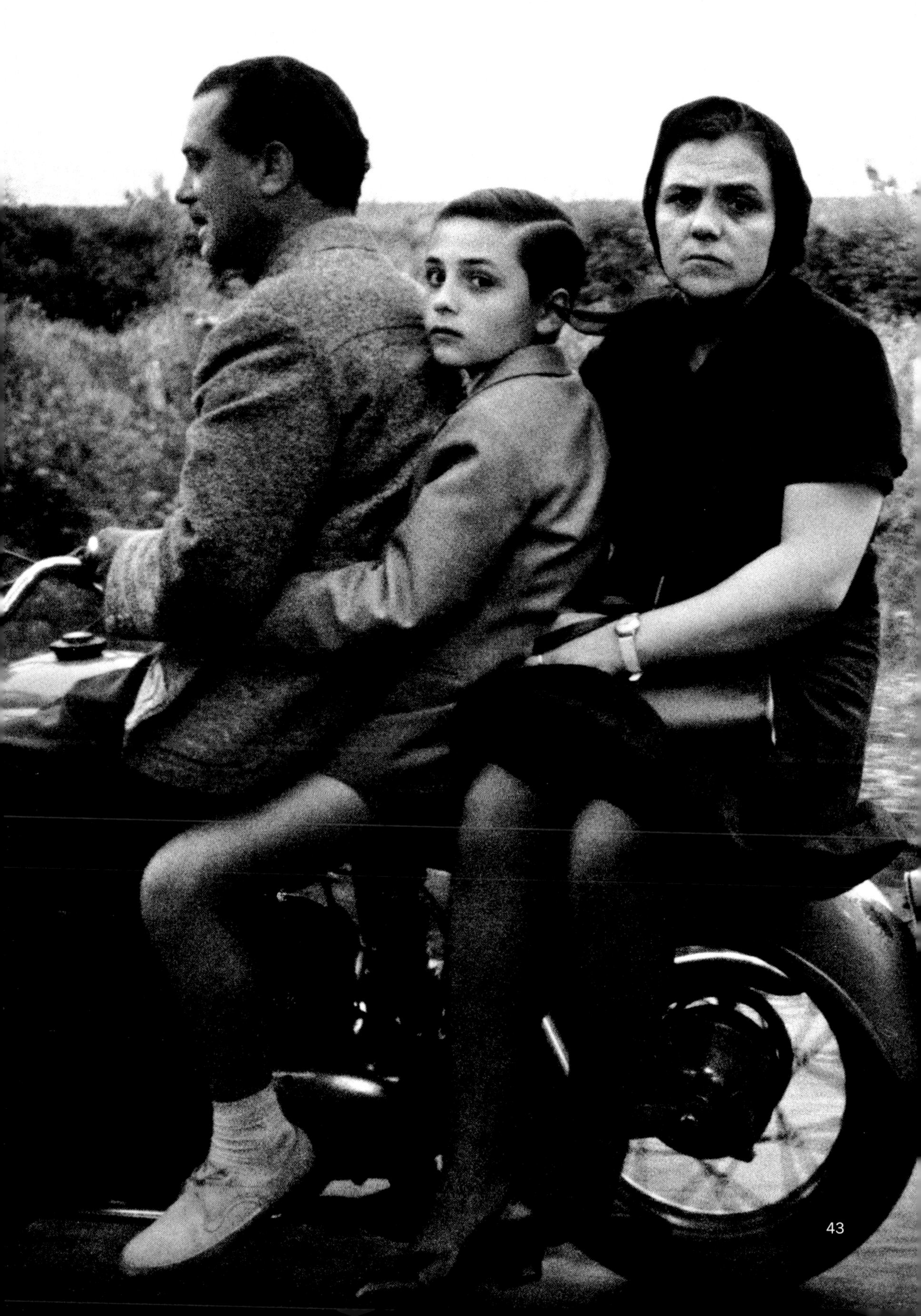

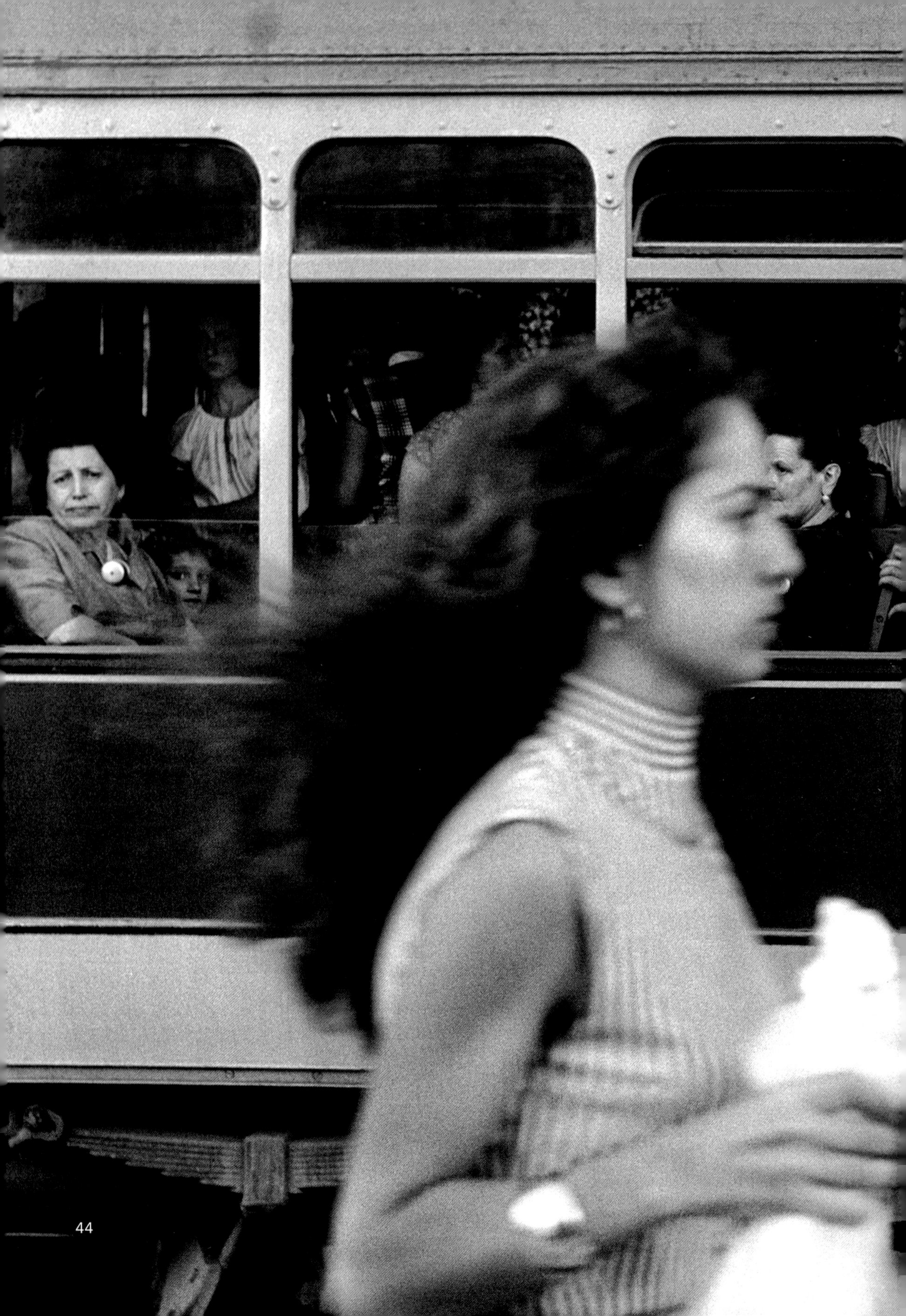

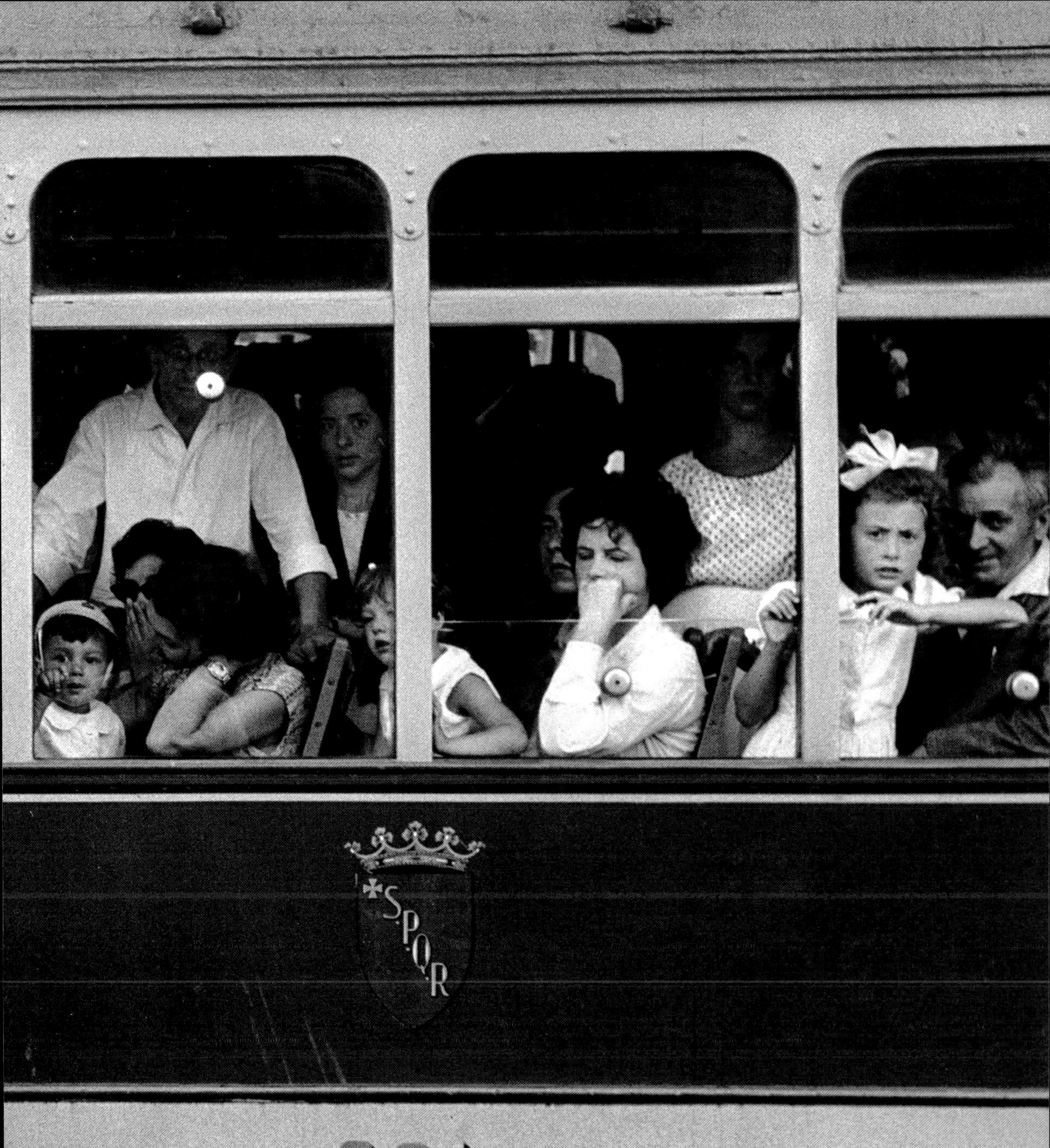
S.P.Q.R
901

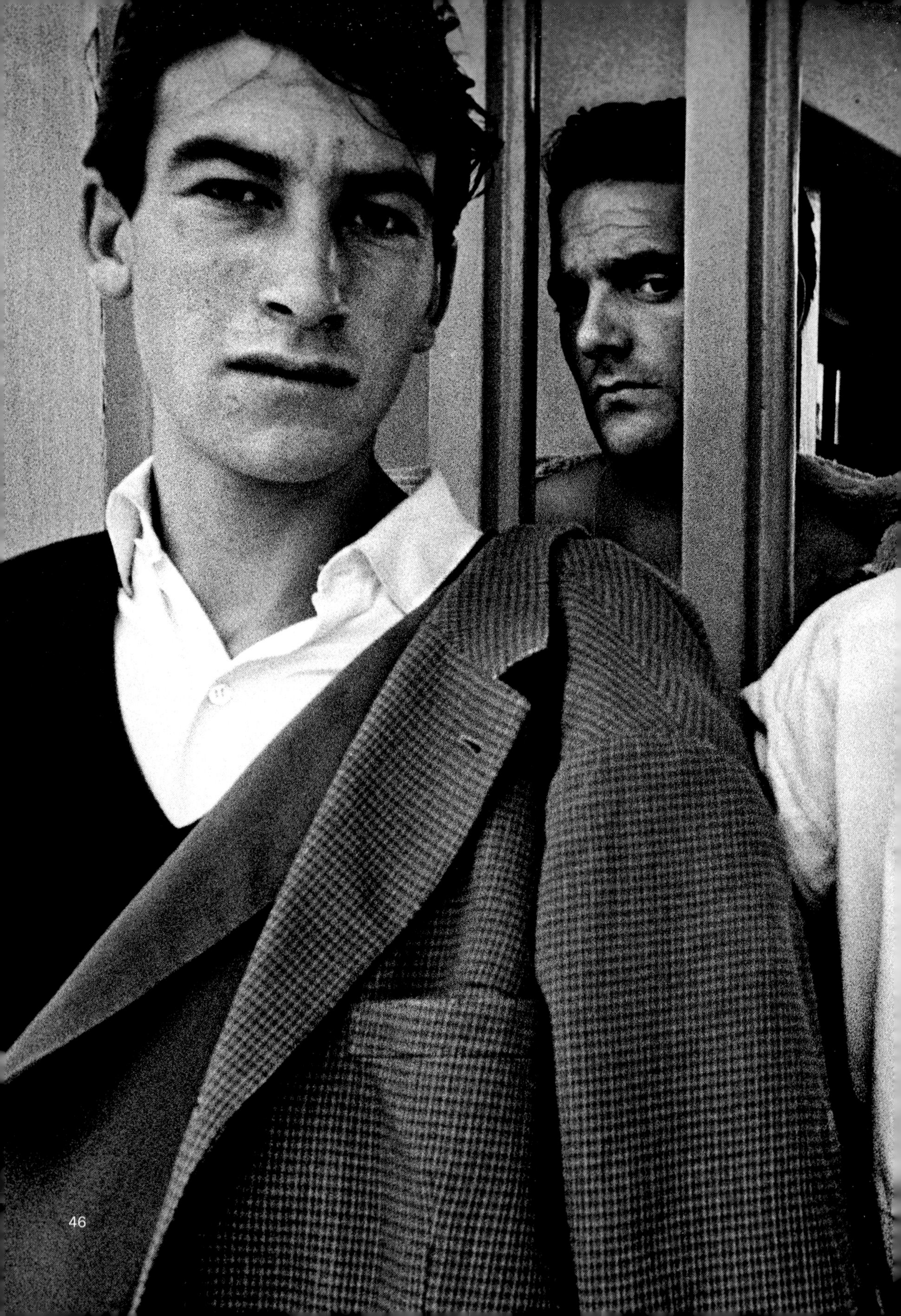

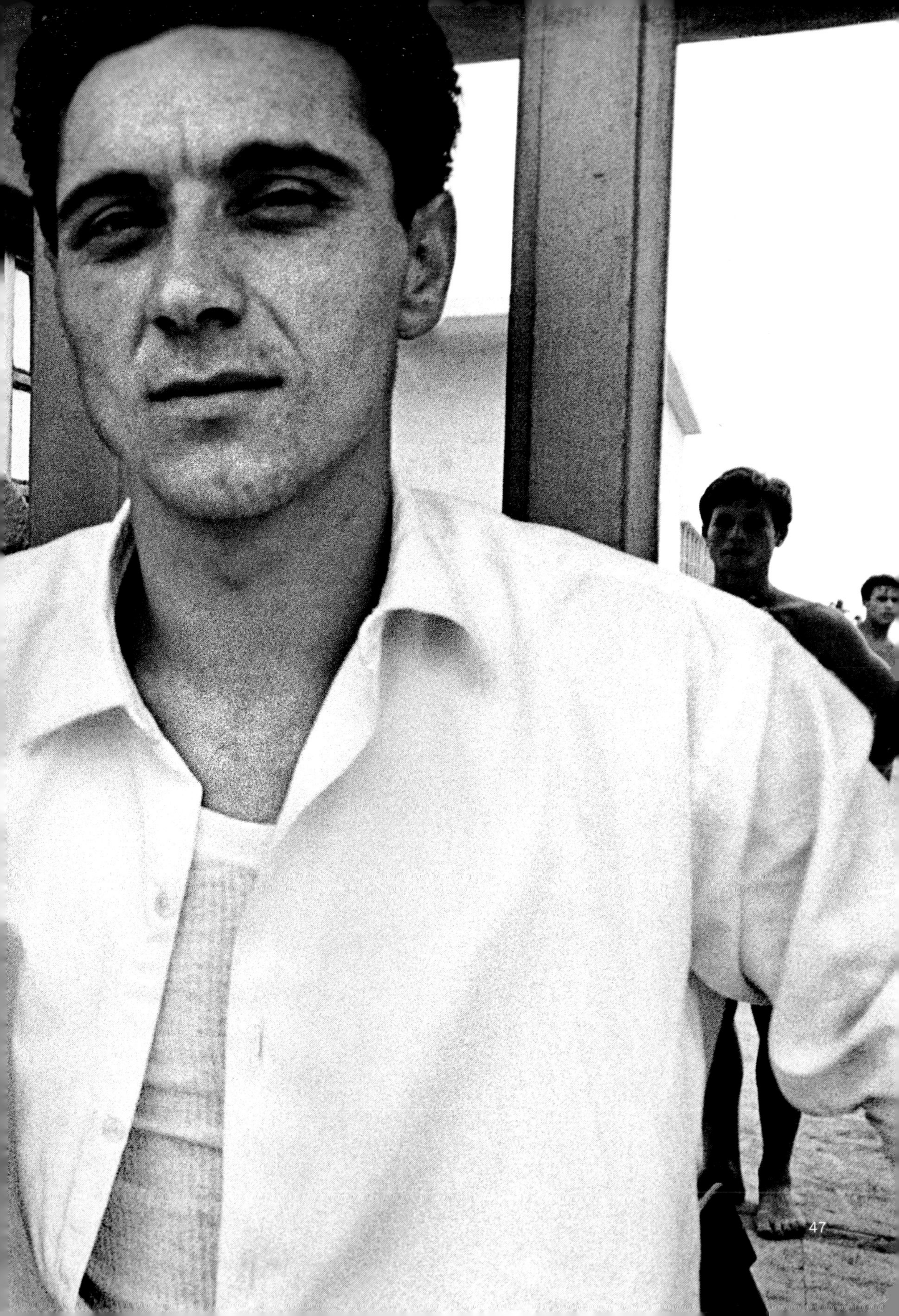

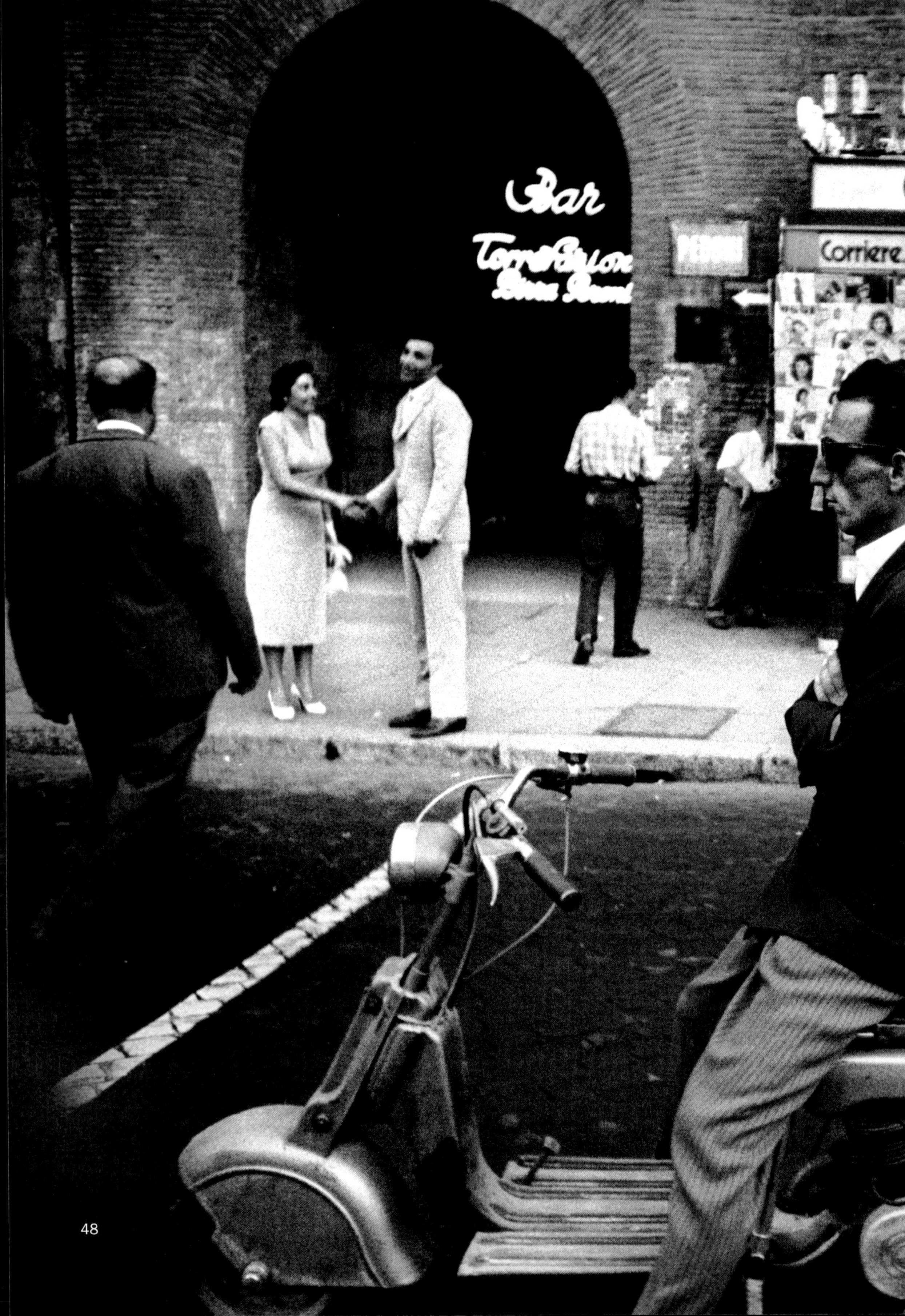

48

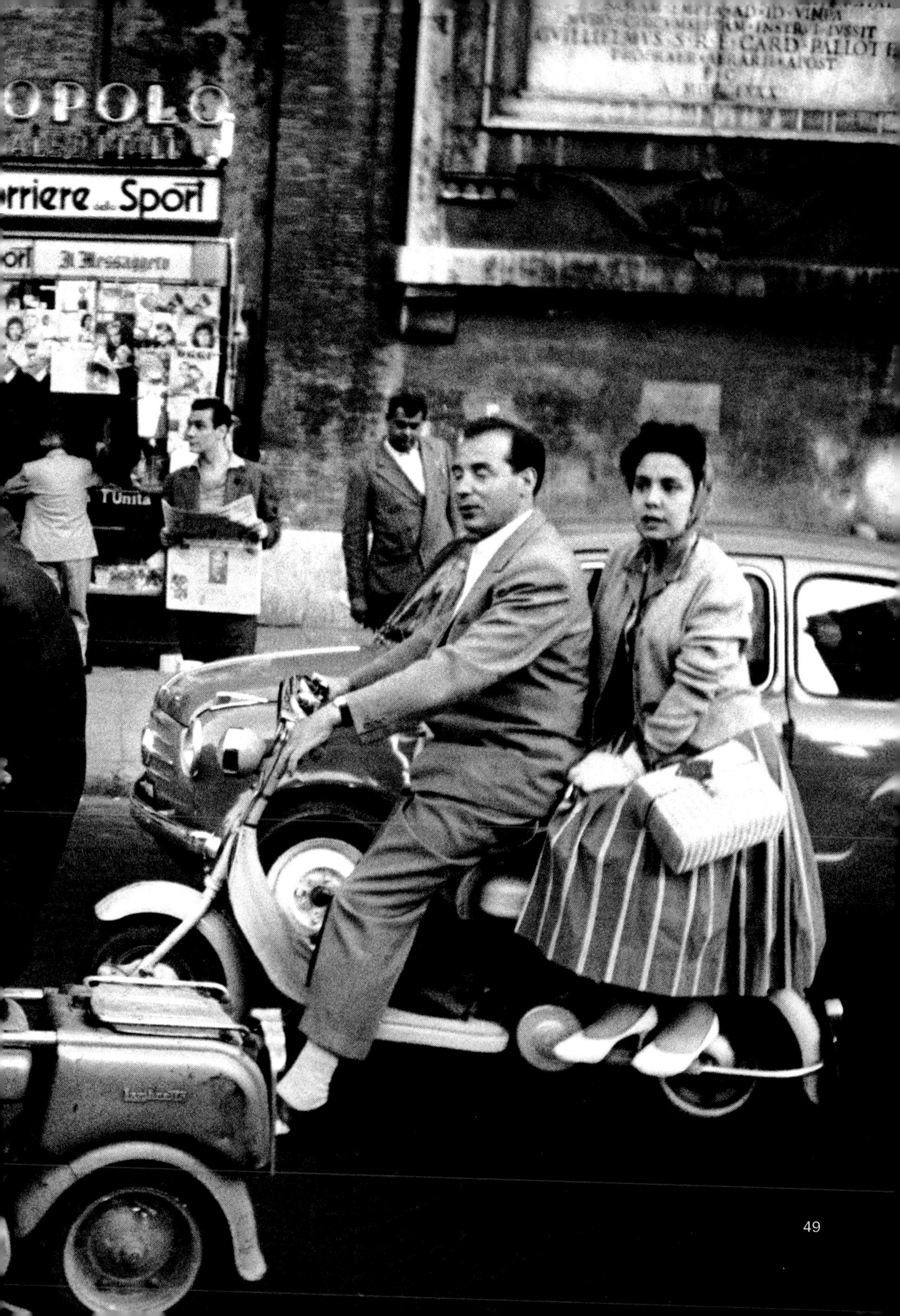

OPOLO
rriere dello Sport
Il Messaggero
l'Unità

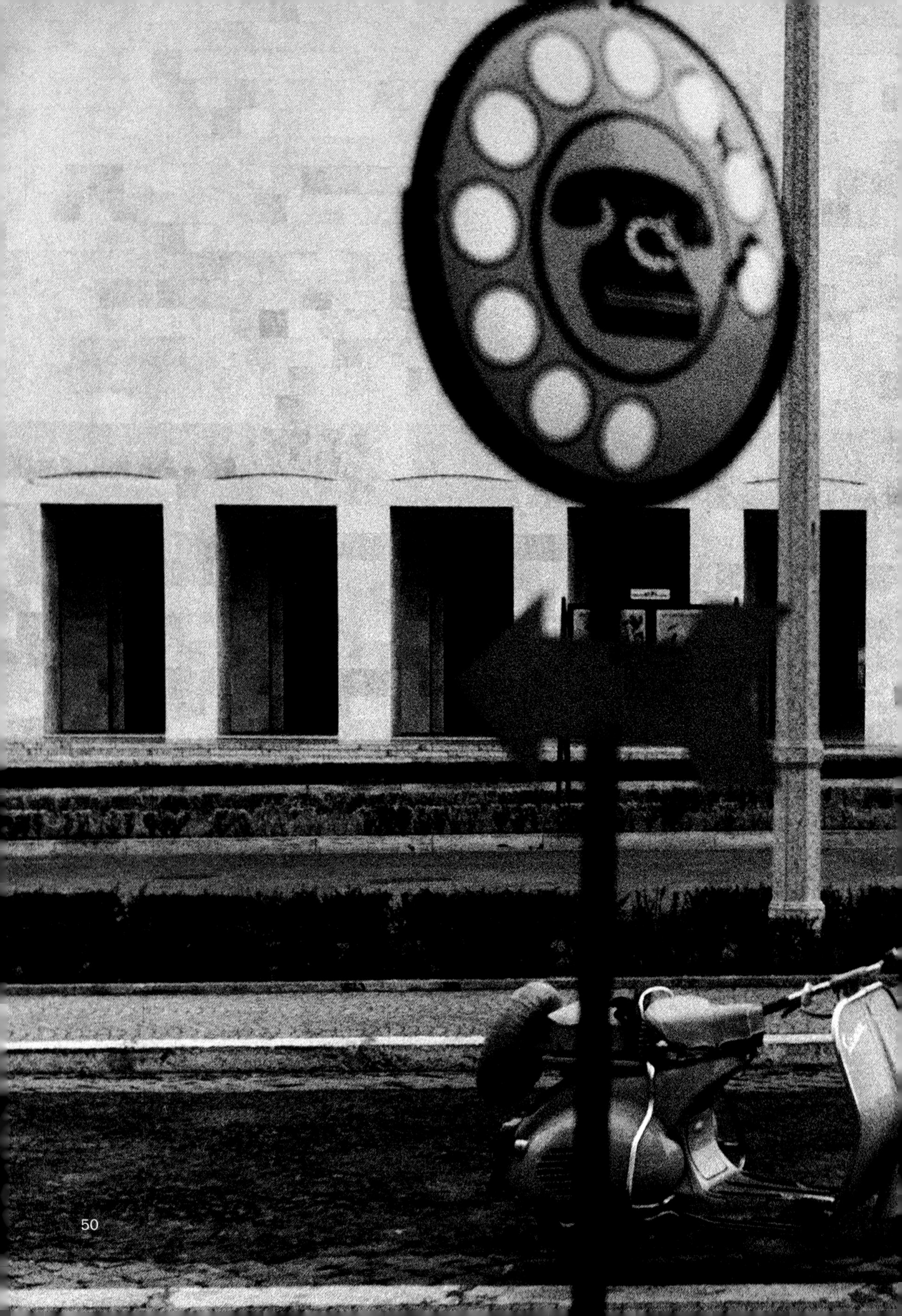

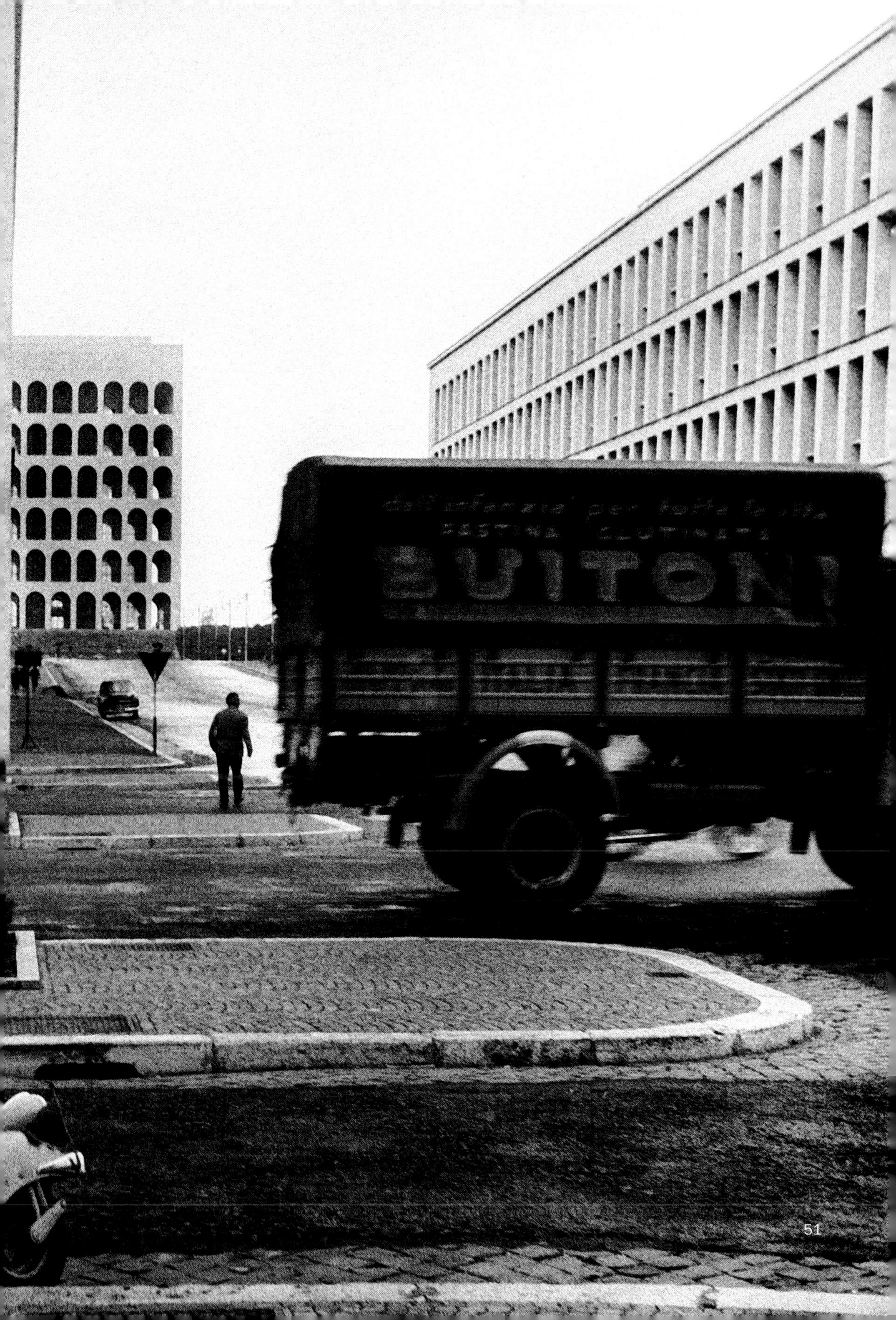
BUITONI

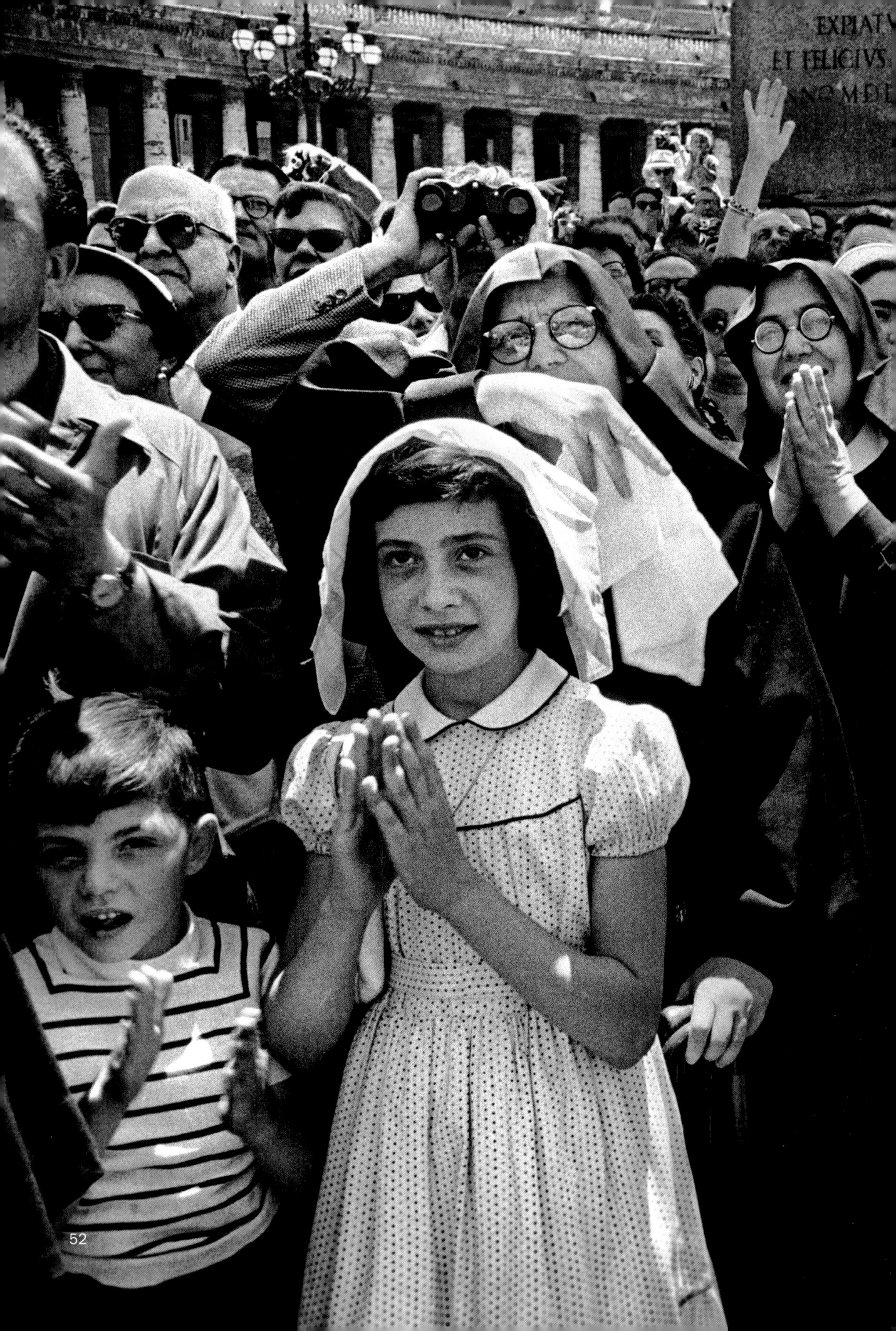
EXPIAT
ET FELICIVS
NO M D

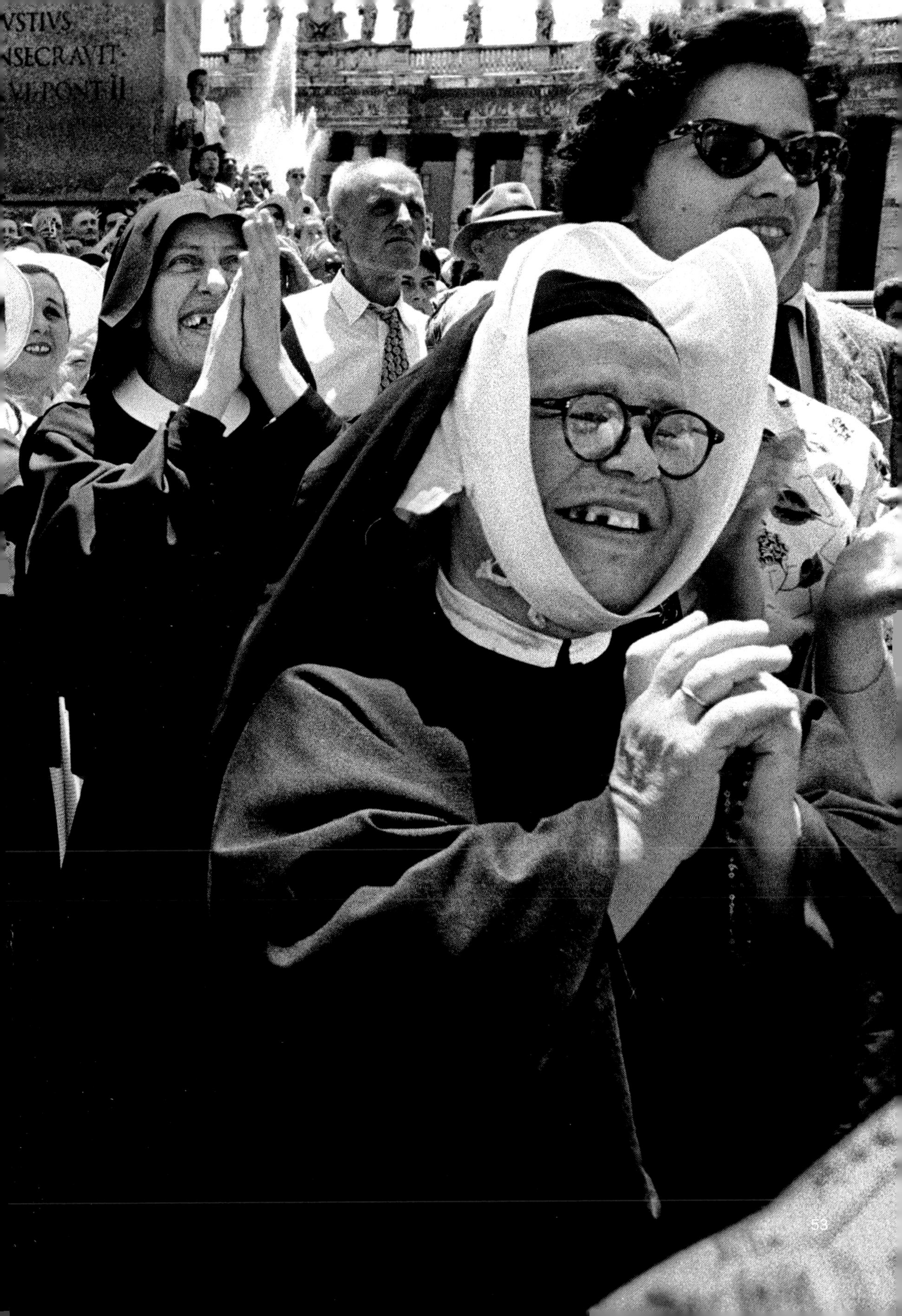
VSTIVS
NSECRAVIT
VI PONT II

МОСКВА

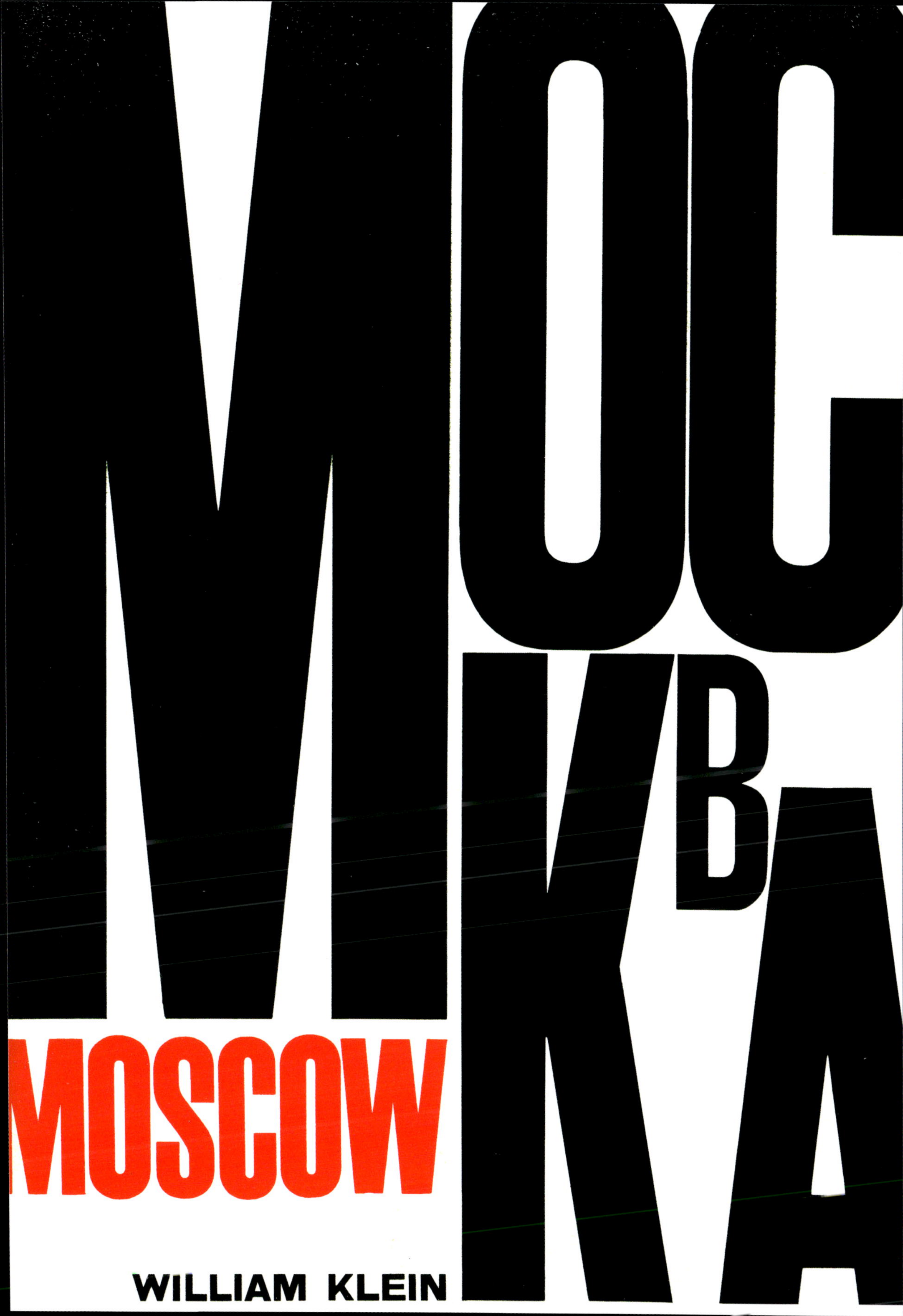

МОСКВА
MOSCOW
WILLIAM KLEIN

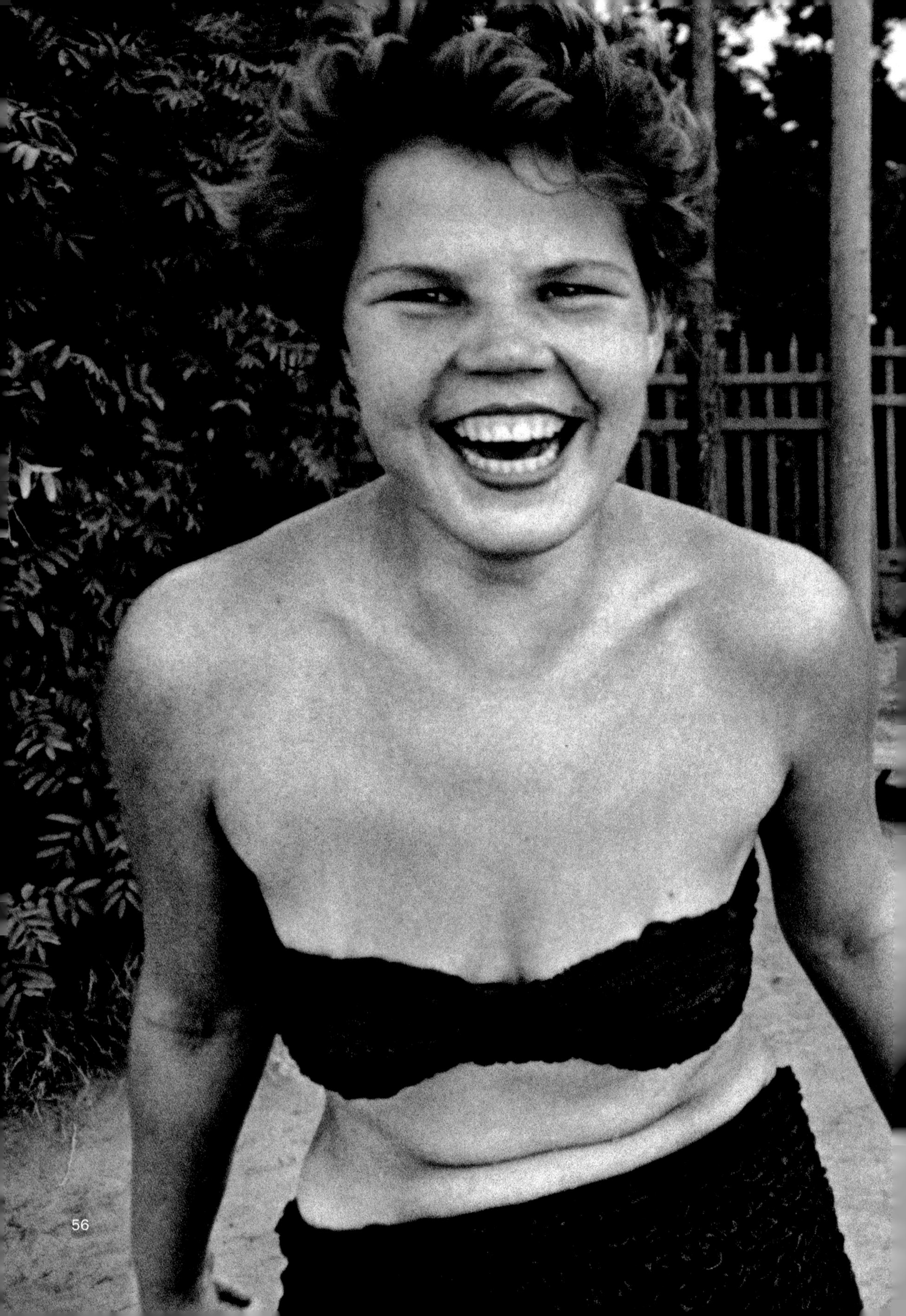

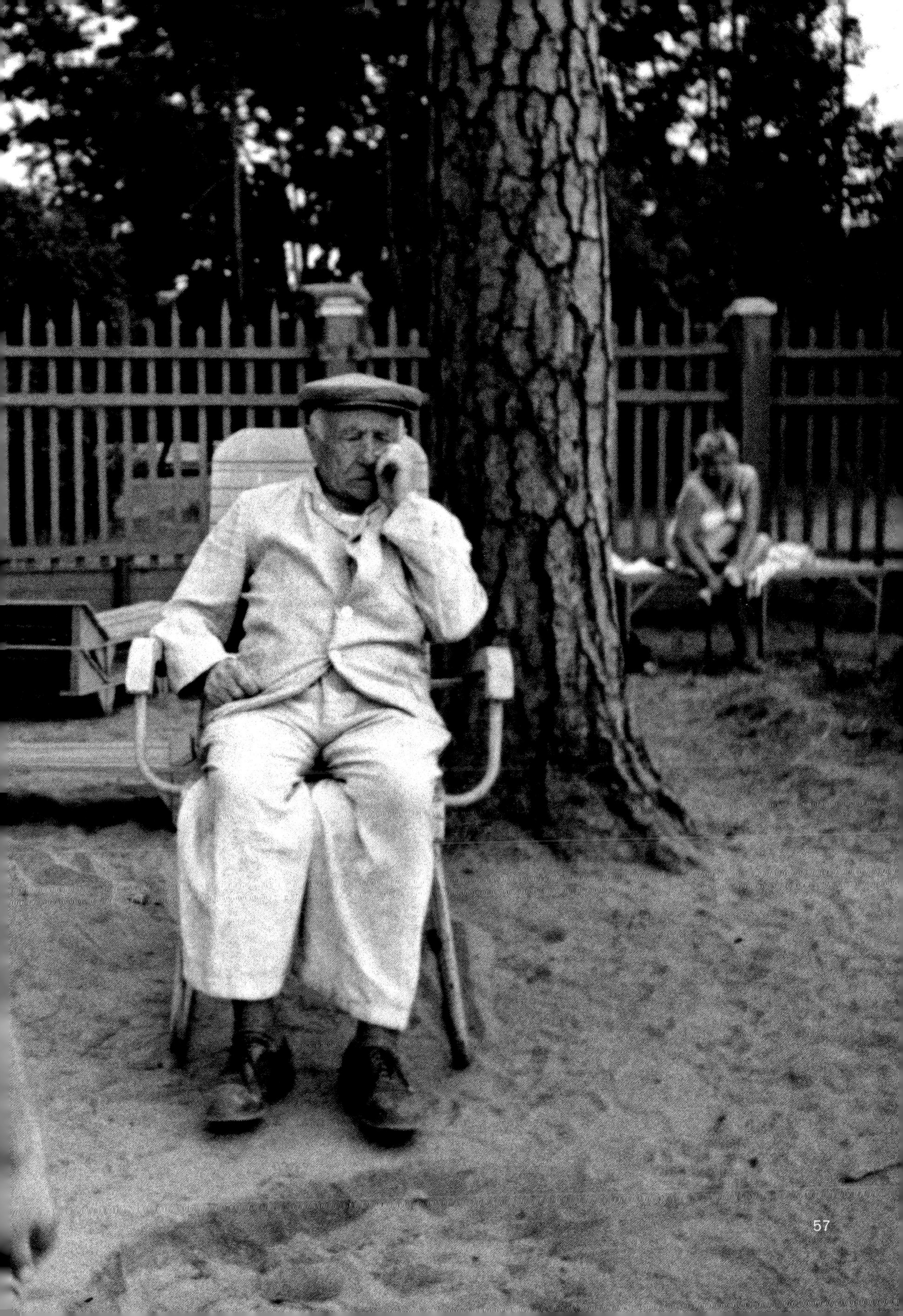

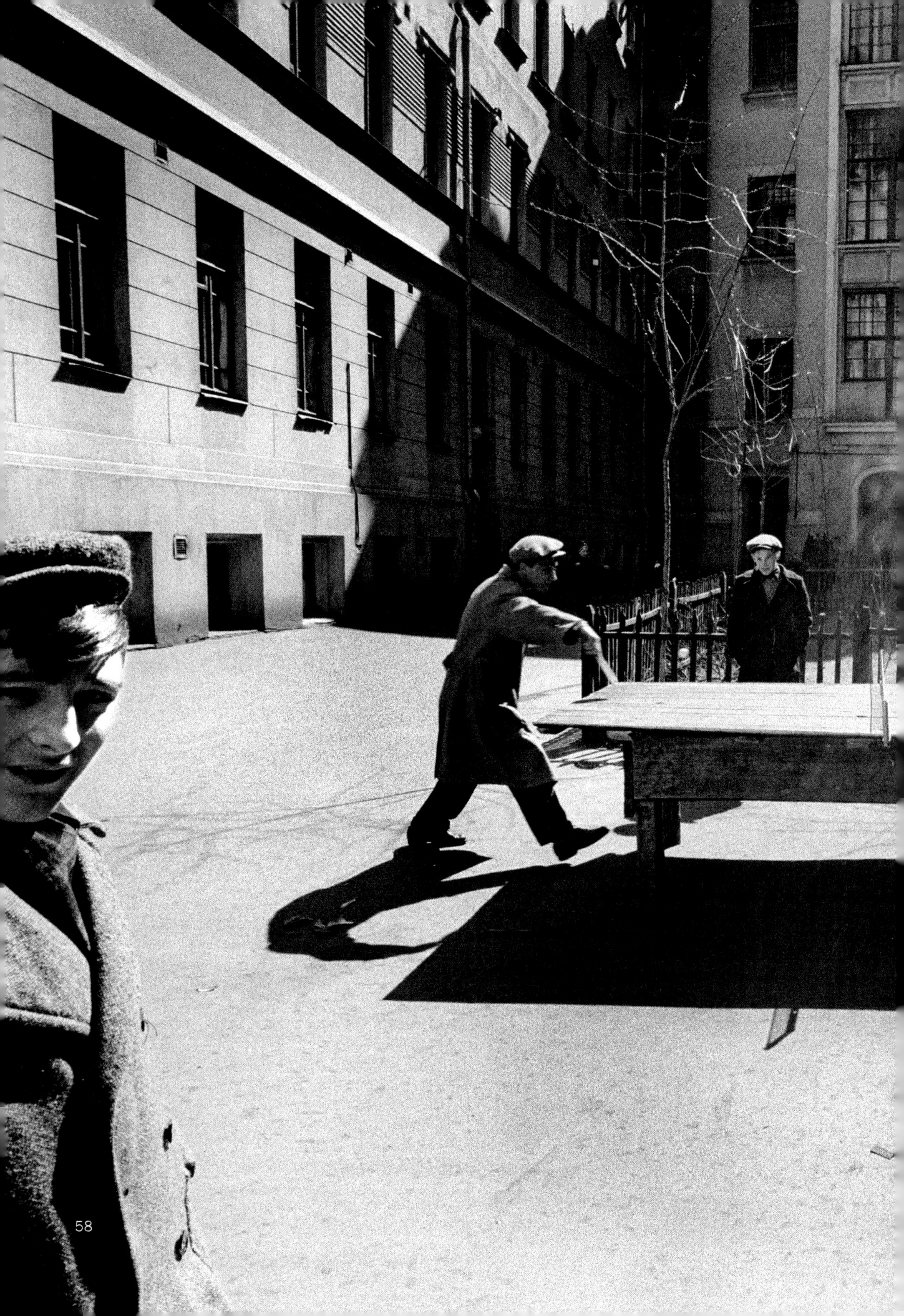

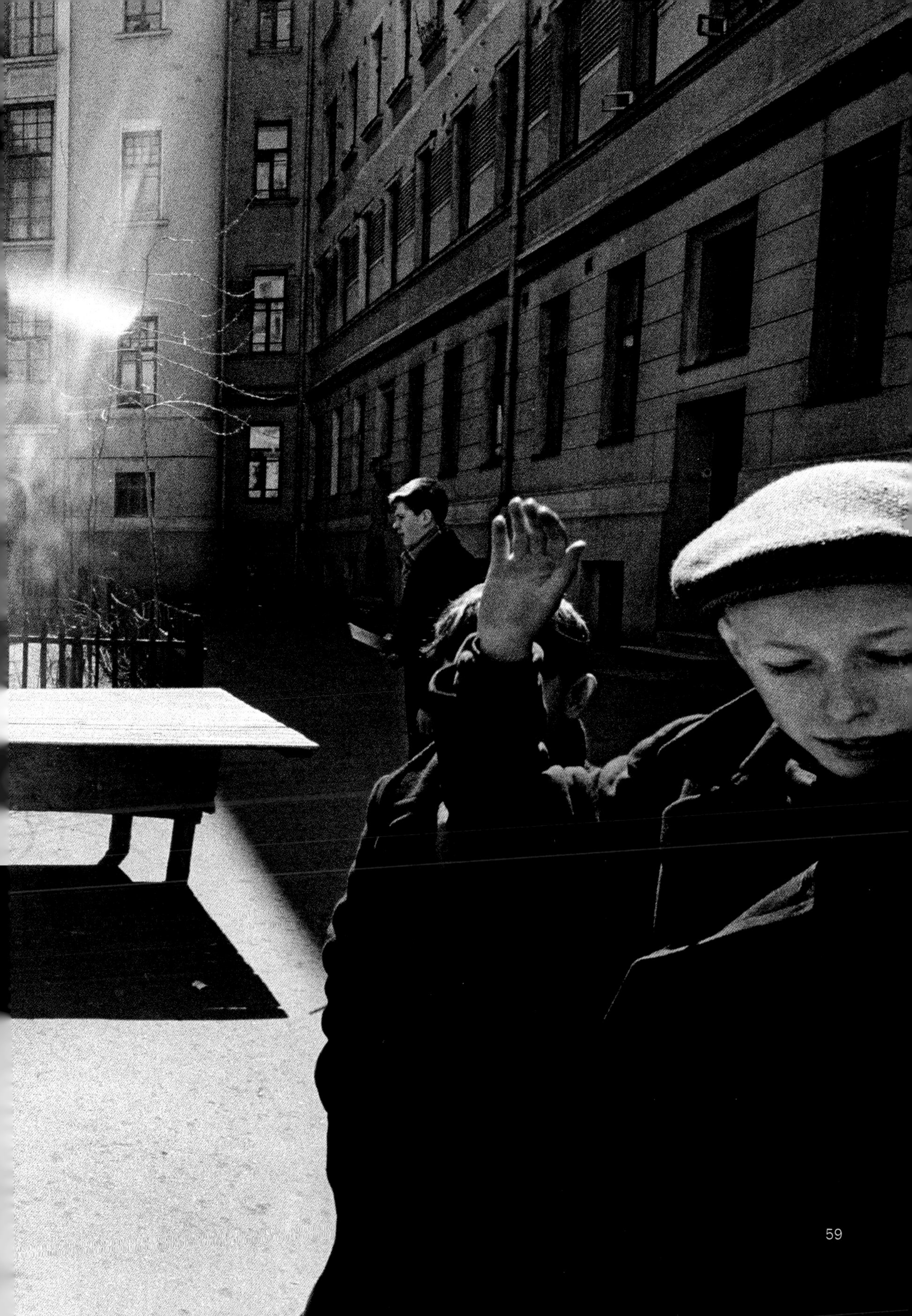

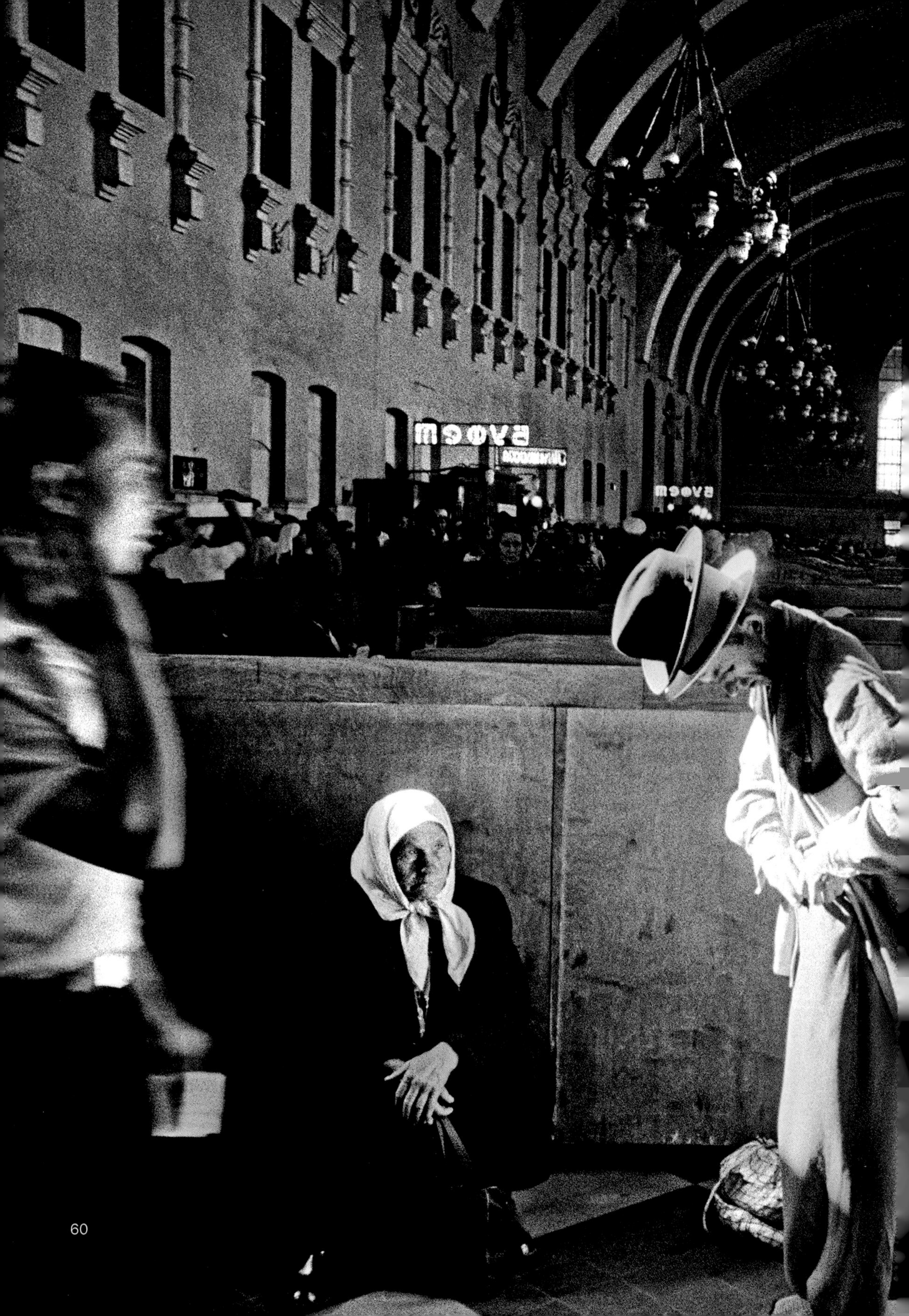

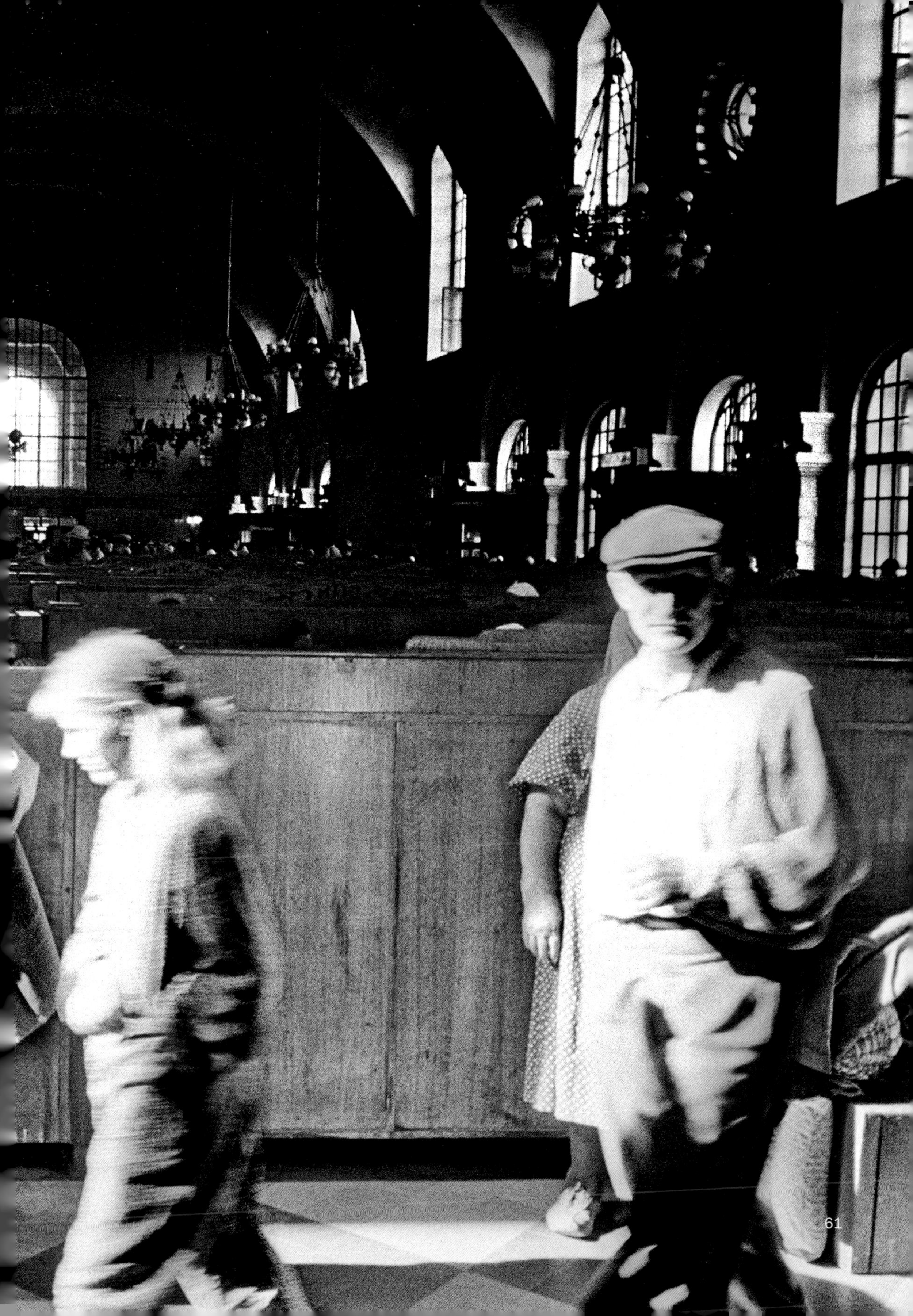

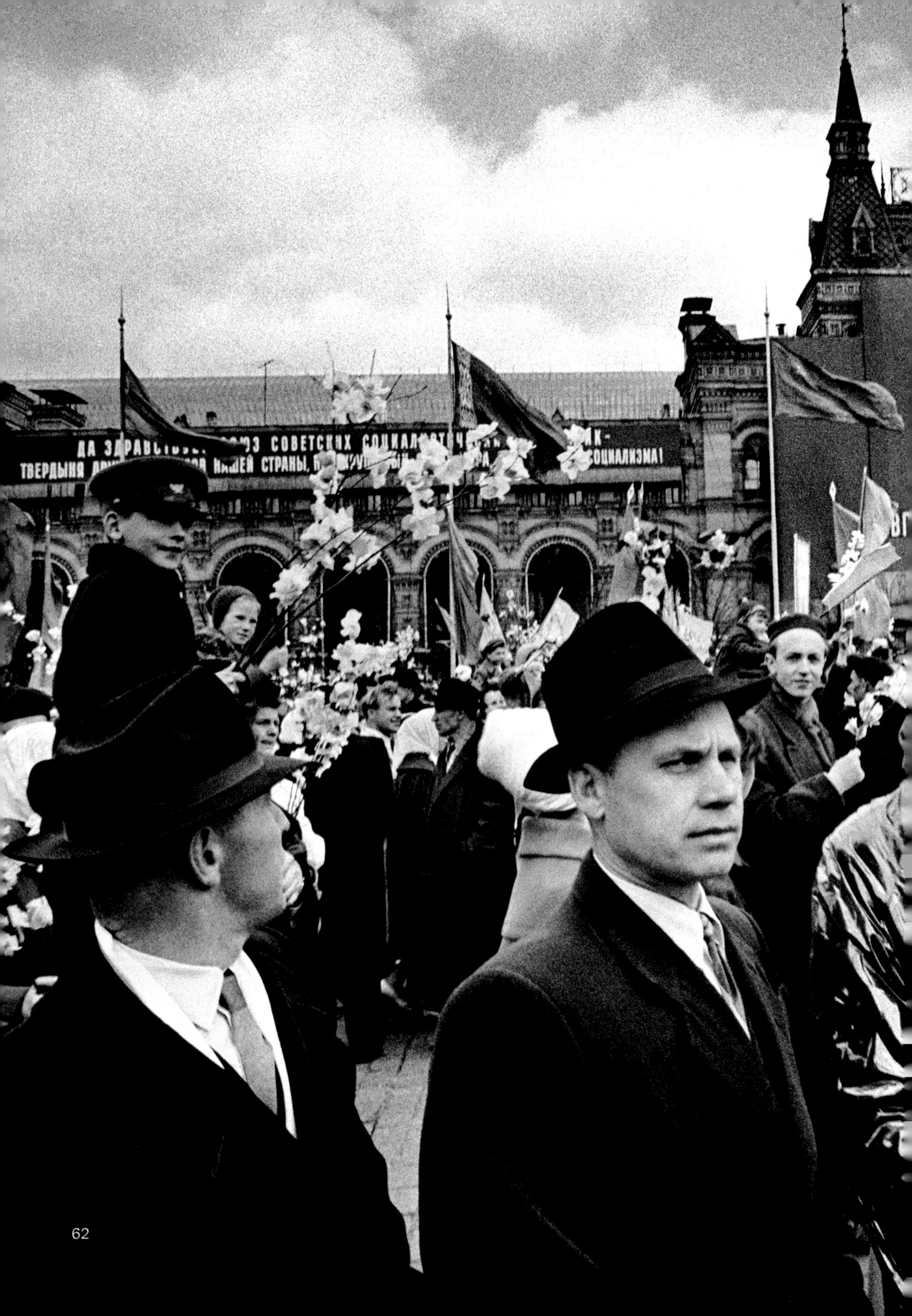
ДА ЗДРАВСТВУЕТ СОЮЗ СОВЕТСКИХ СОЦИАЛИСТИЧЕСКИХ ... К СОЦИАЛИЗМА!
ТВЕРДЫНЯ ... НАШЕЙ СТРАНЫ, ...

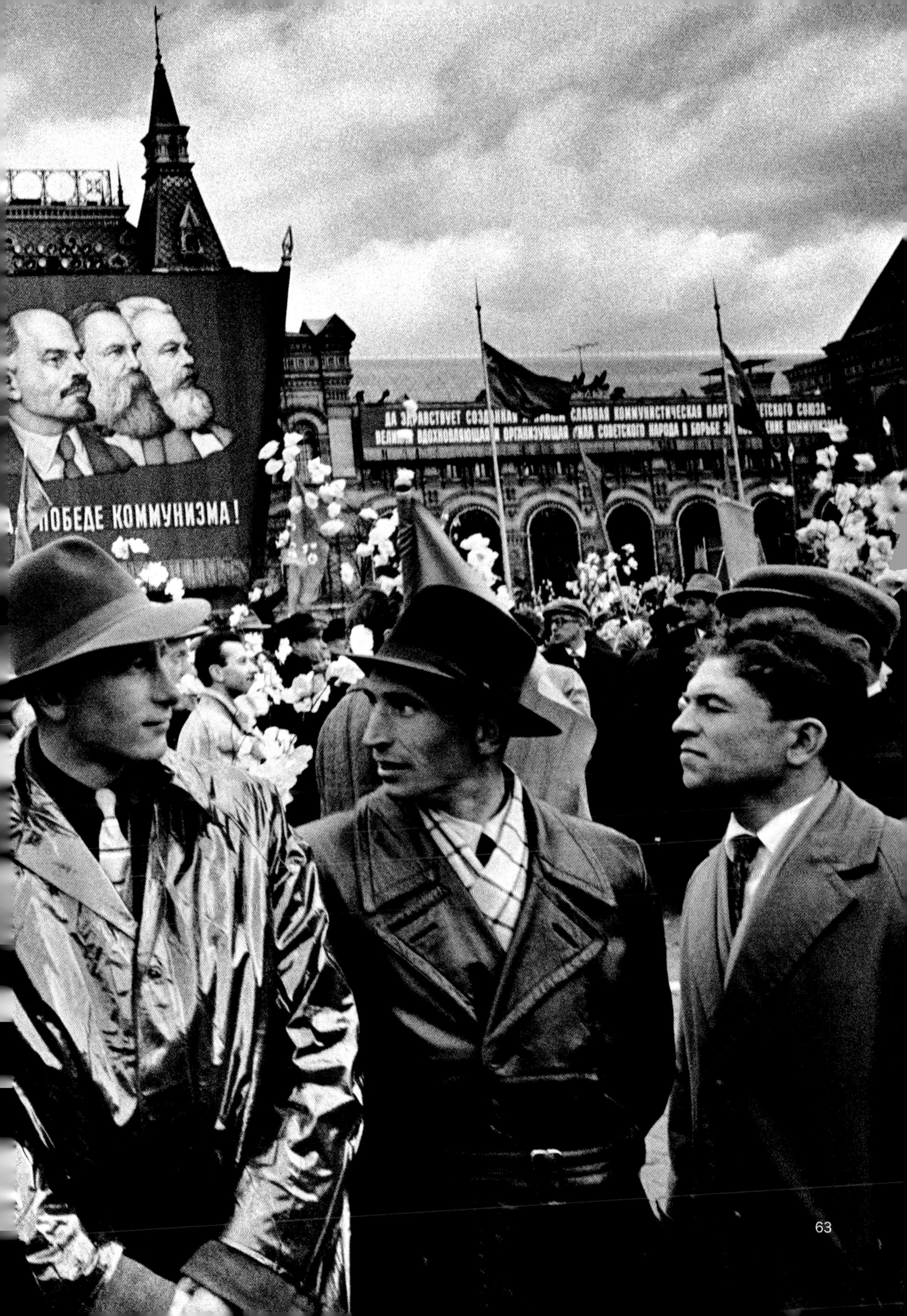

ПОБЕДЕ КОММУНИЗМА!
ДА ЗДРАВСТВУЕТ СОЗДАННАЯ ... СЛАВНАЯ КОММУНИСТИЧЕСКАЯ ПАРТ... ЕТСКОГО СОЮЗА
ВЕЛИ... ВДОХНОВЛЯЮЩАЯ И ОРГАНИЗУЮЩАЯ СИЛА СОВЕТСКОГО НАРОДА В БОРЬБЕ ЗА ... НИЕ КОММУНИЗМА

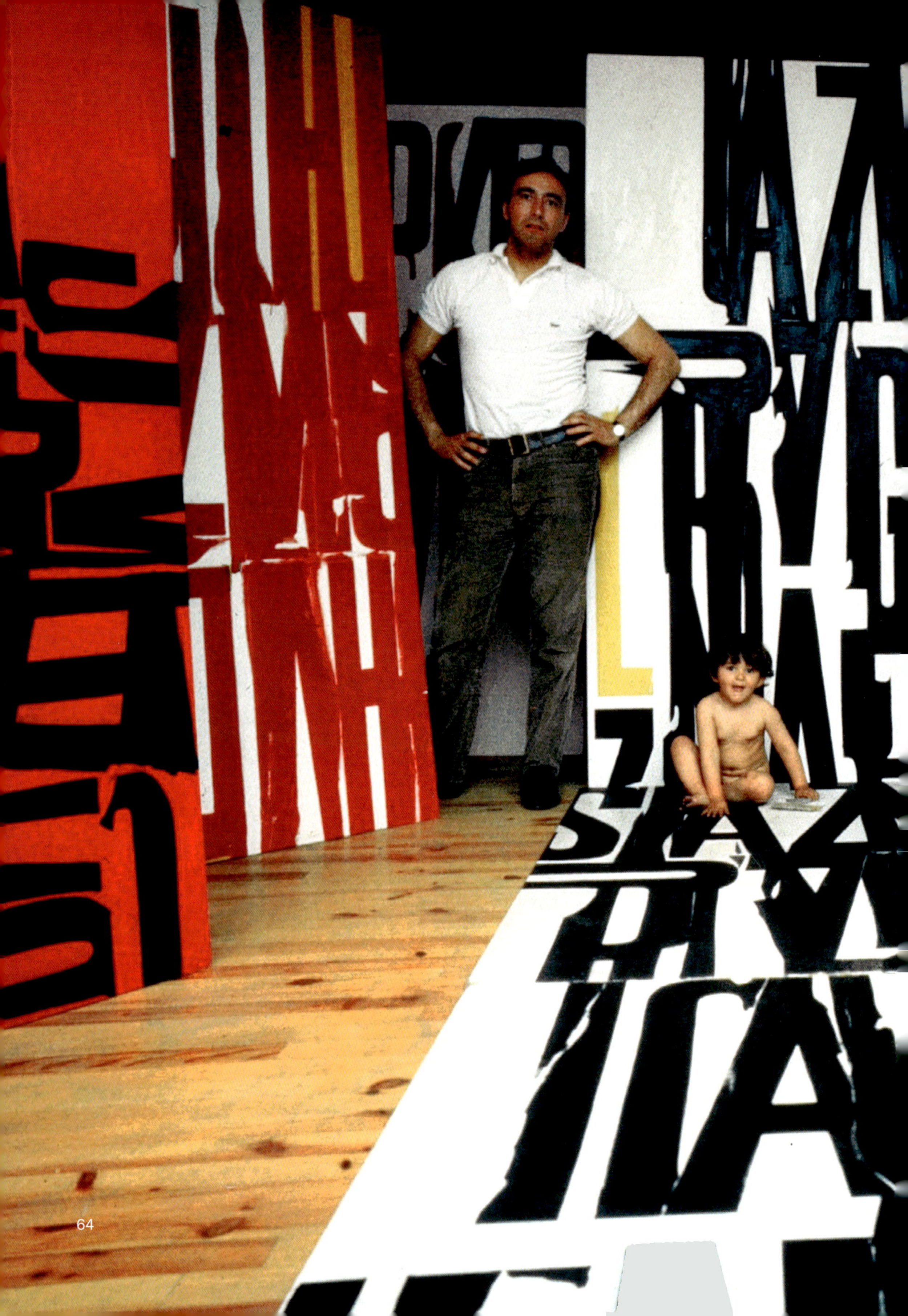

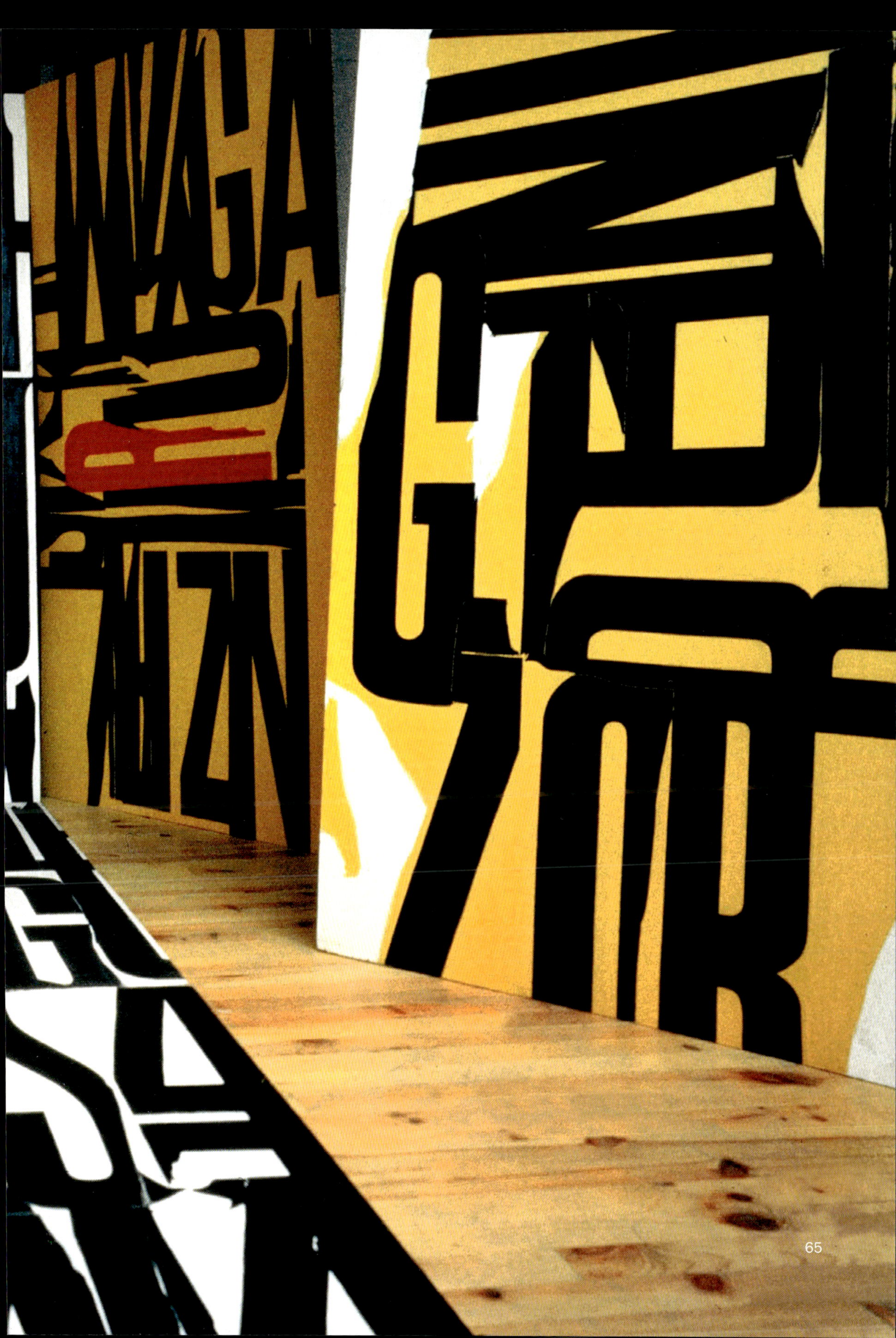

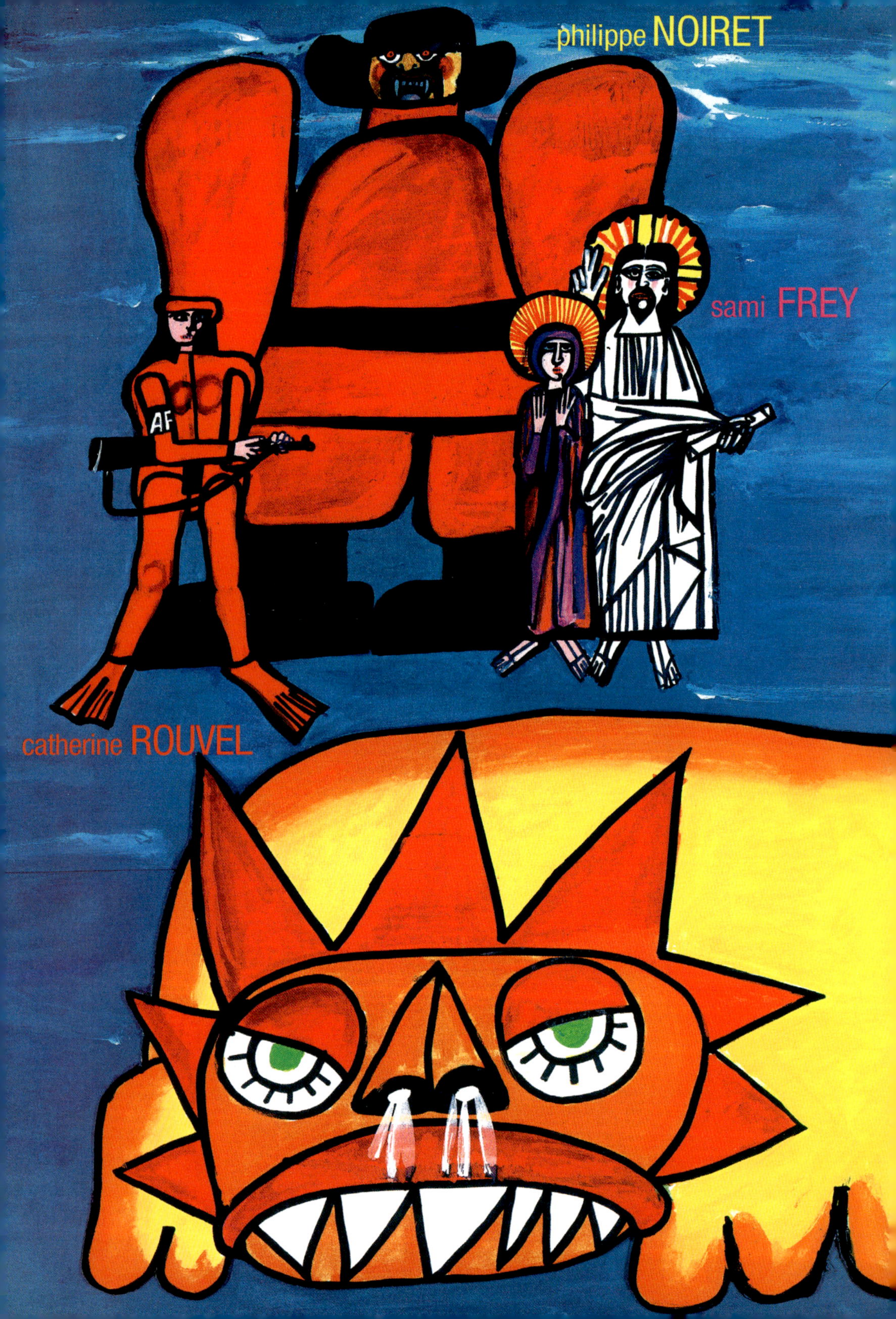
philippe NOIRET
sami FREY
catherine ROUVEL

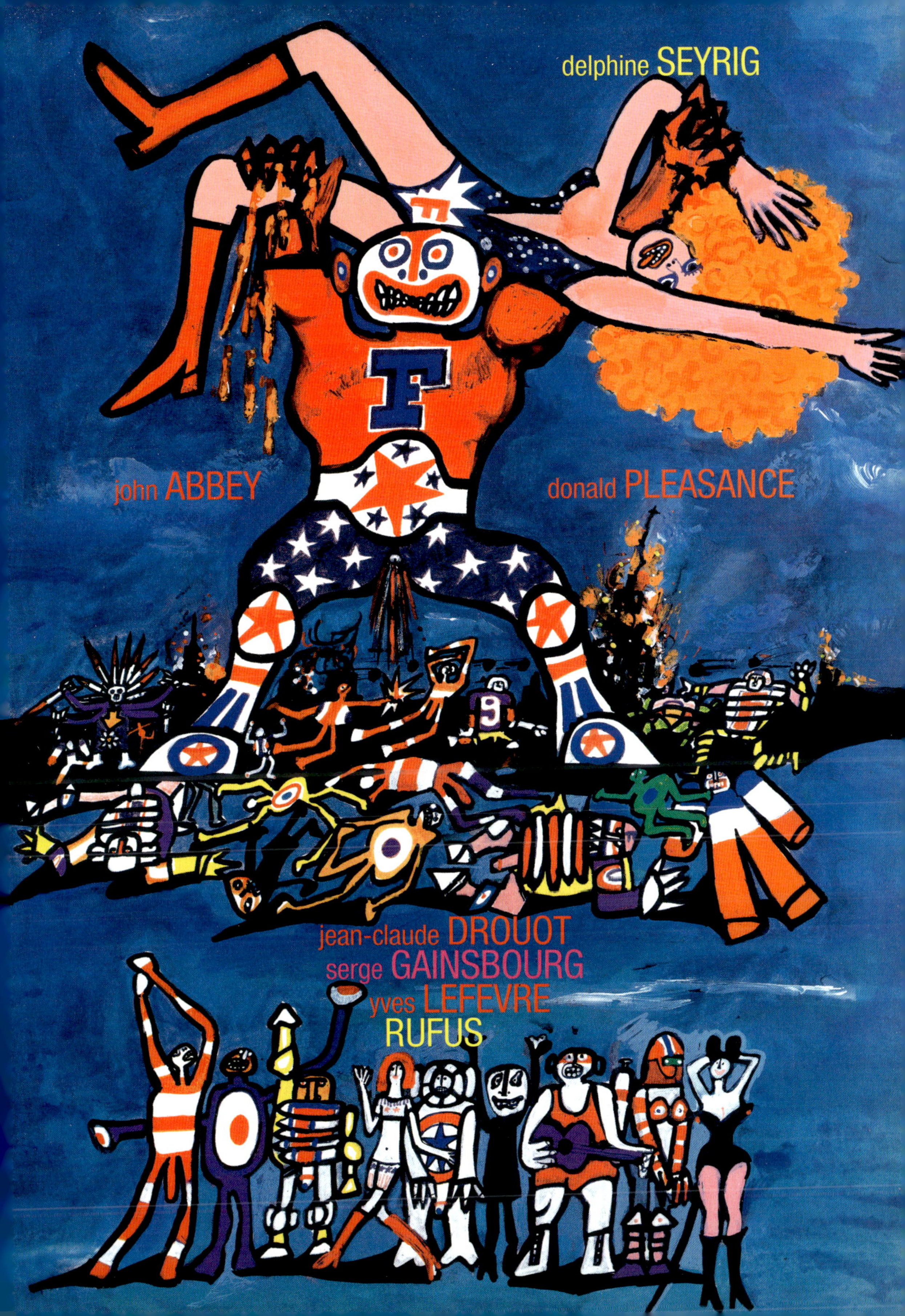
delphine SEYRIG
john ABBEY
donald PLEASANCE
jean-claude DROUOT
serge GAINSBOURG
yves LEFÈVRE
RUFUS

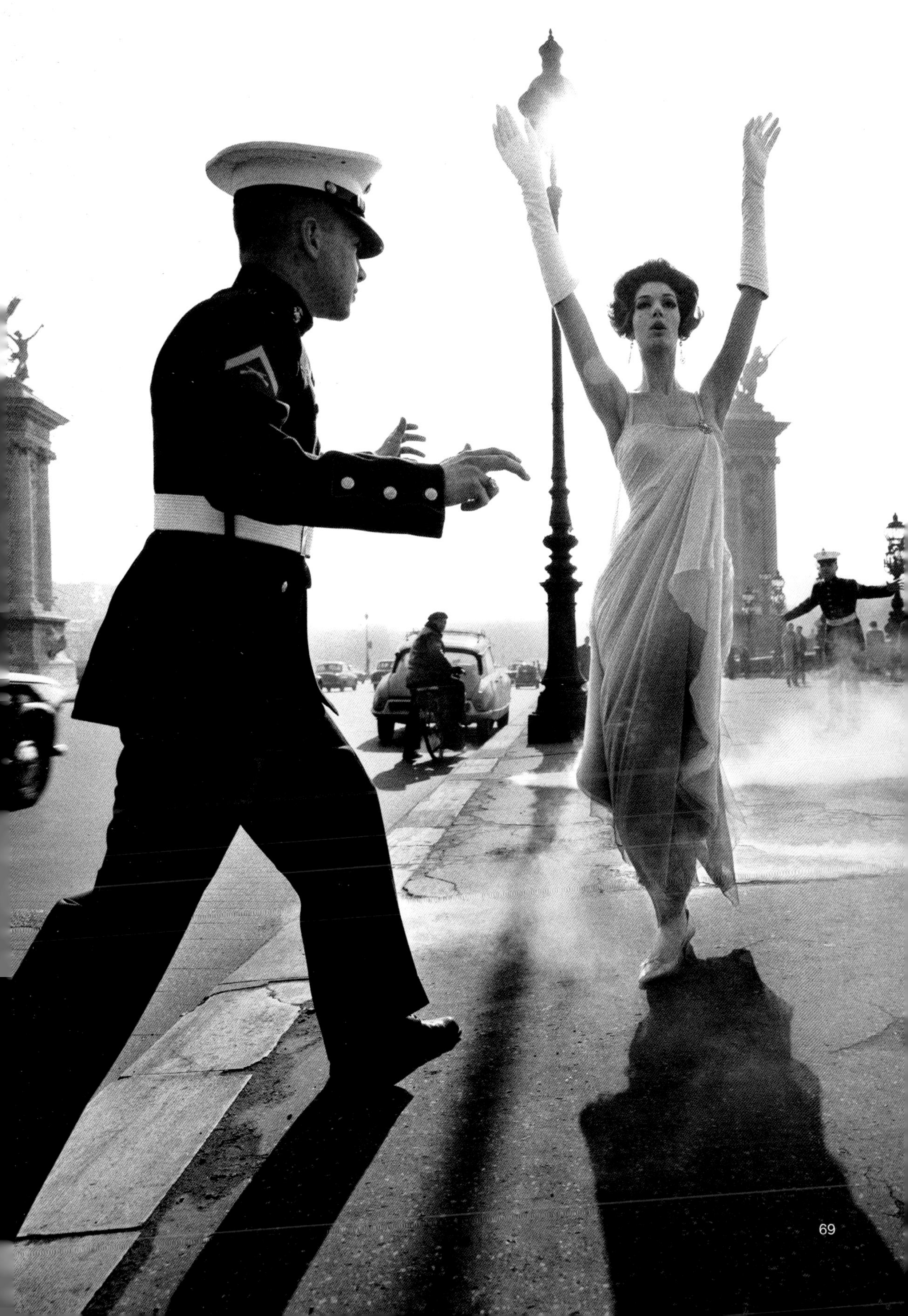

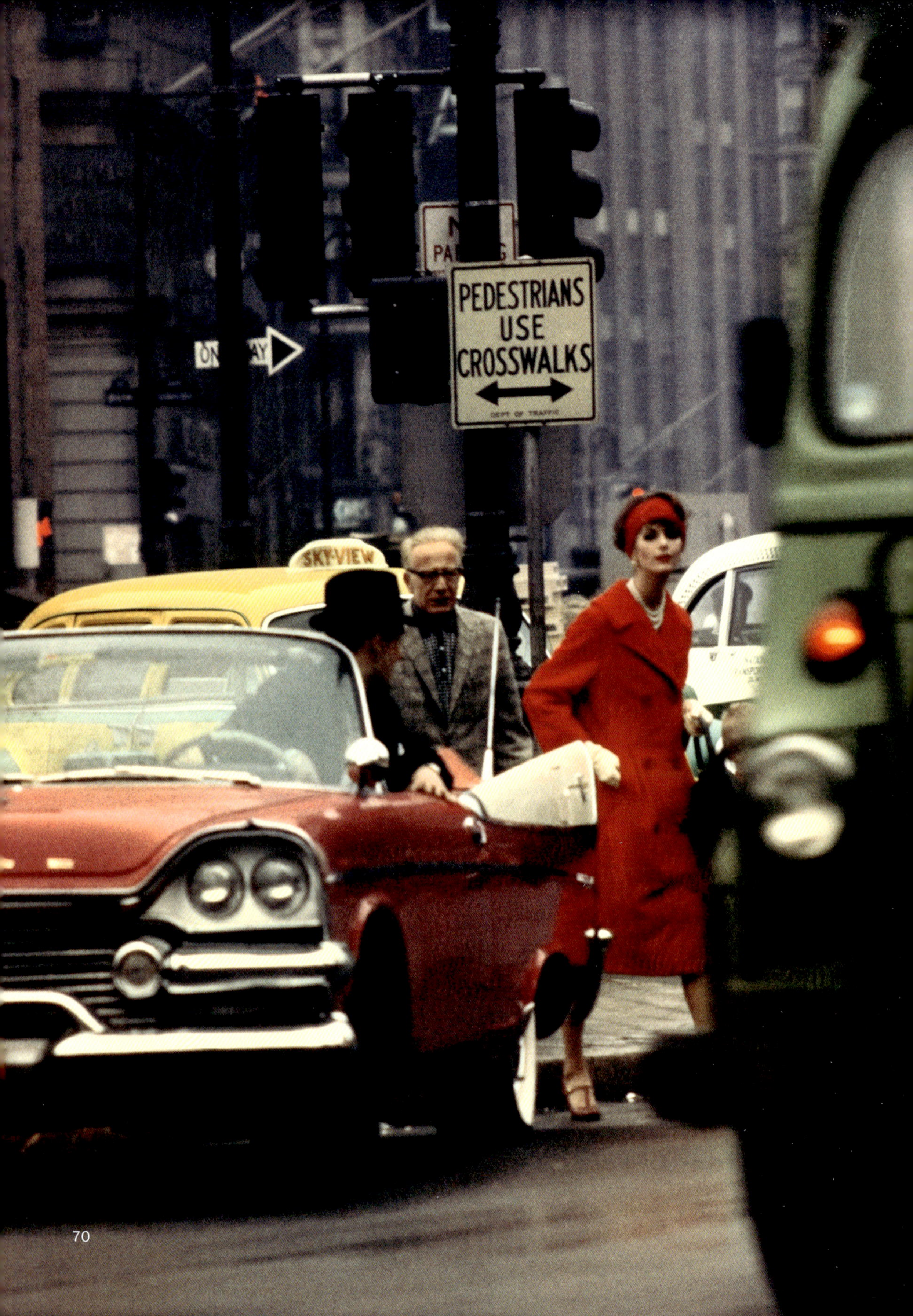
ONE WAY
PEDESTRIANS
USE
CROSSWALKS
DEPT OF TRAFFIC
SKY-VIEW

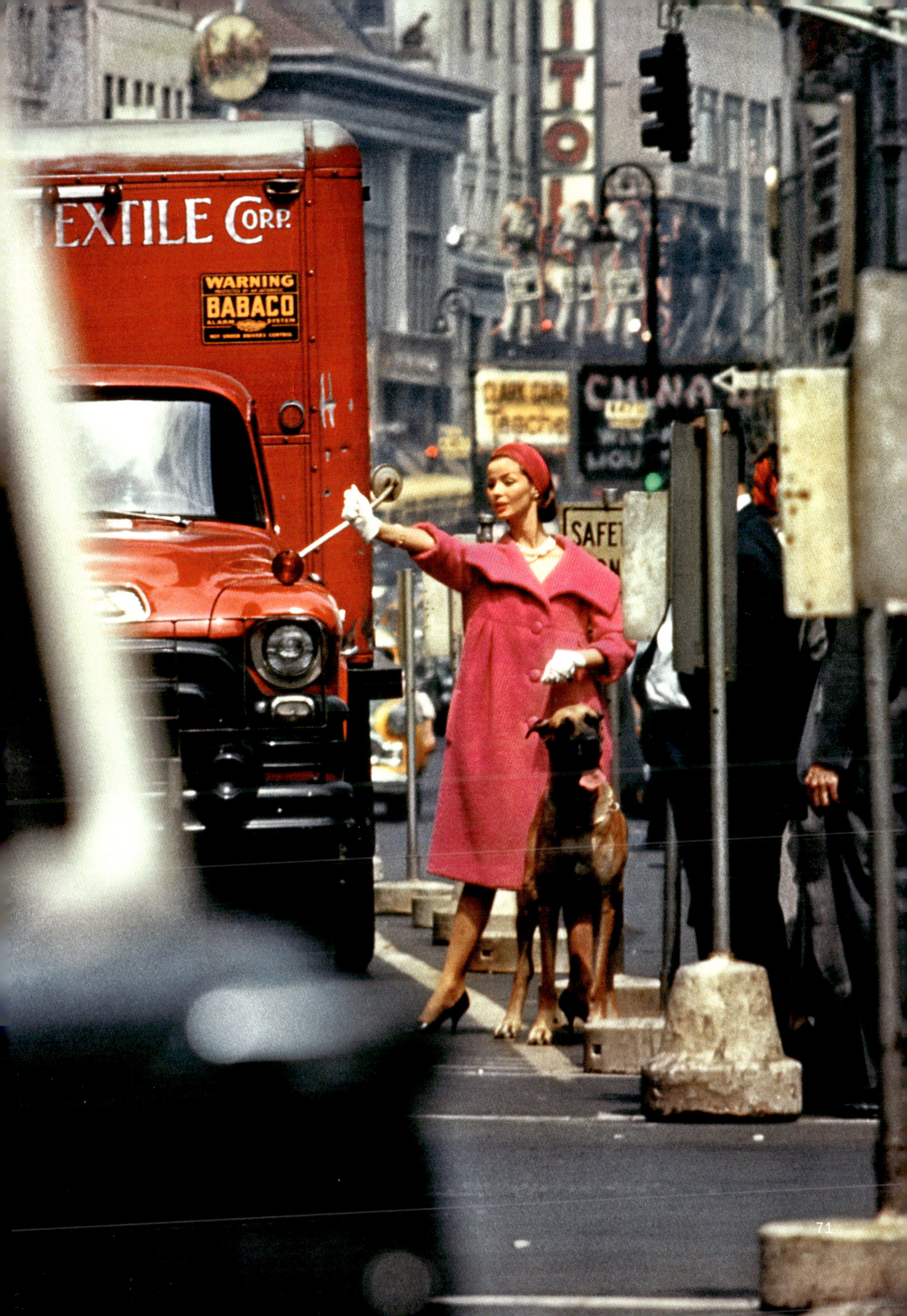
EXTILE CORP.
WARNING
BABACO
ALARM SYSTEM
SAFE

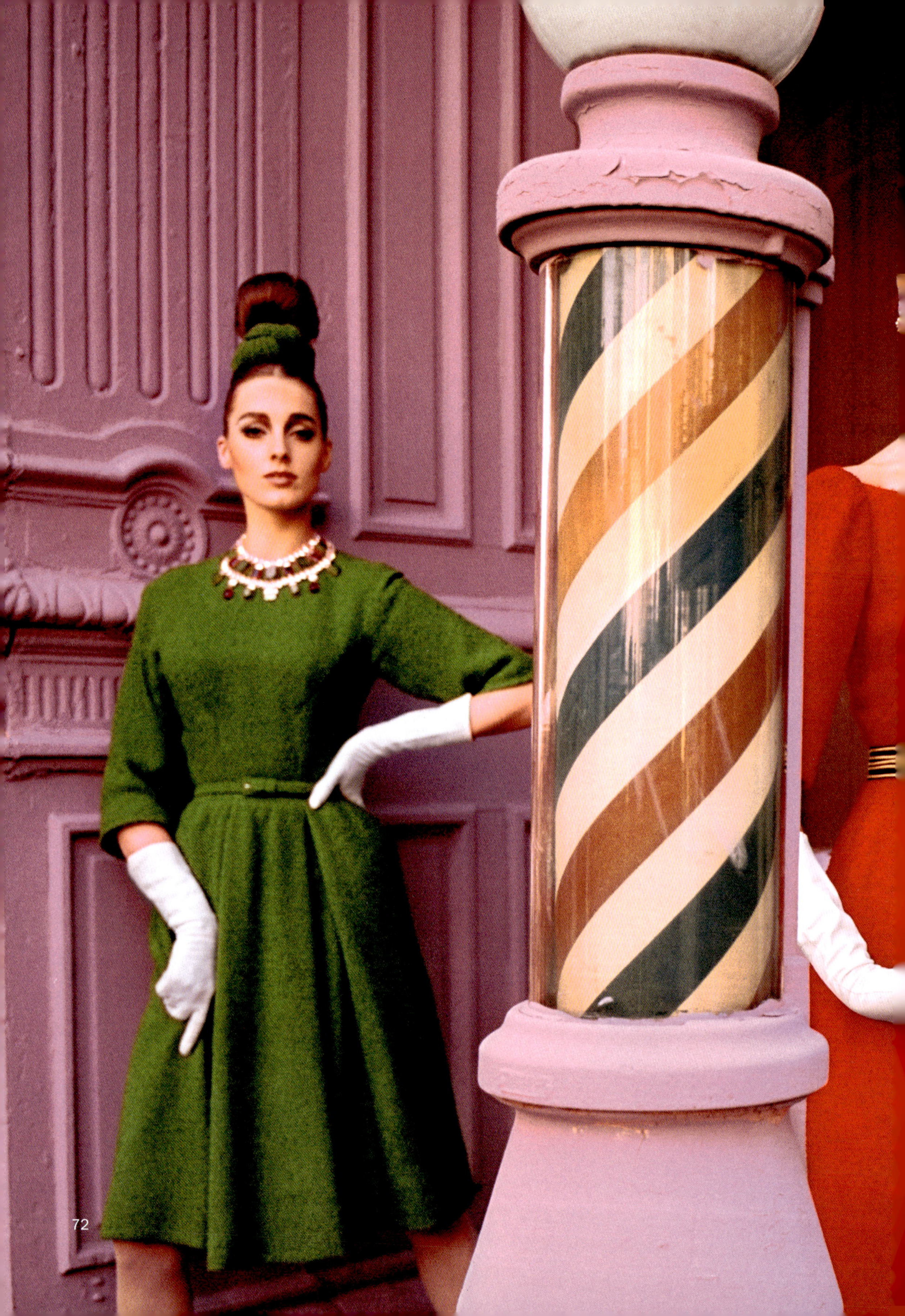

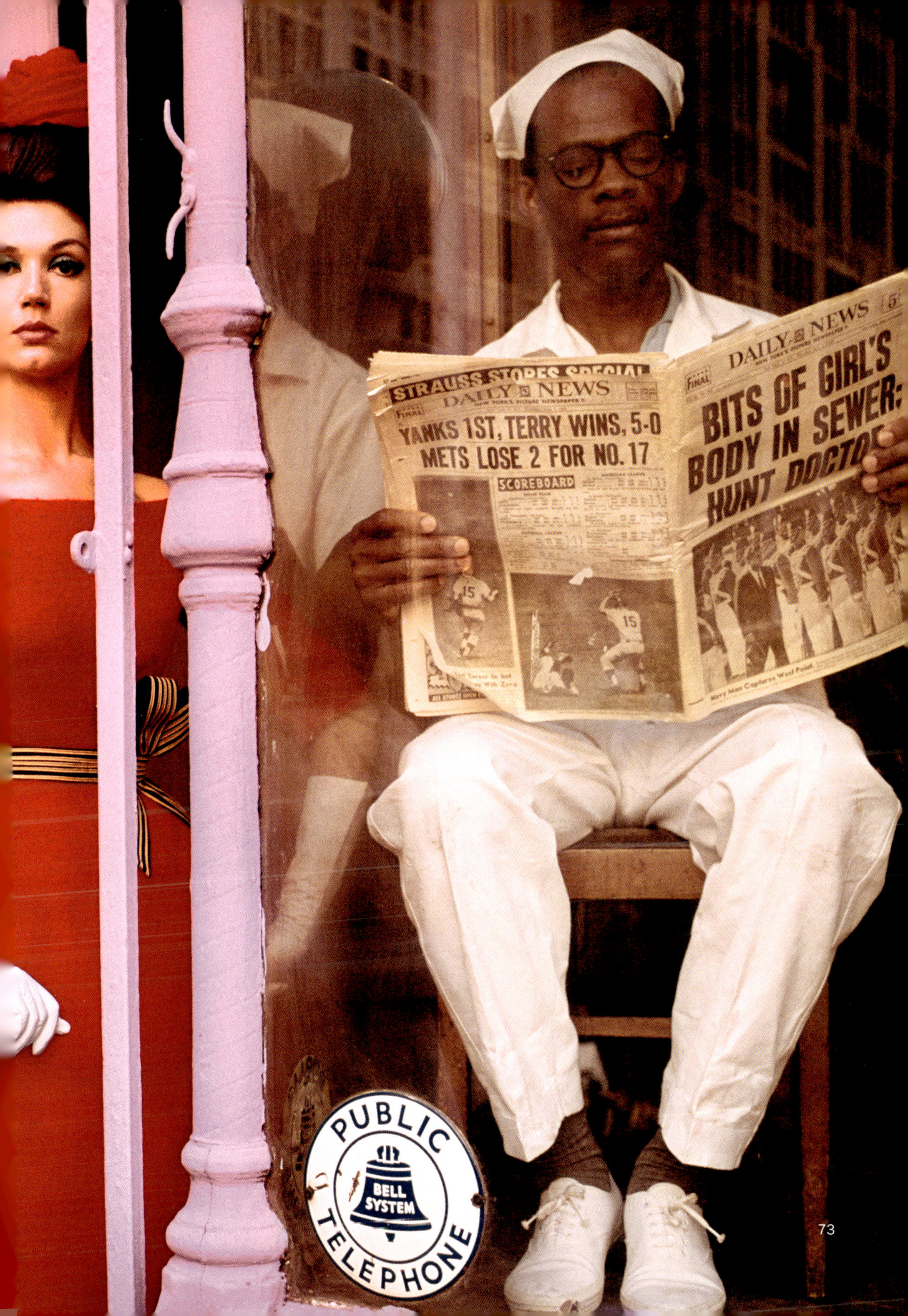

STRAUSS STORES SPECIAL
DAILY NEWS
NEW YORK'S PICTURE NEWSPAPER
FINAL
YANKS 1ST, TERRY WINS, 5-0
METS LOSE 2 FOR NO. 17
SCOREBOARD
DAILY NEWS
5¢
Final
BITS OF GIRL'S
BODY IN SEWER:
HUNT DOCTOR
PUBLIC TELEPHONE
BELL SYSTEM

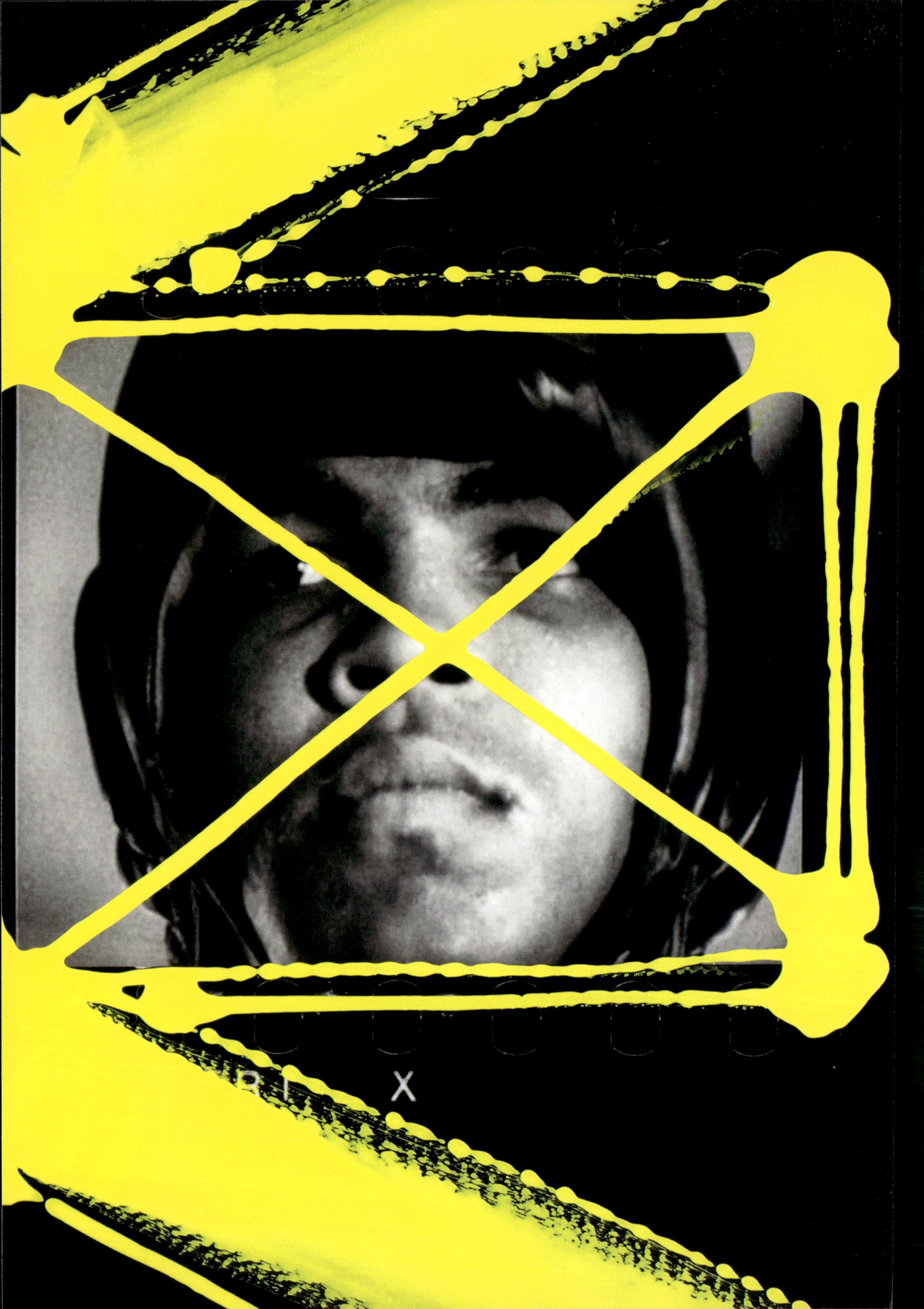
RIX X

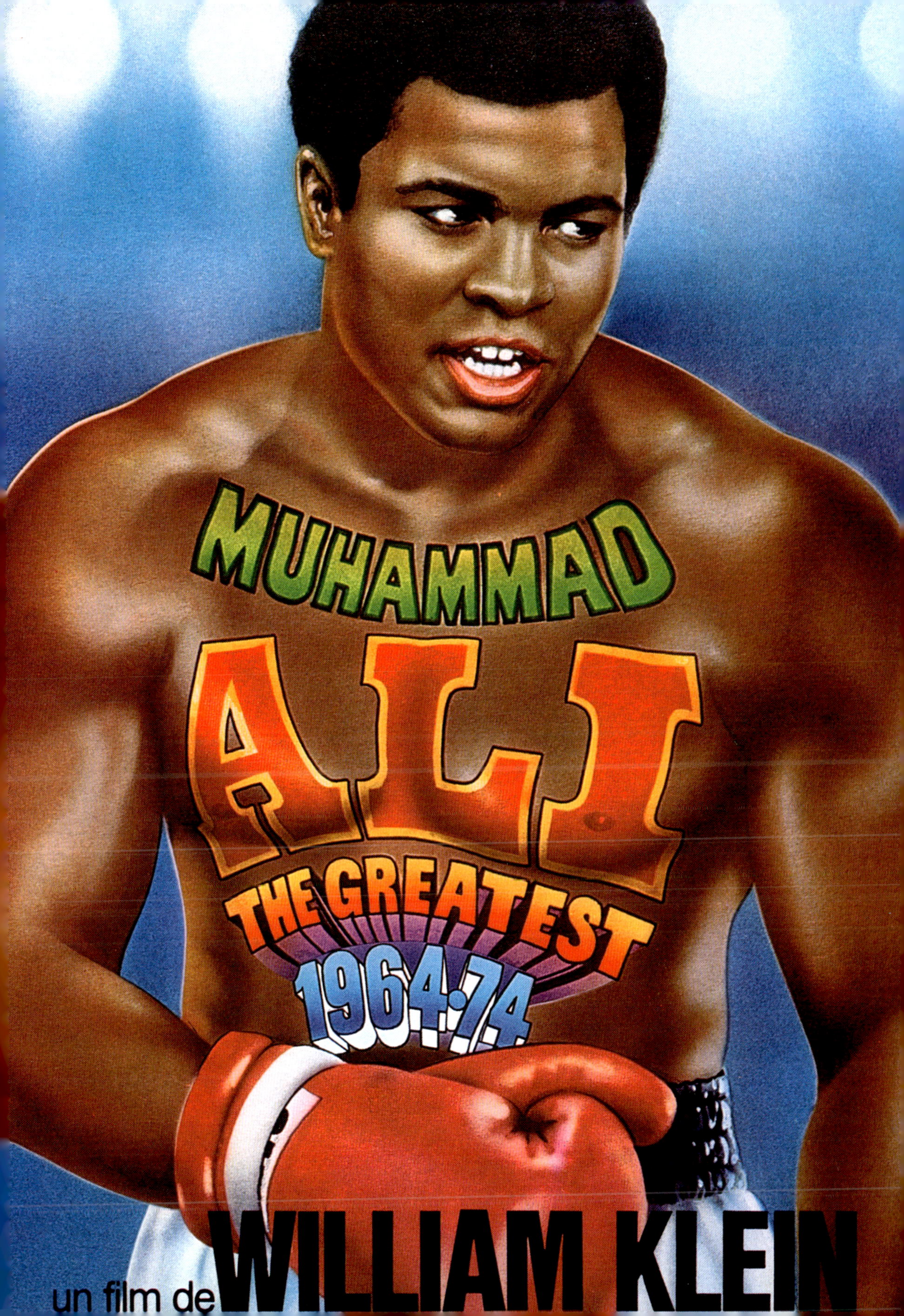

MUHAMMAD
ALI
THE GREATEST
1964-74
WILLIAM KLEIN
un film de

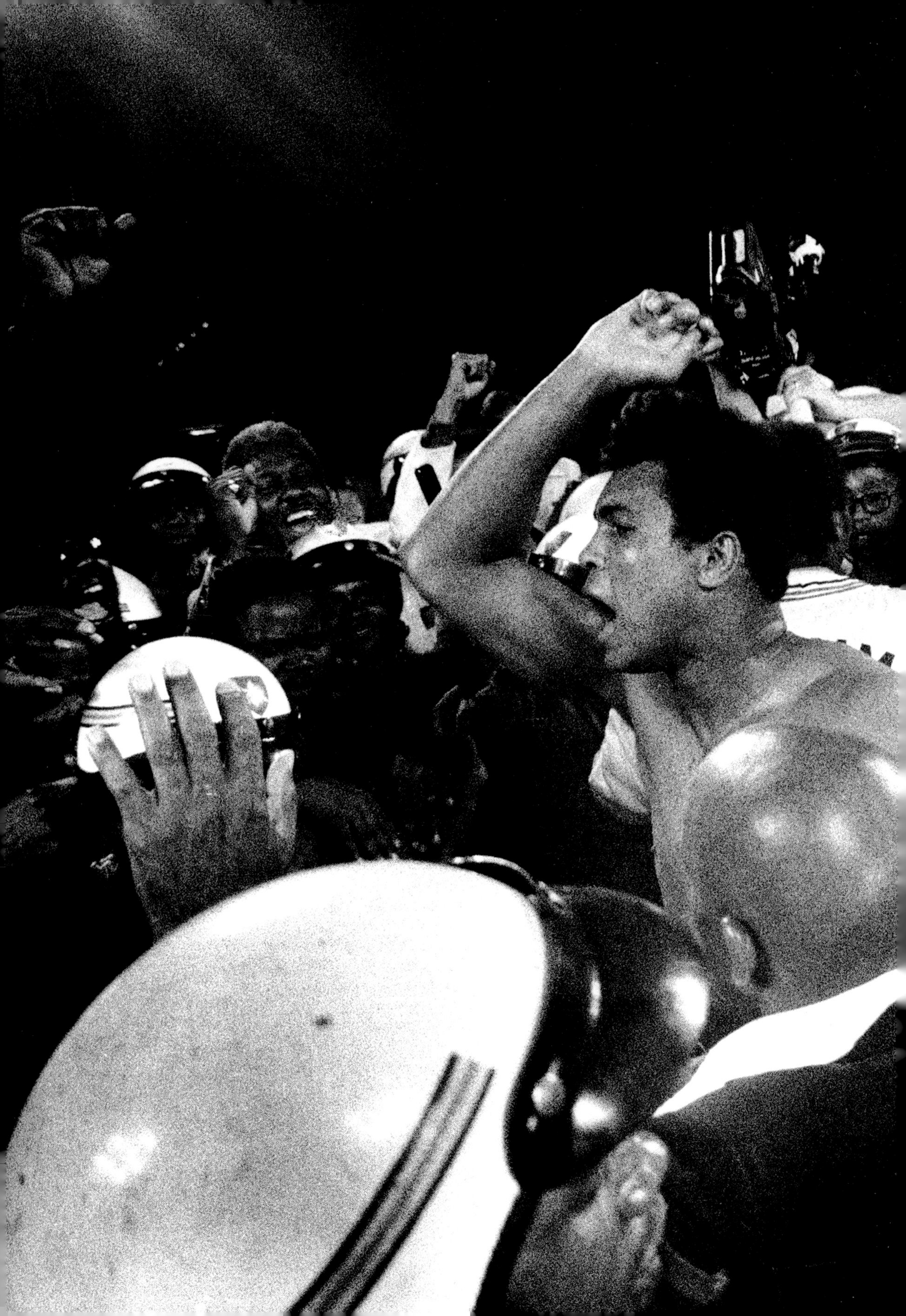

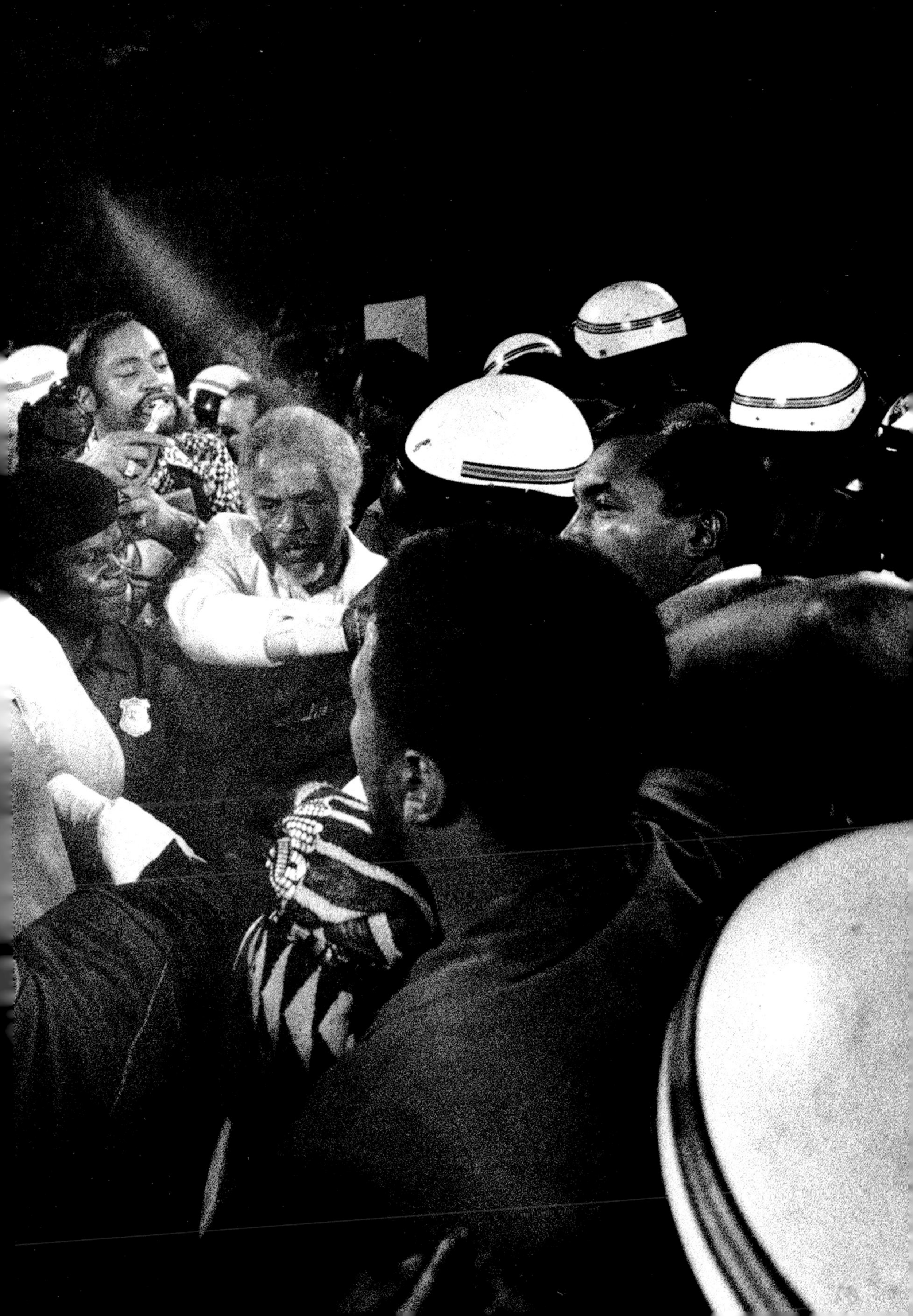

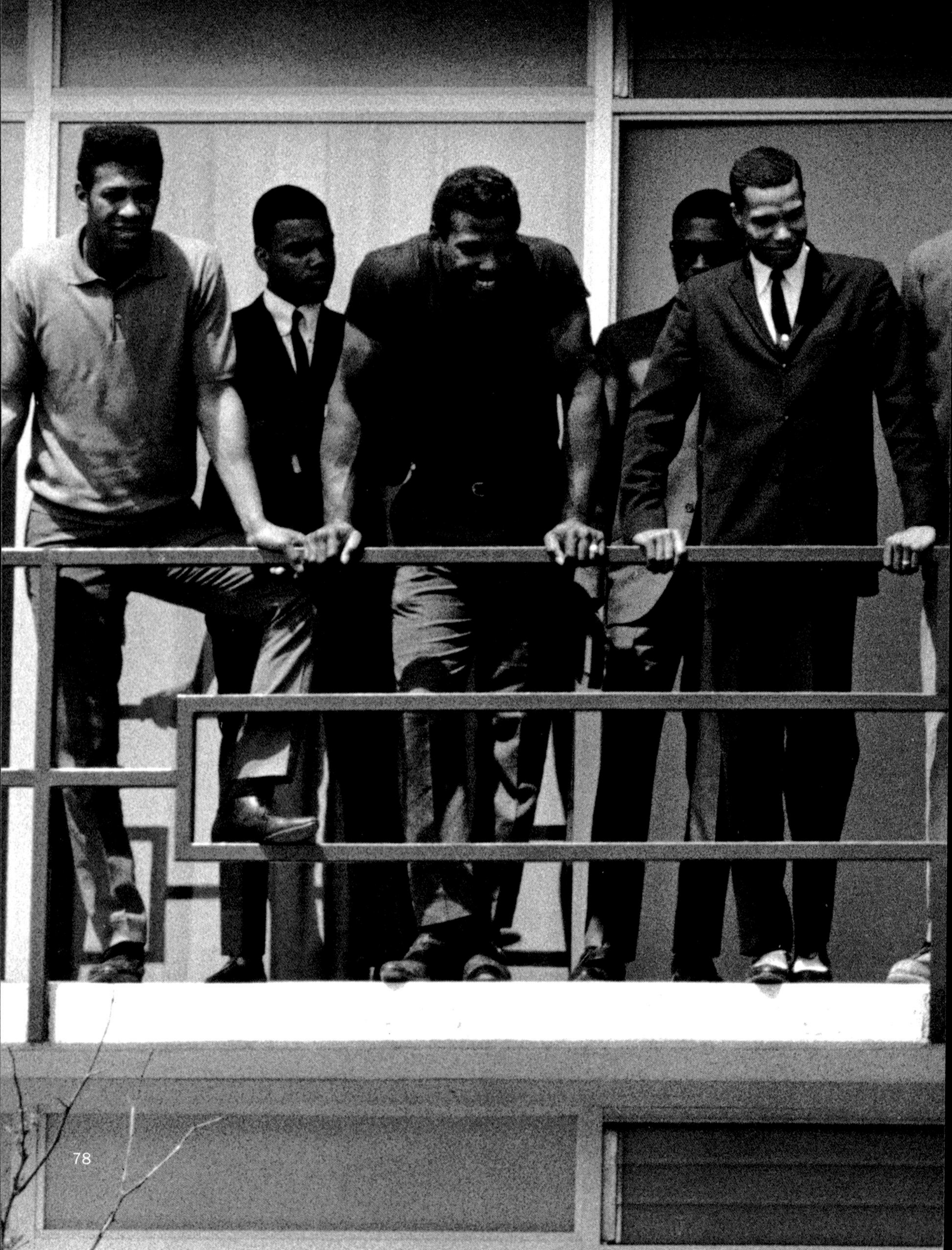

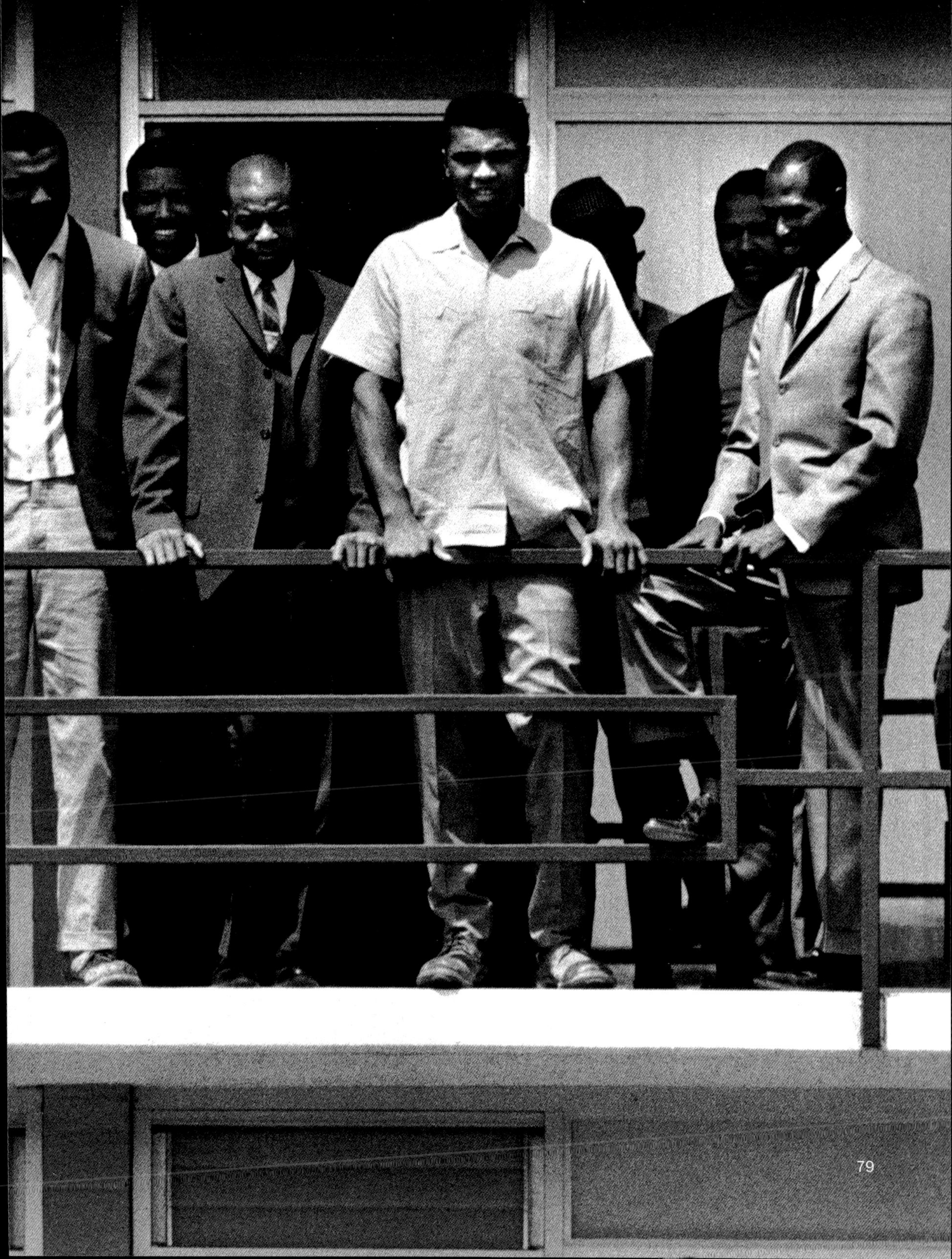

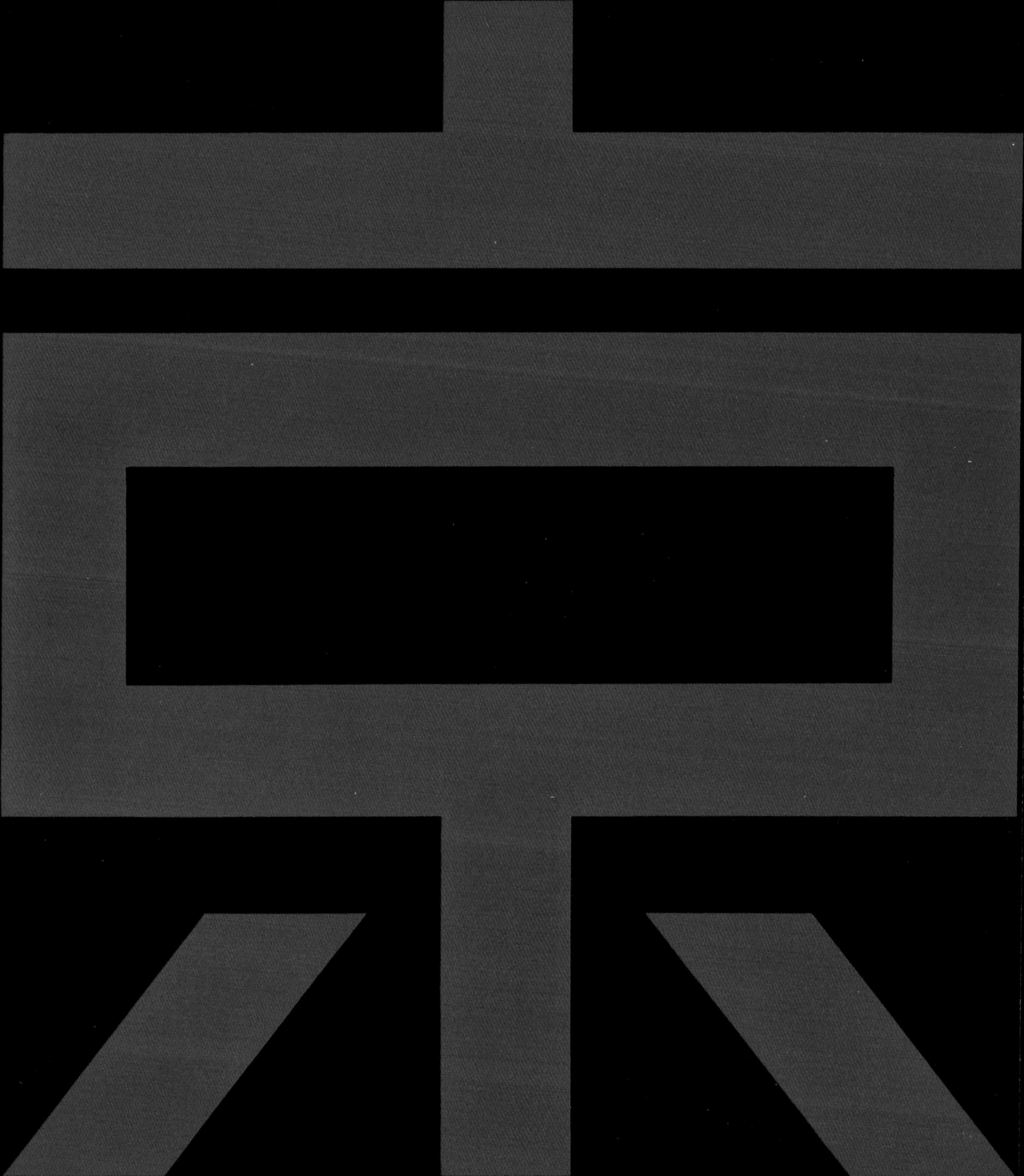

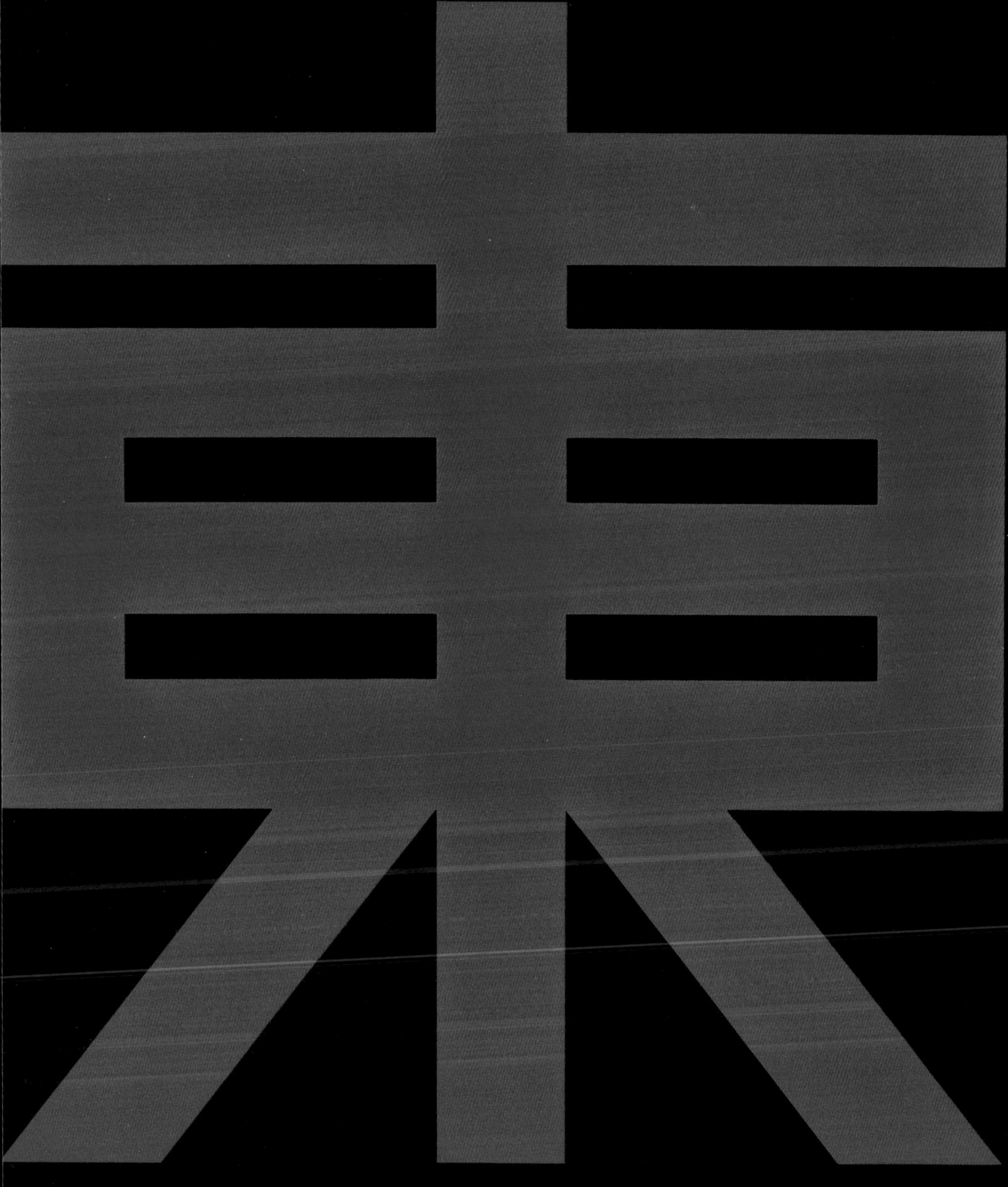

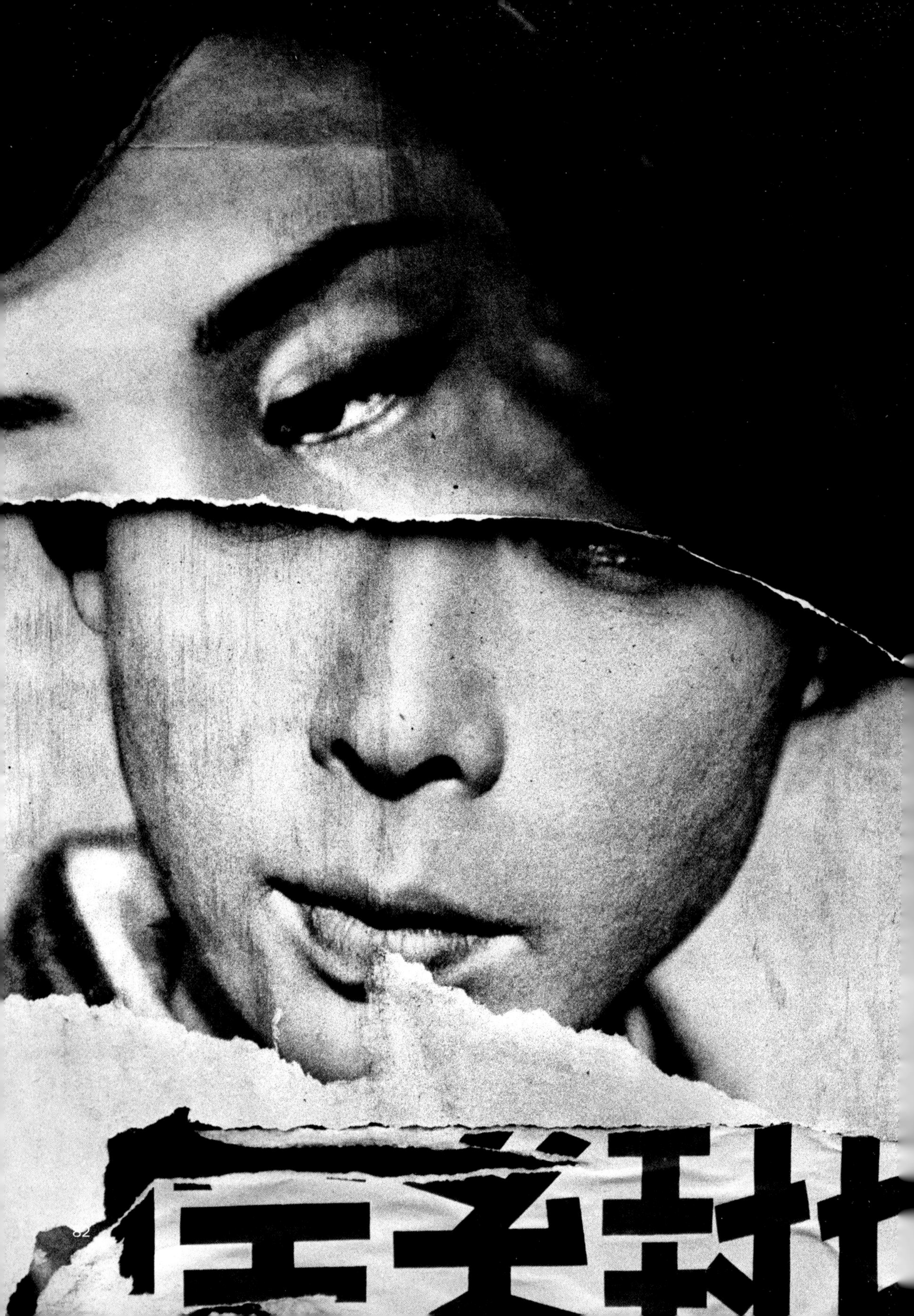
82

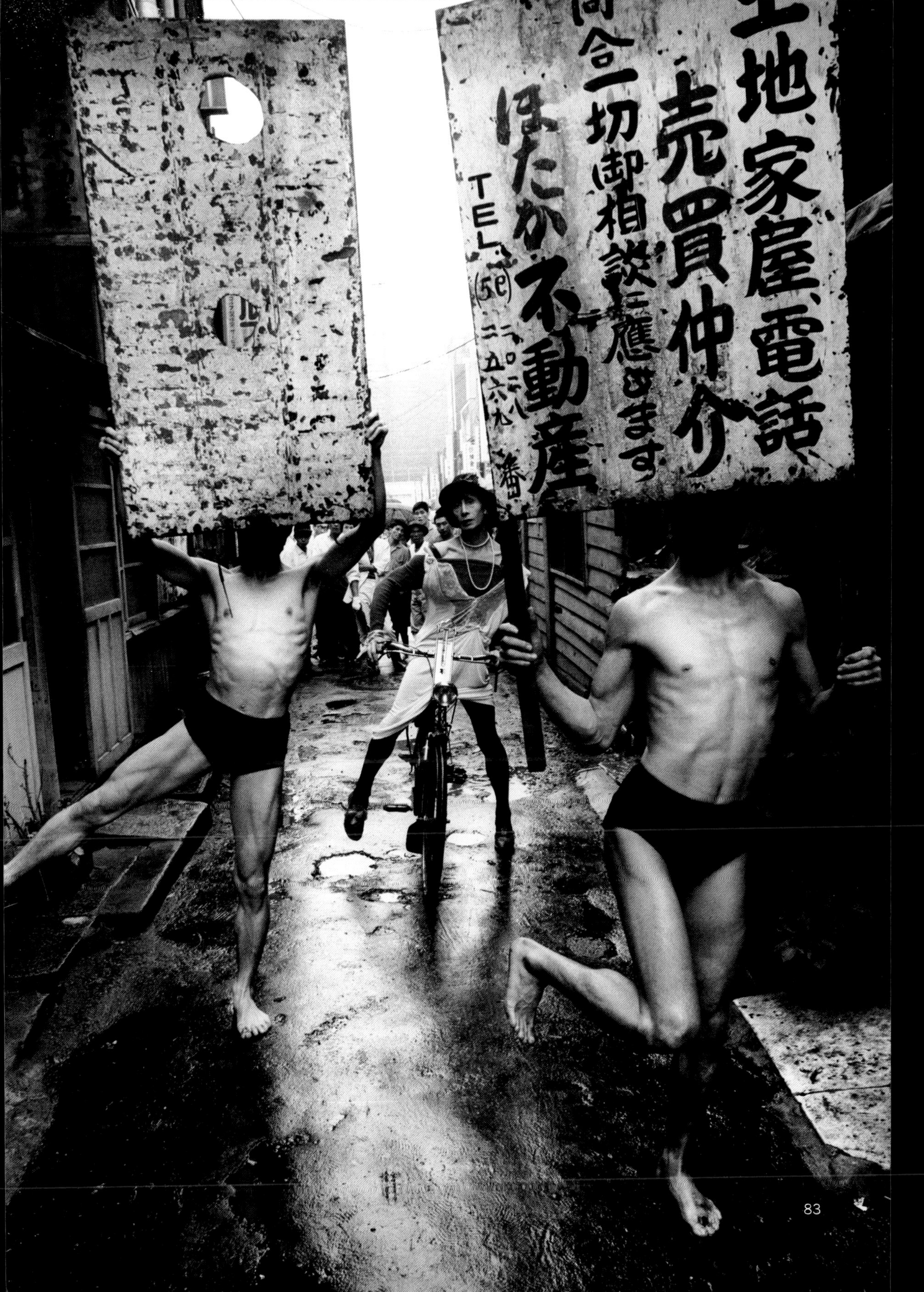
土地、家屋、電話
土地売買仲介
同合一切御相談に應じます
ほたか不動産
TEL.(5e)二五六八一番

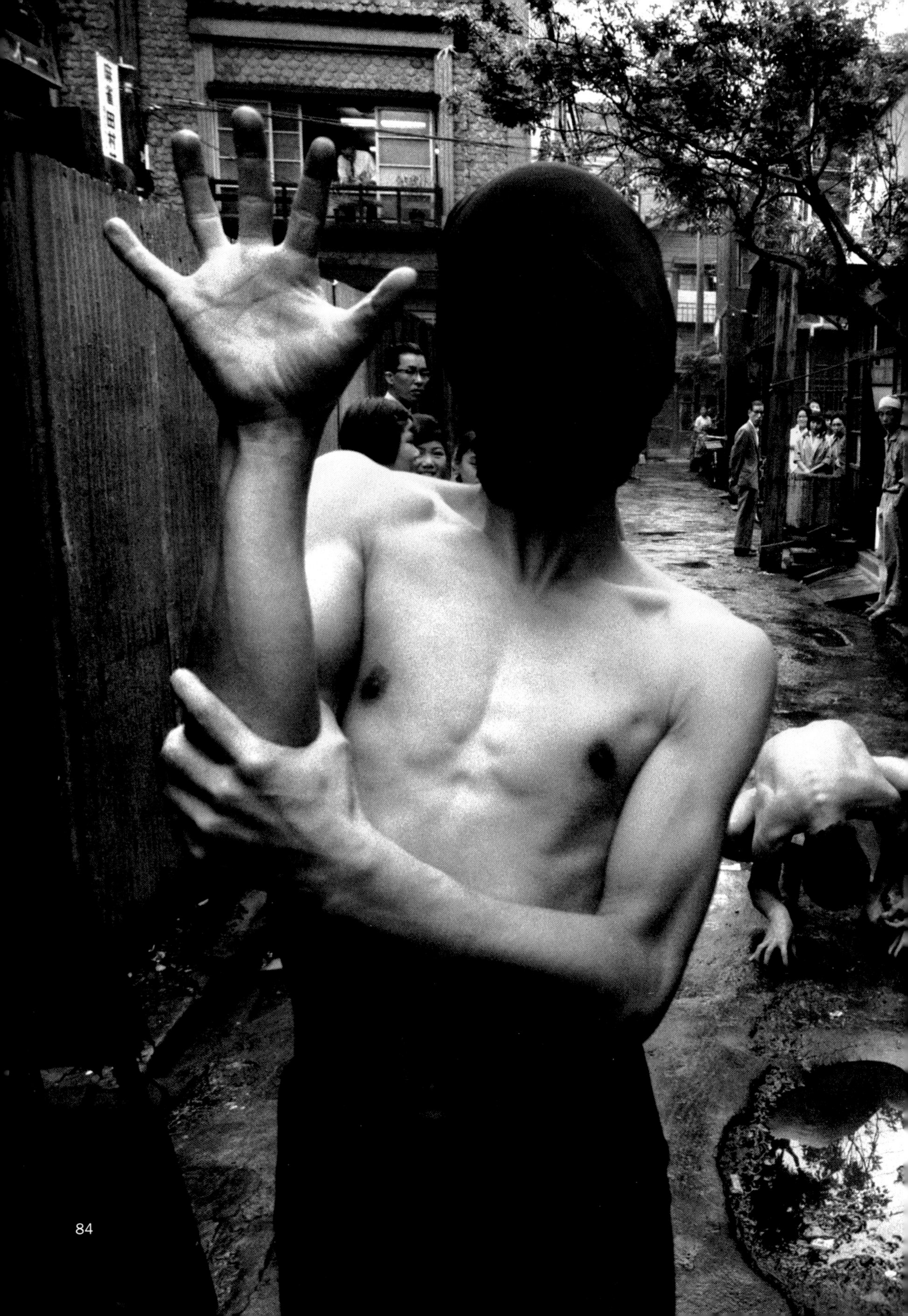

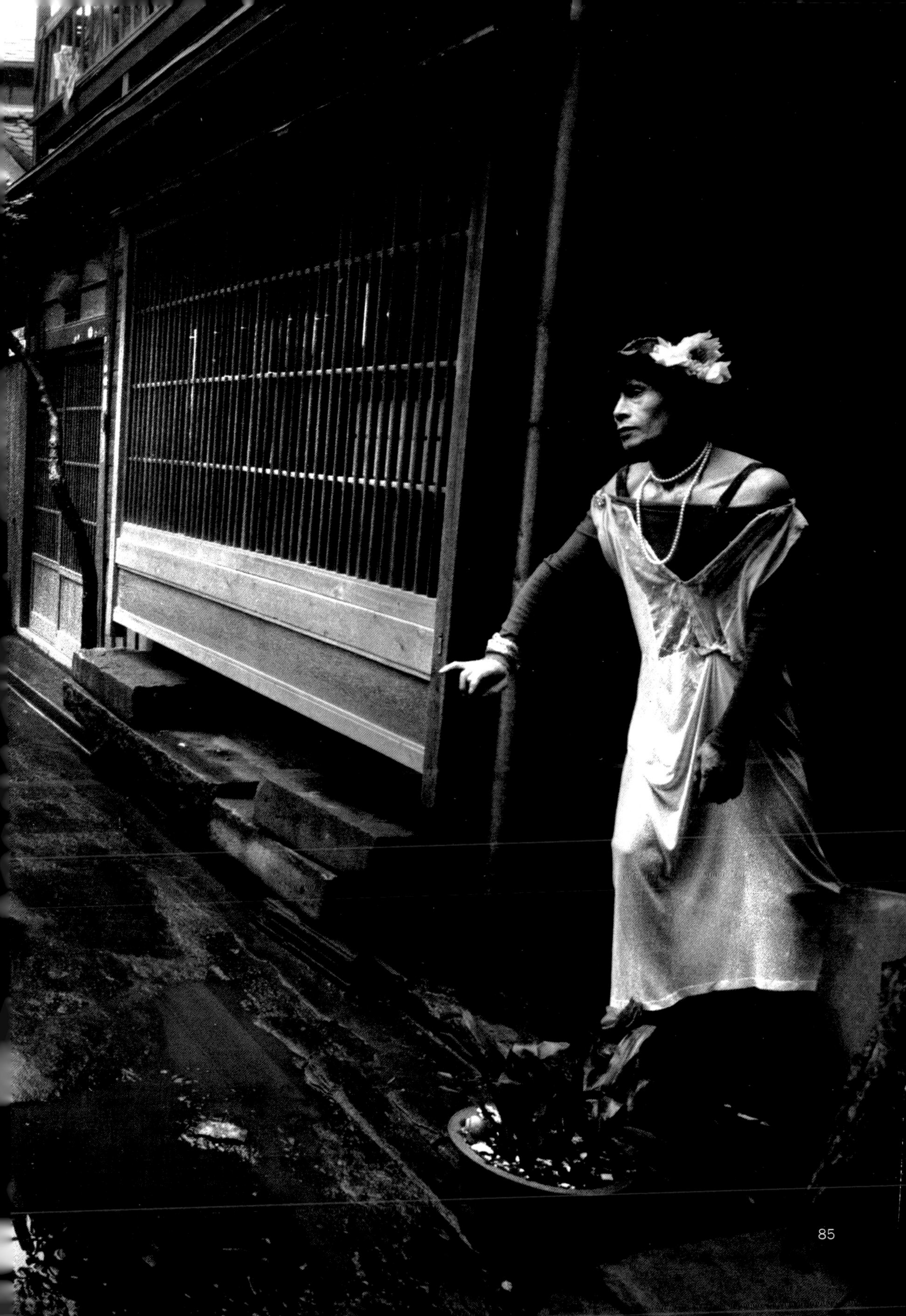

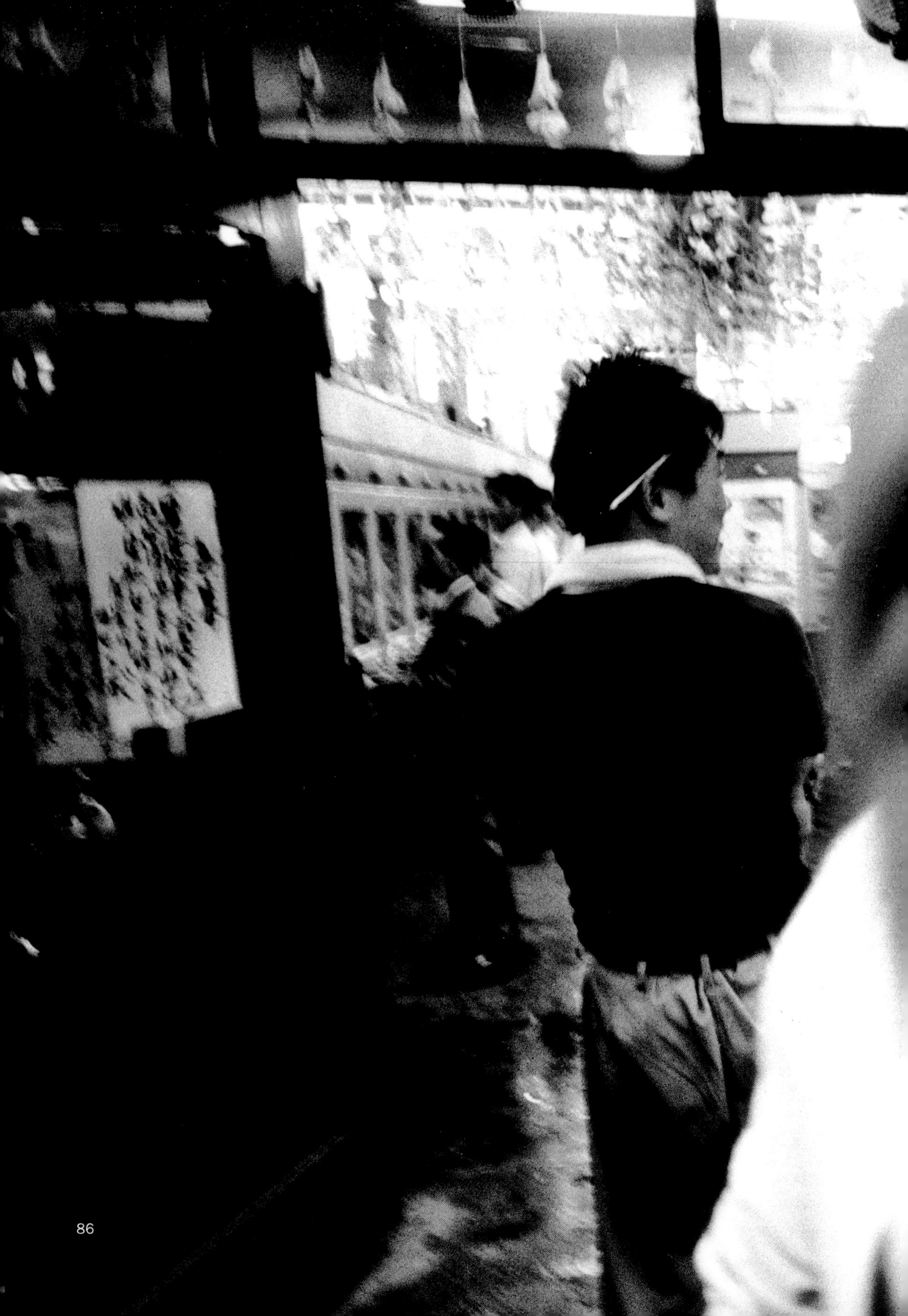

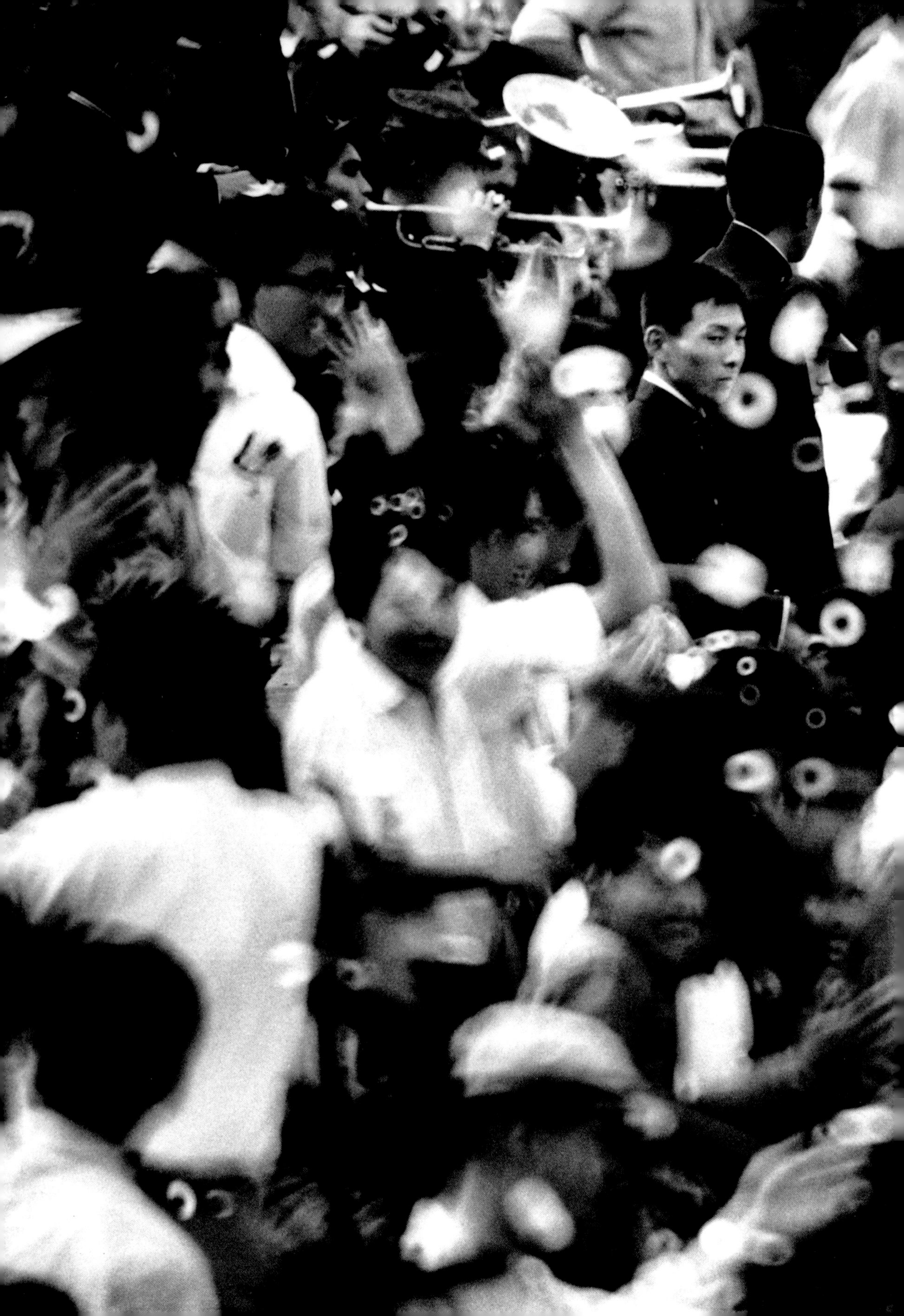

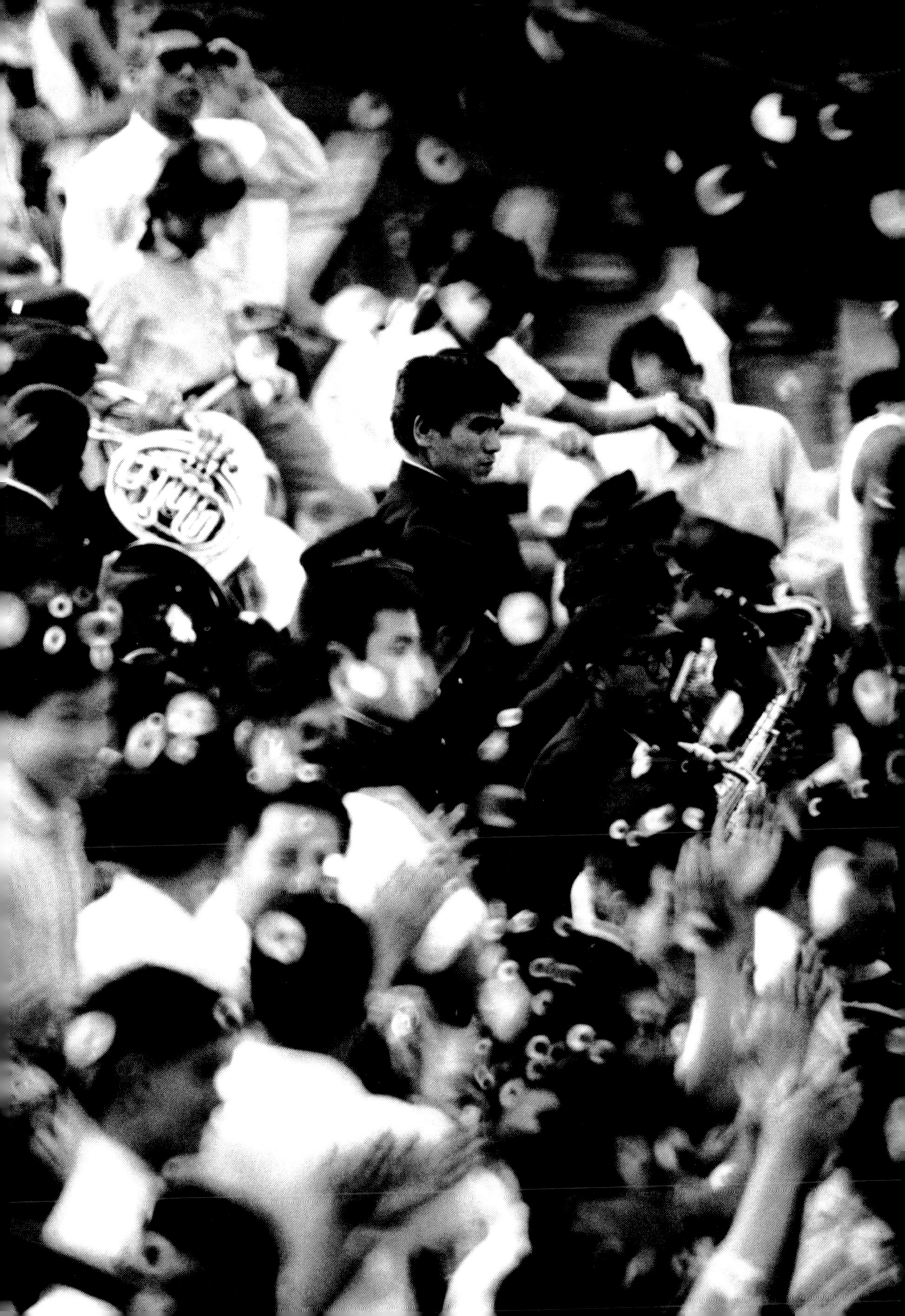

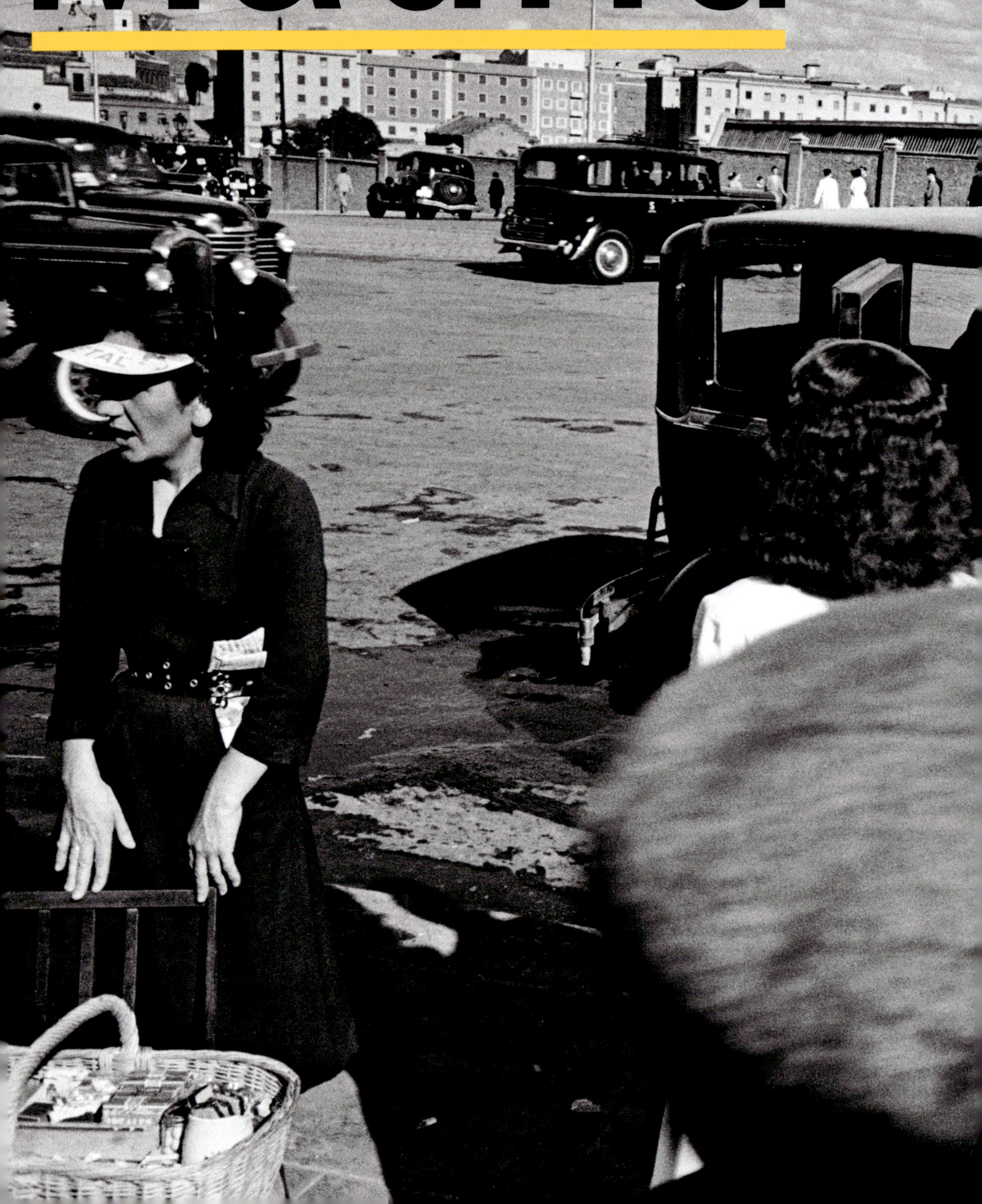

Madrid

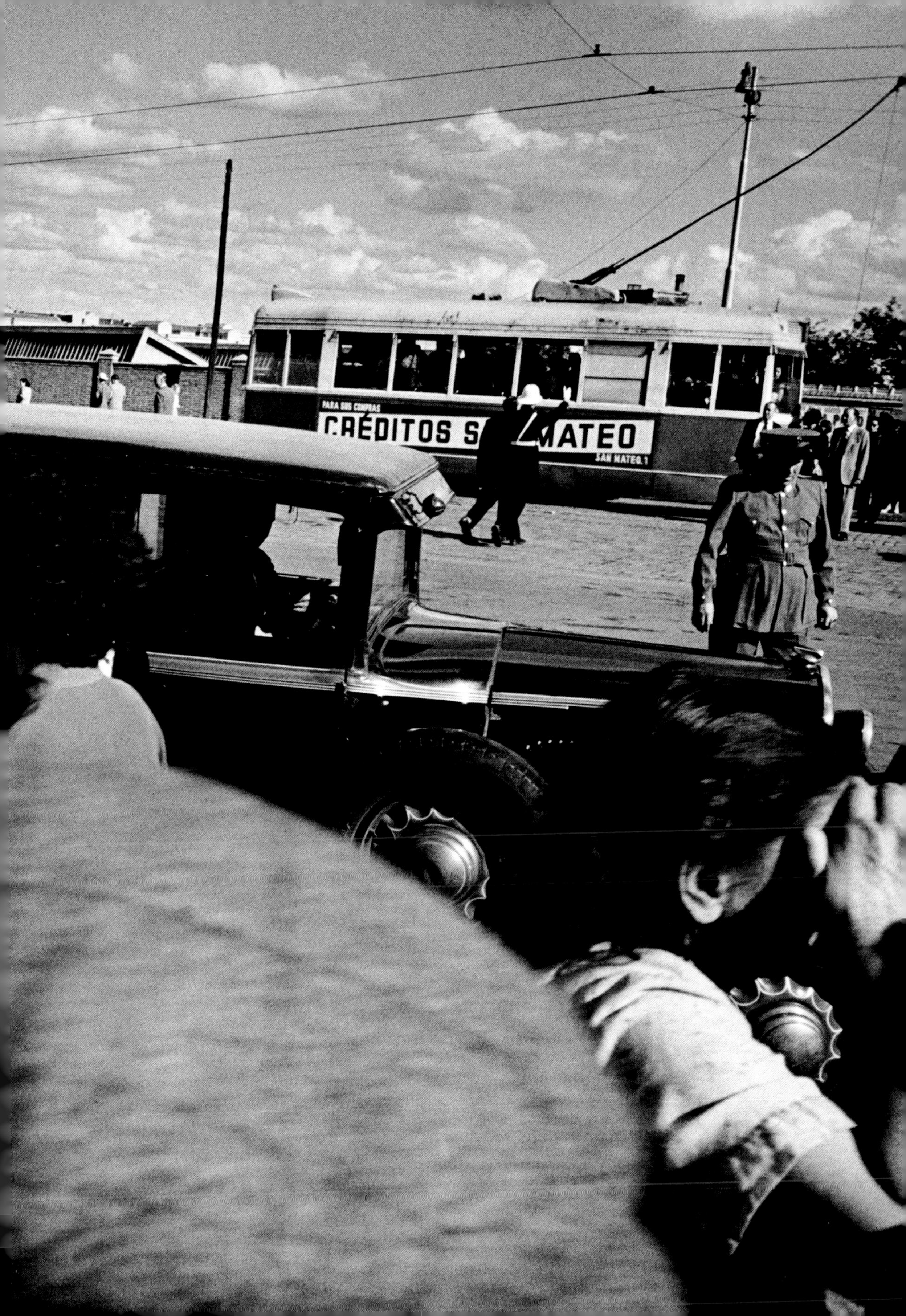
PARA SUS COMPRAS
CRÉDITOS SAN MATEO
SAN MATEO, 1

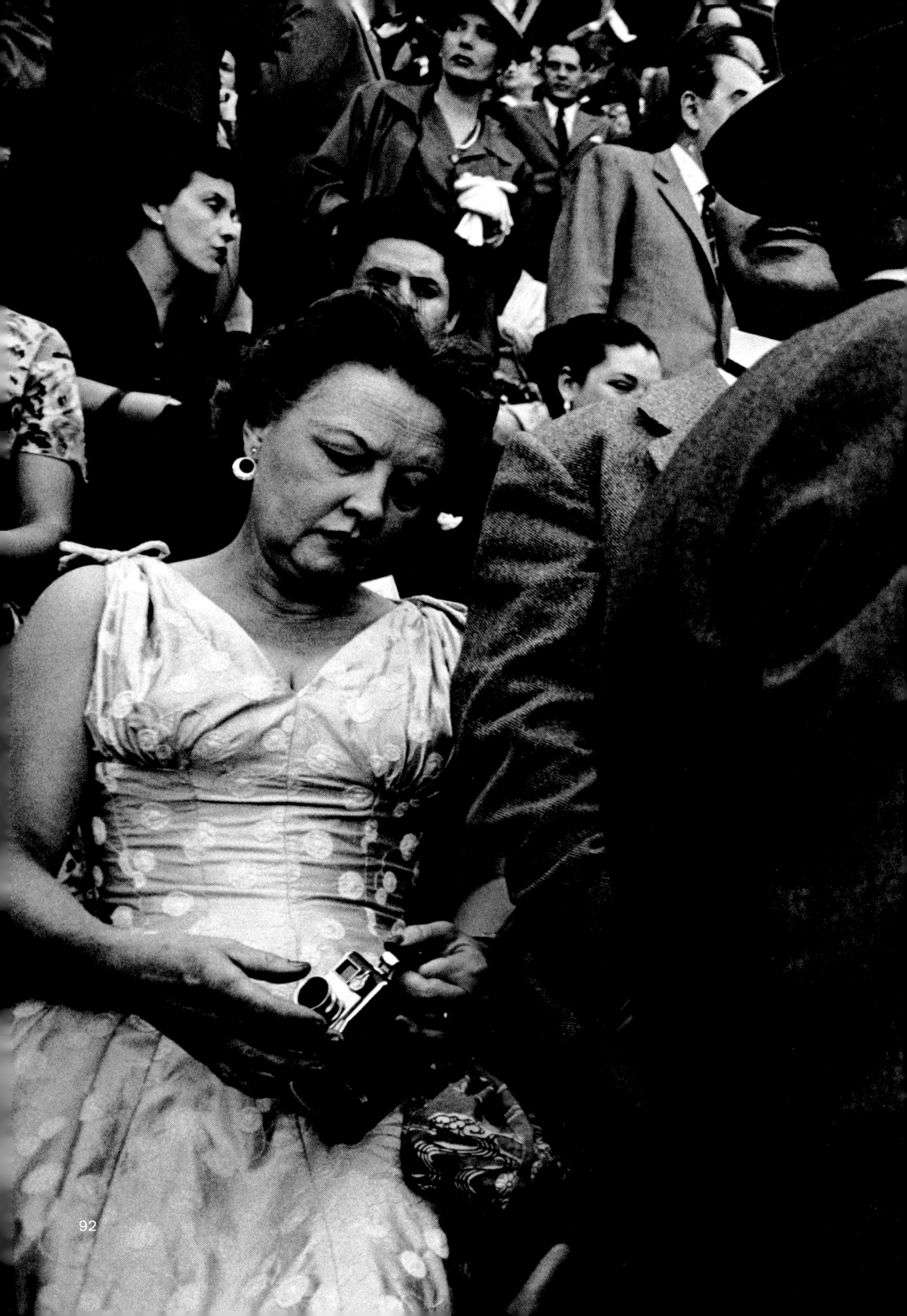

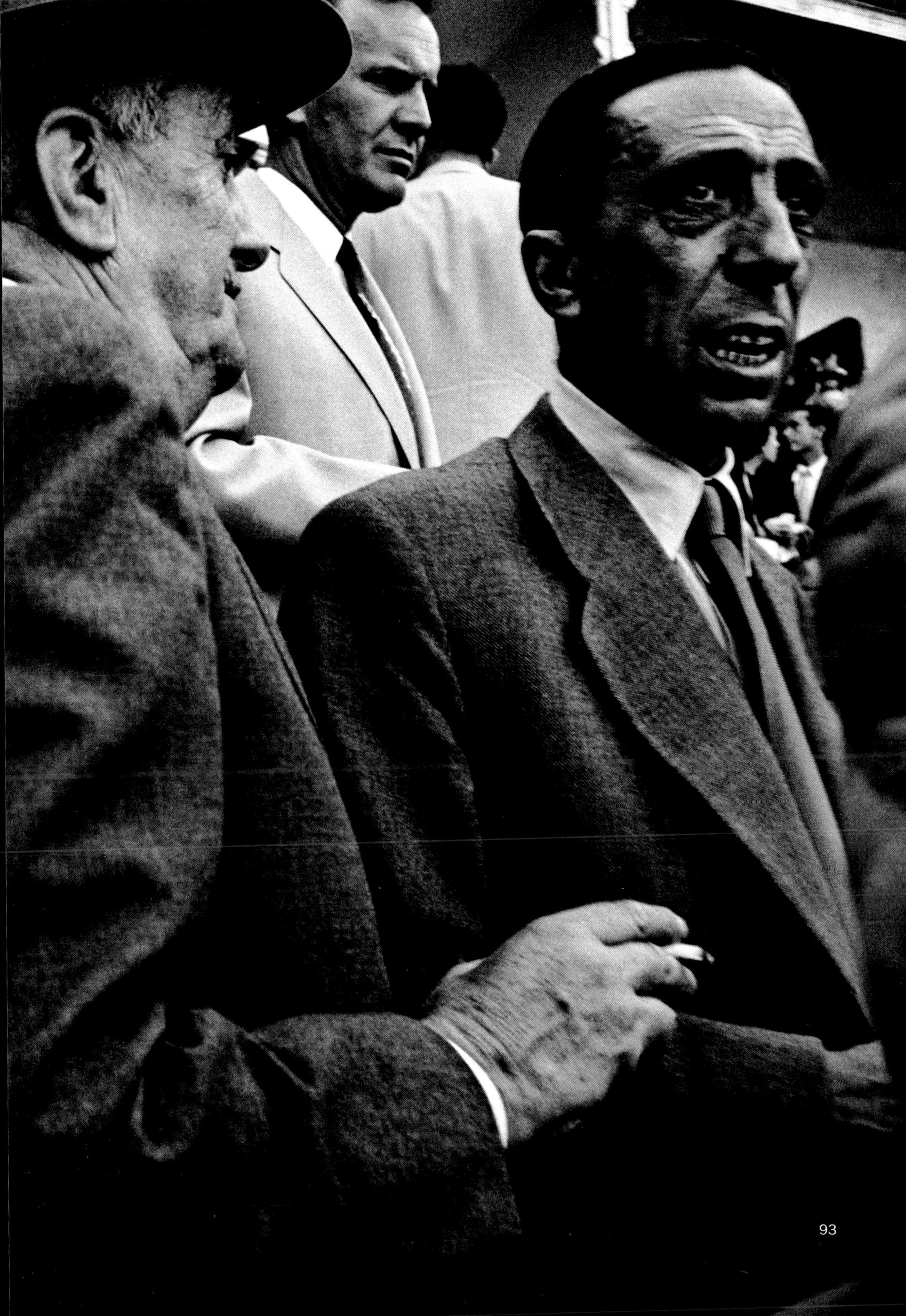

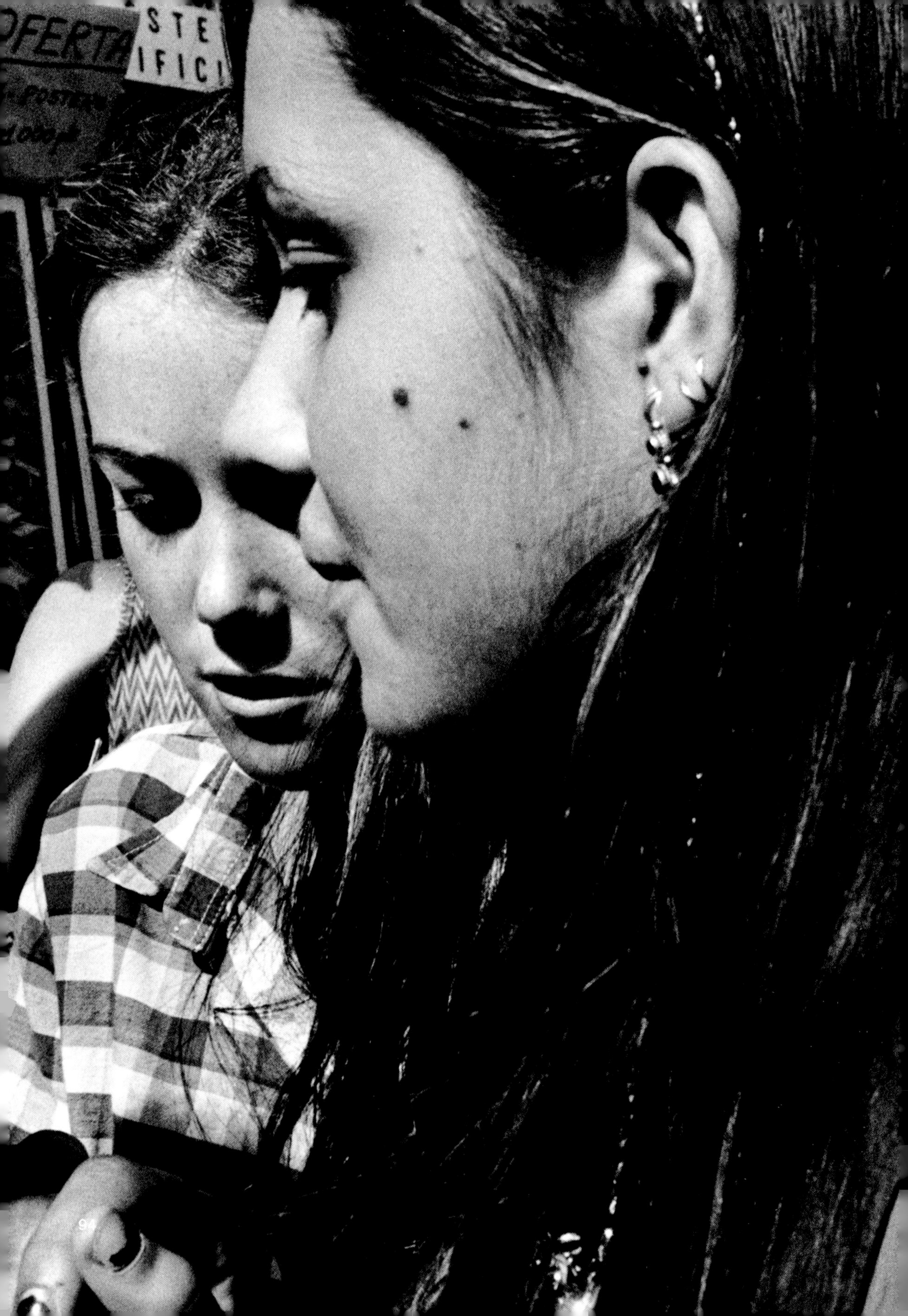
OFERTA
STE
IFICI

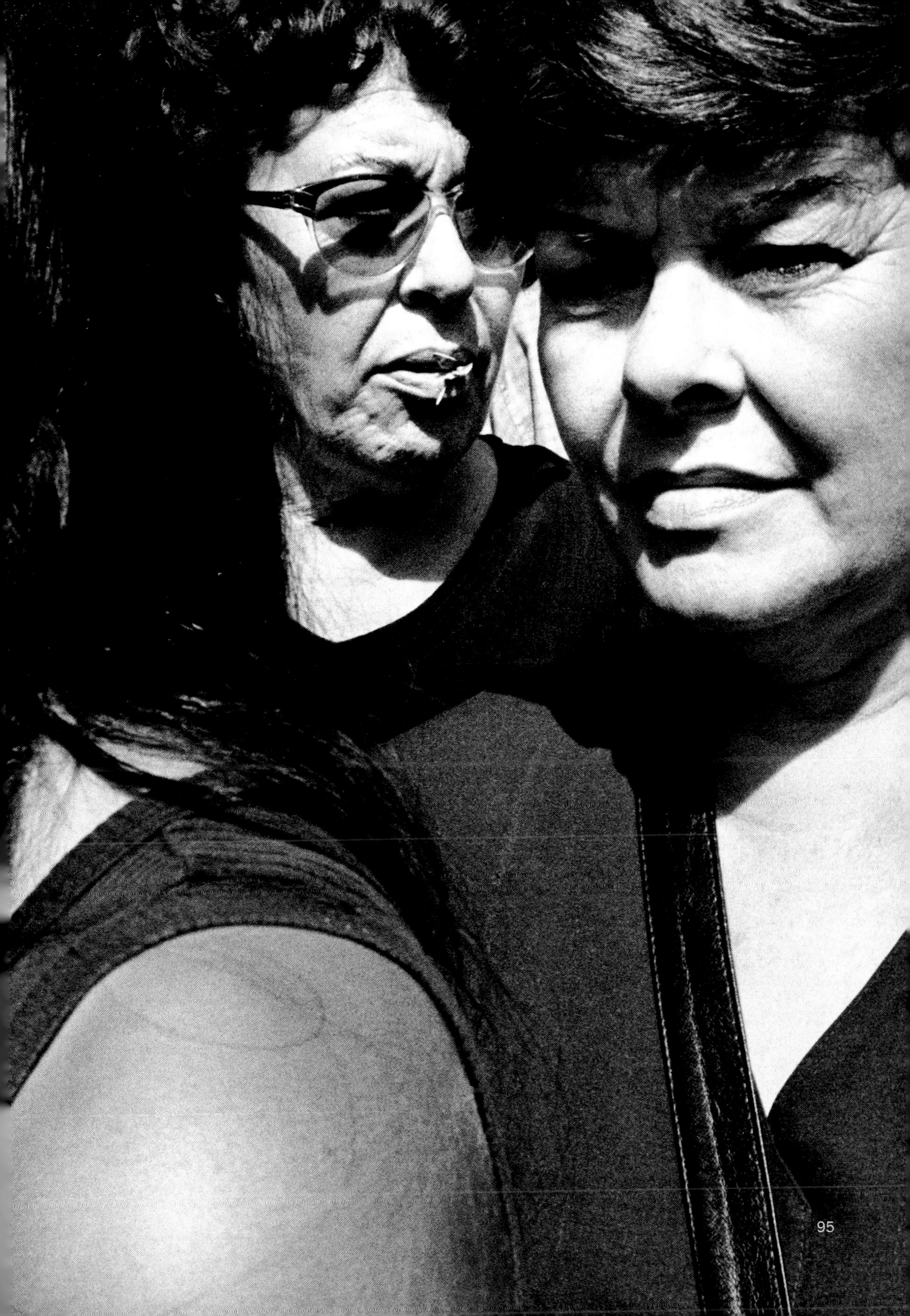

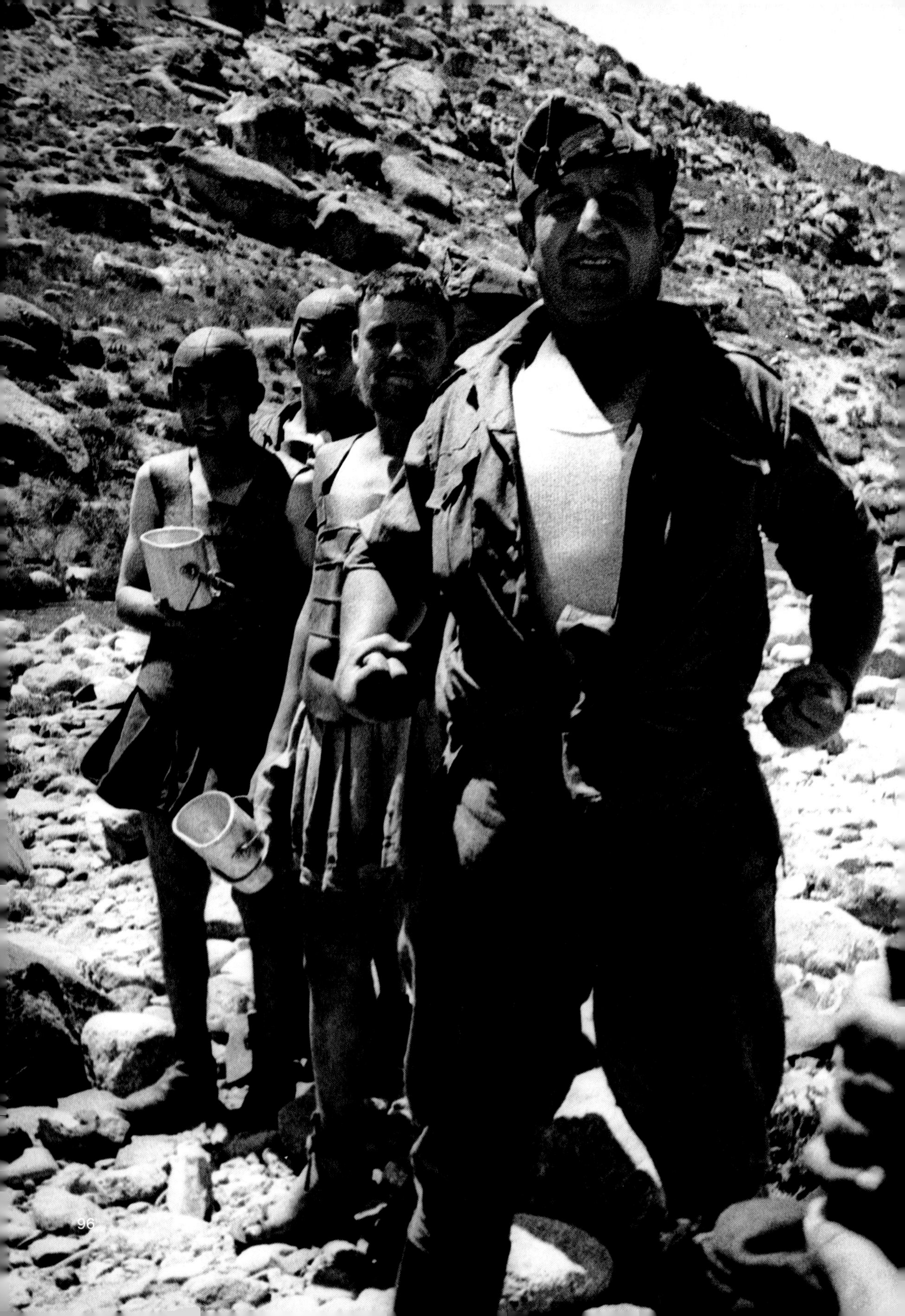

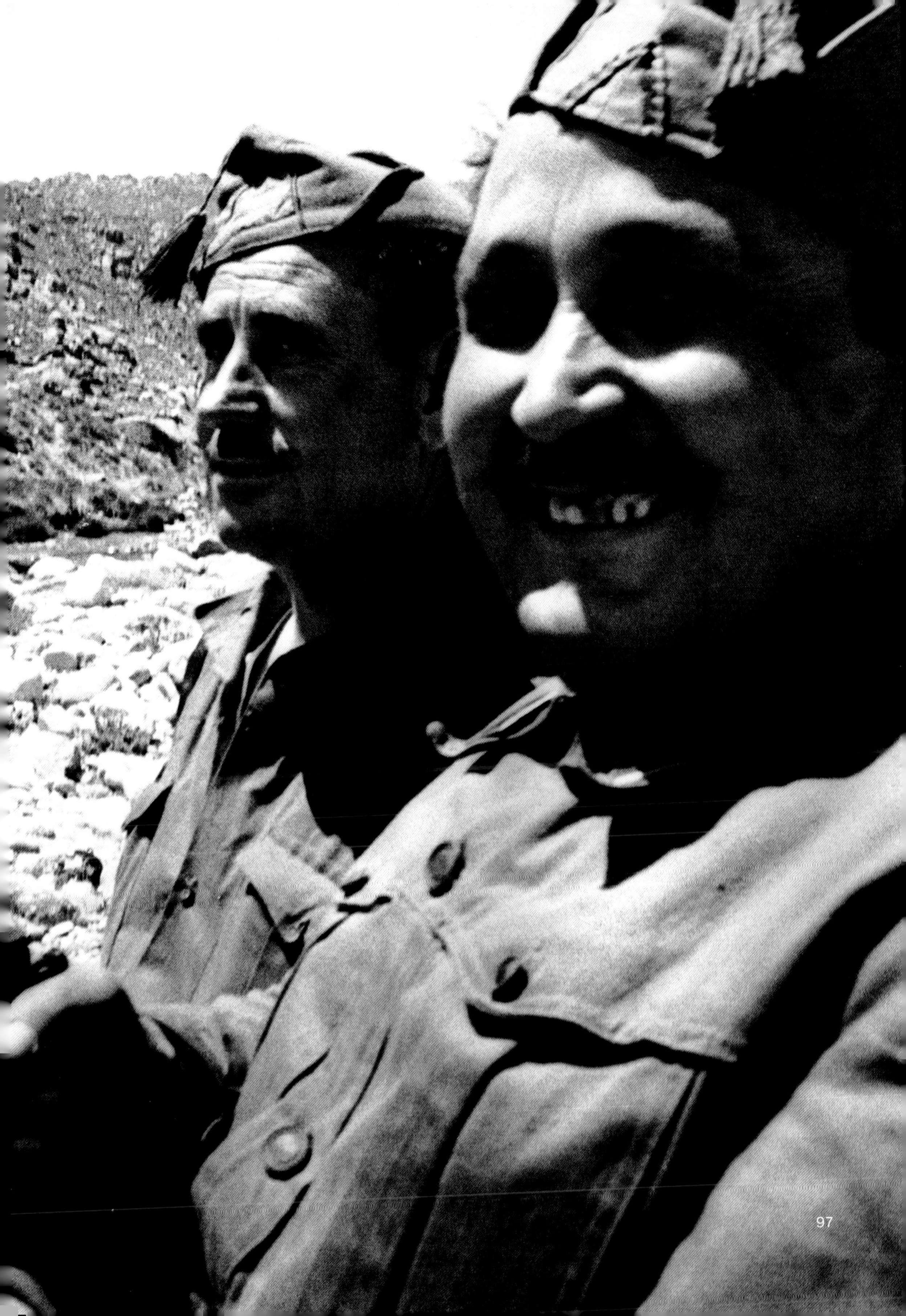

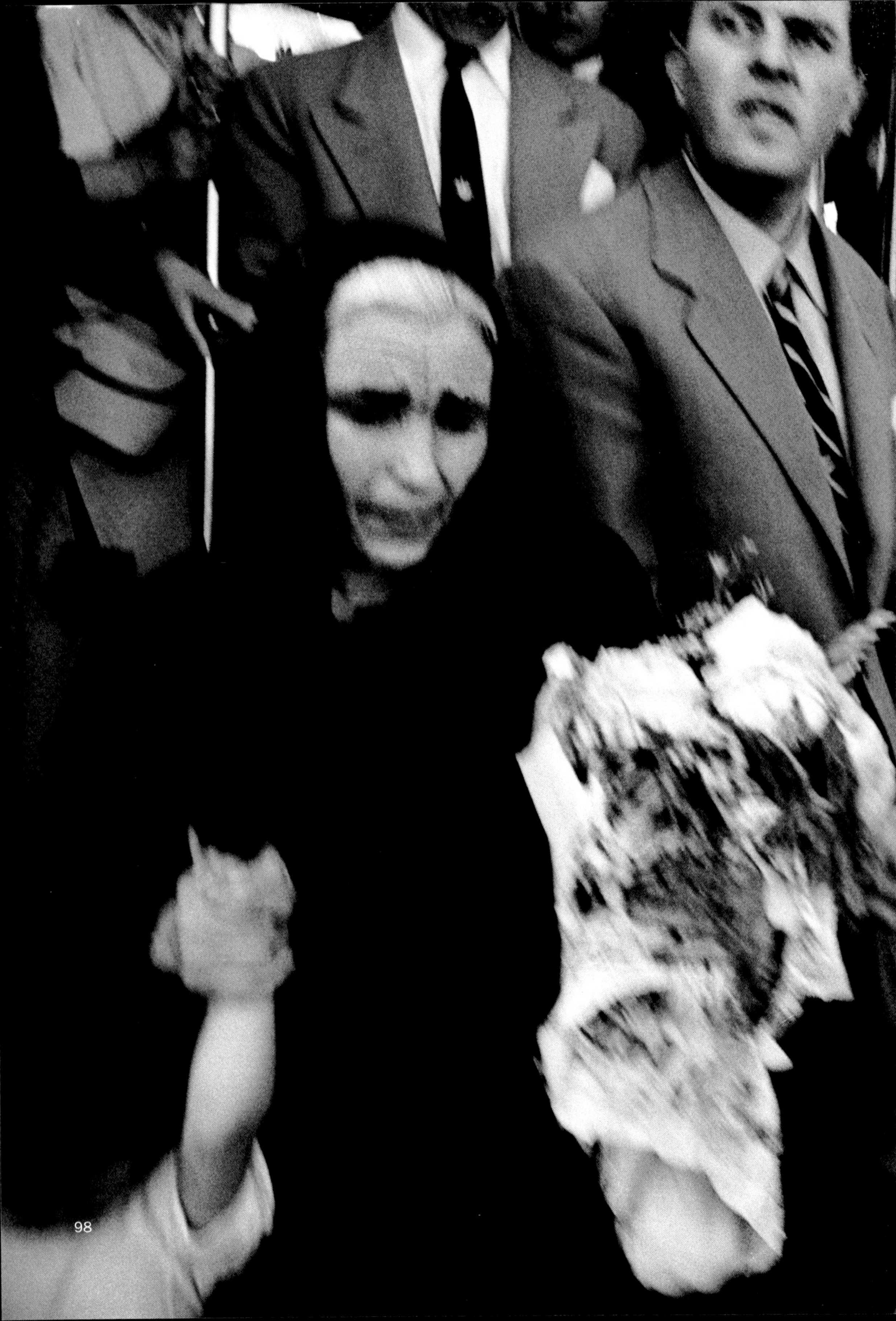

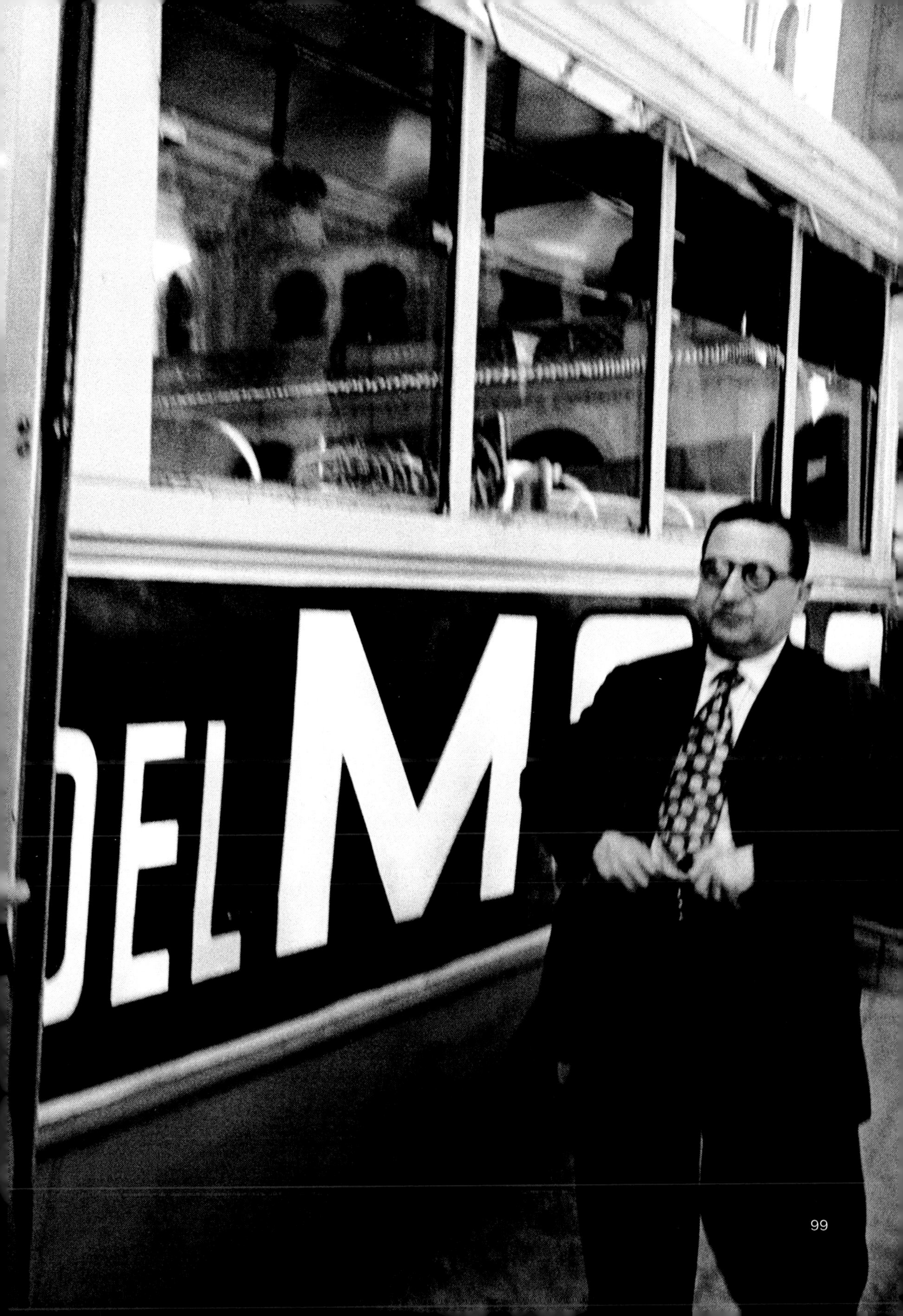

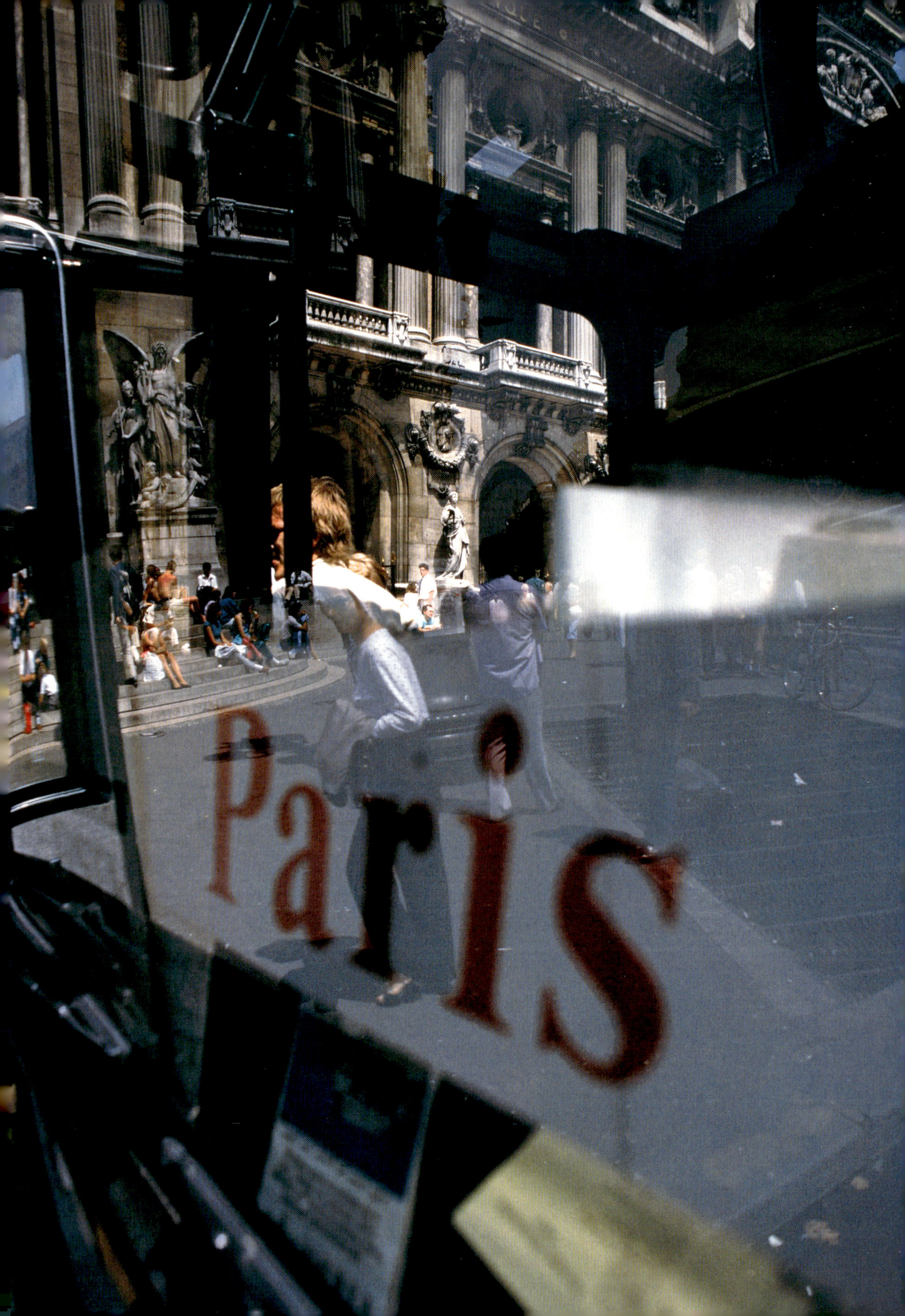
Paris

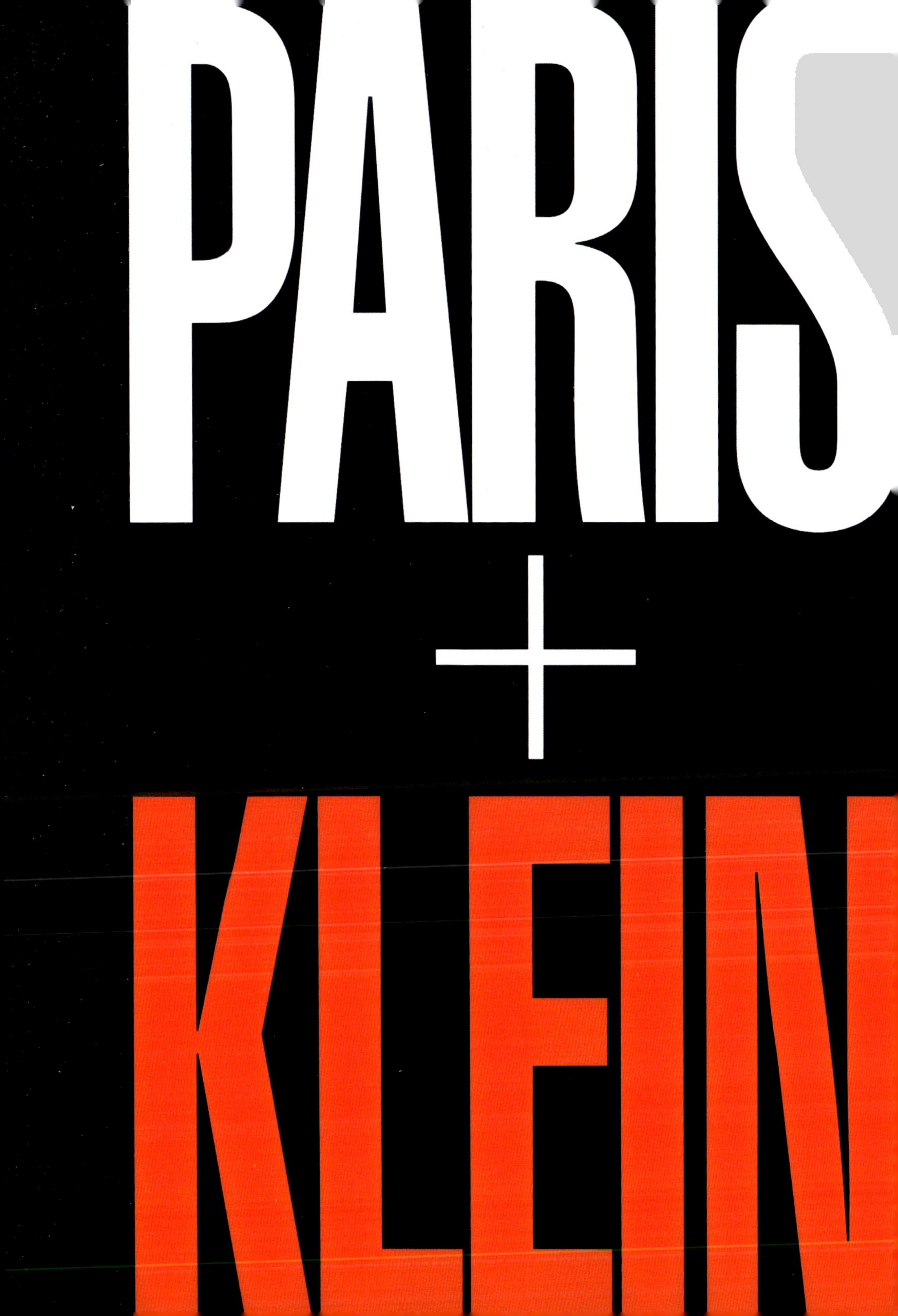

PARIS
+
KLEIN

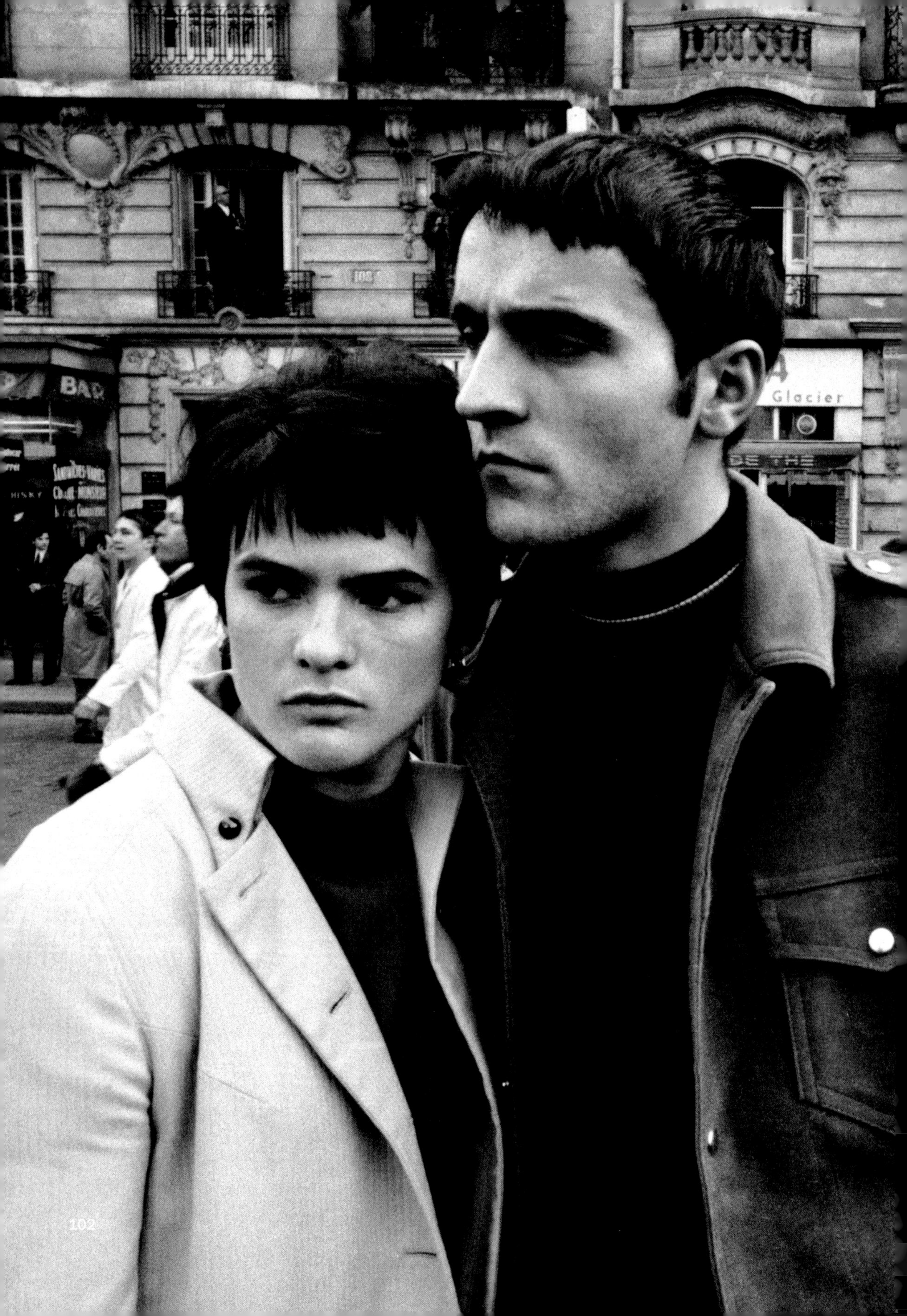

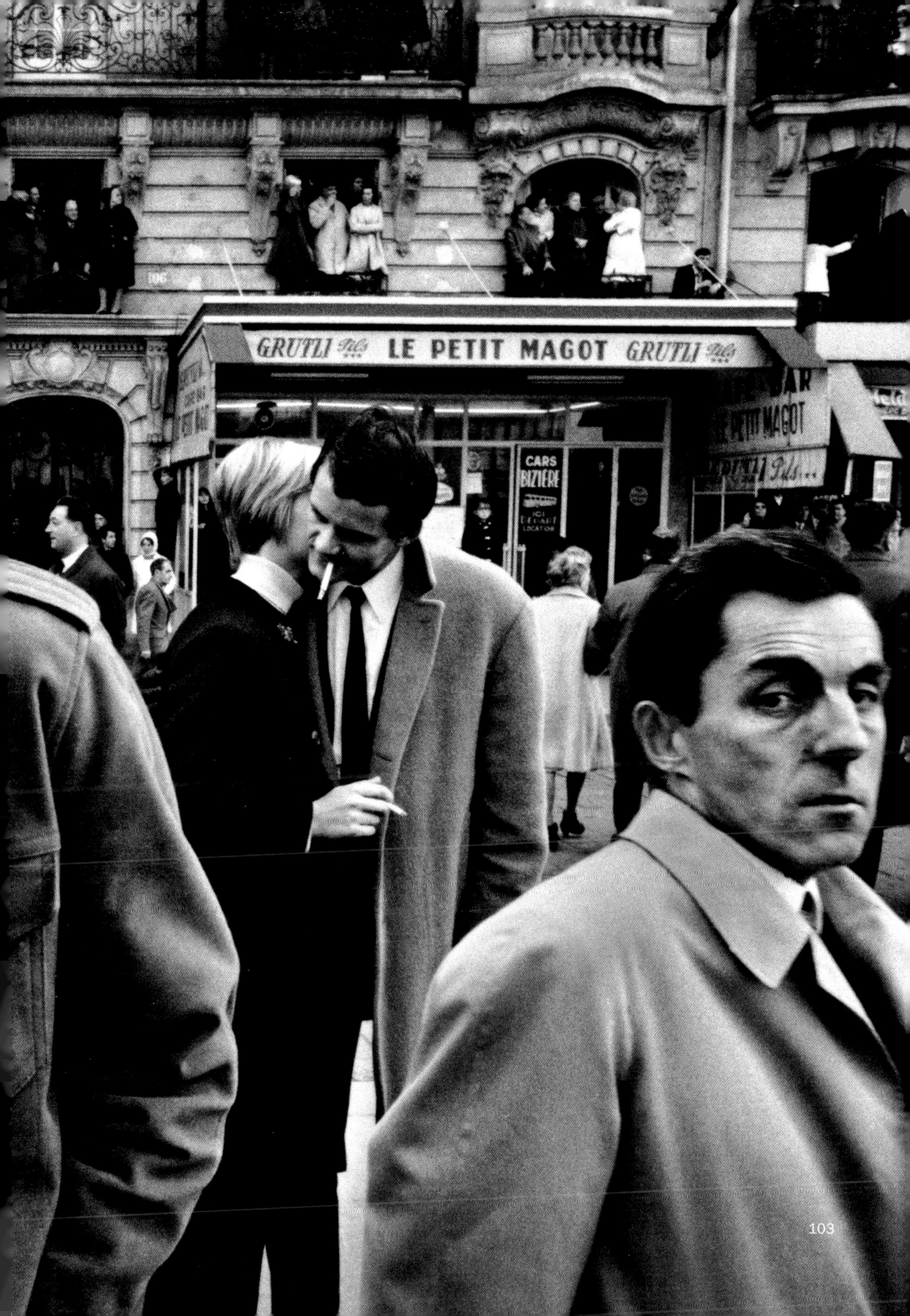

GRUTLI   LE PETIT MAGOT   GRUTLI
CARS
BIZIERE
ICI
DEPART
LOCATION

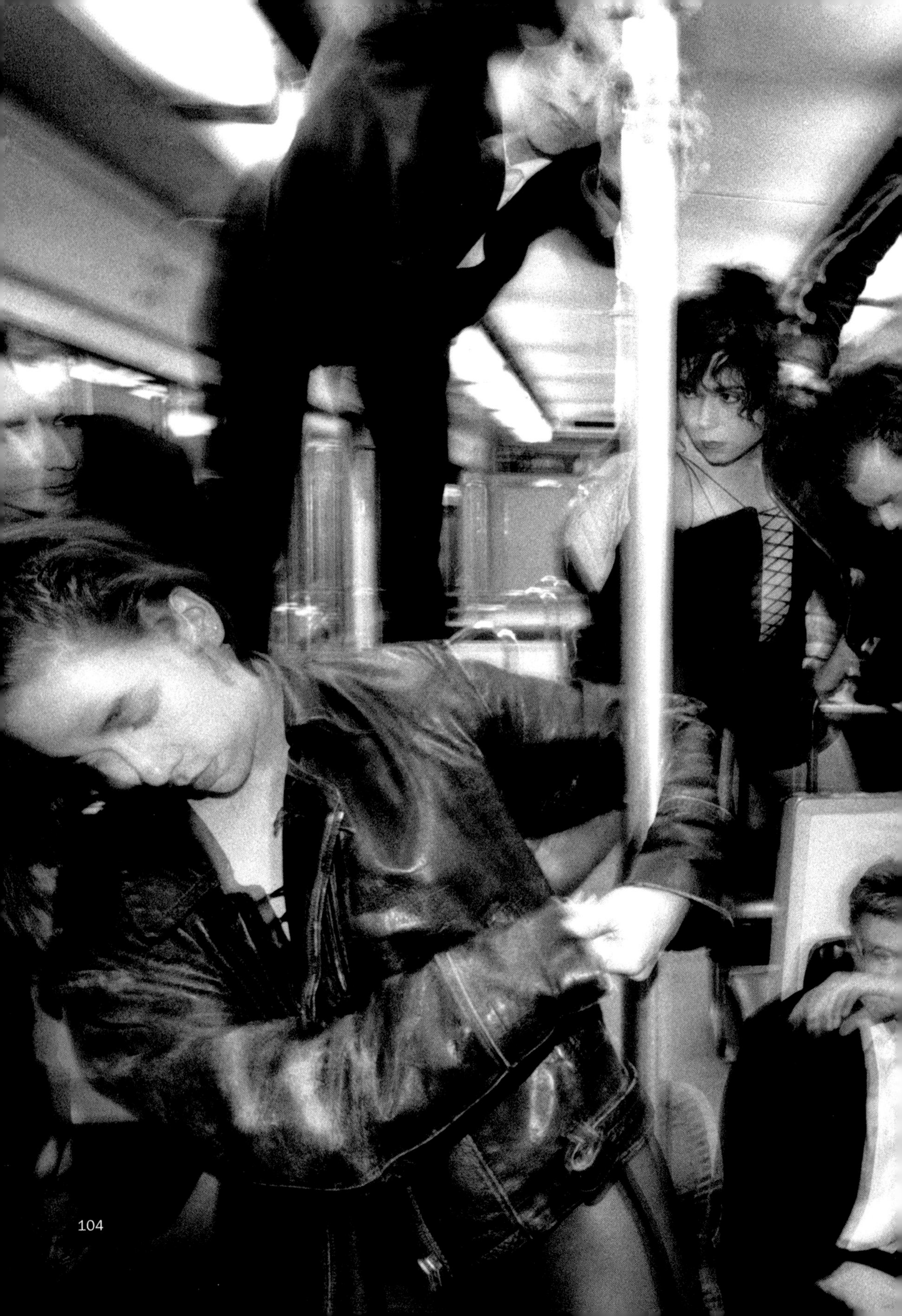

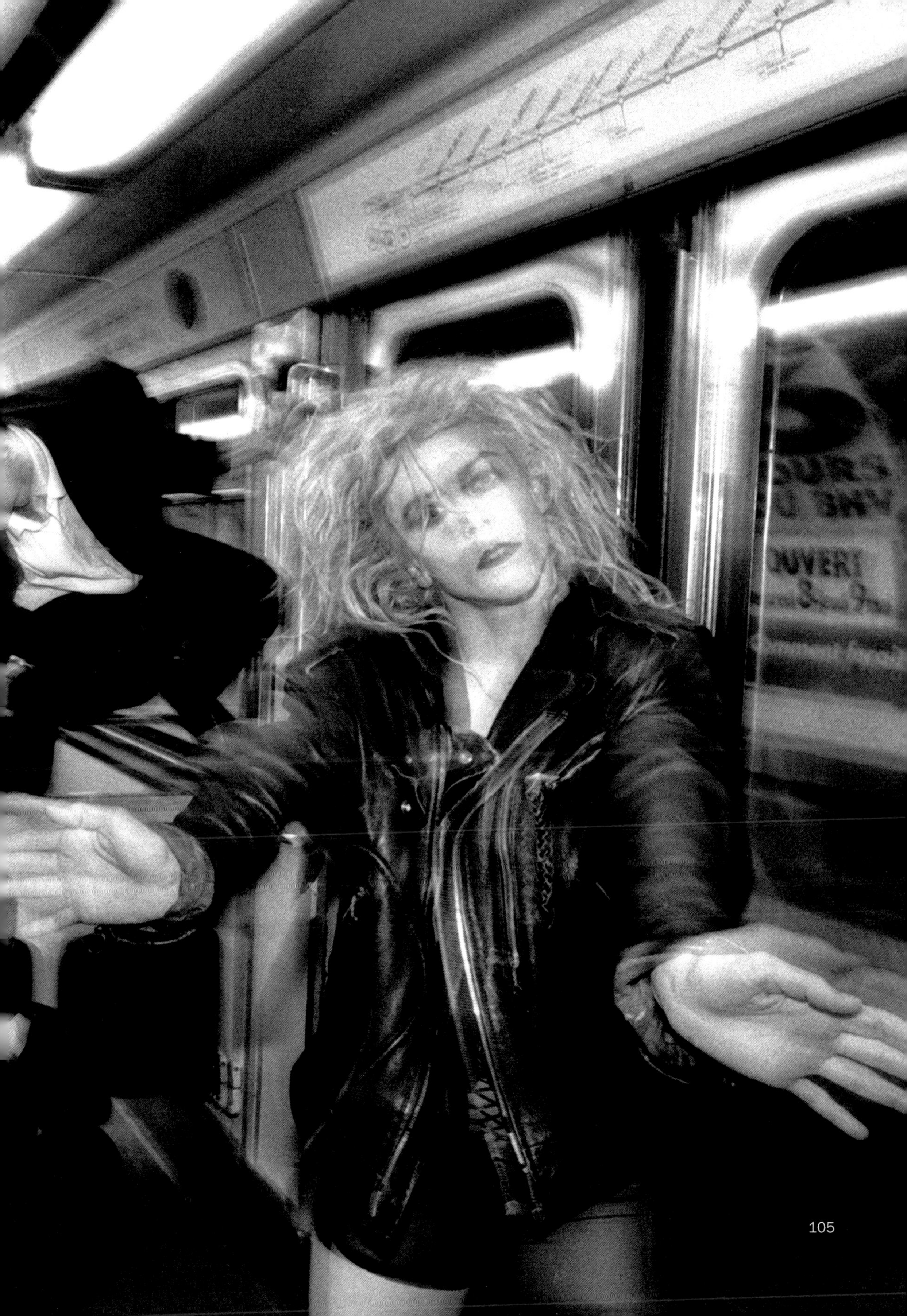

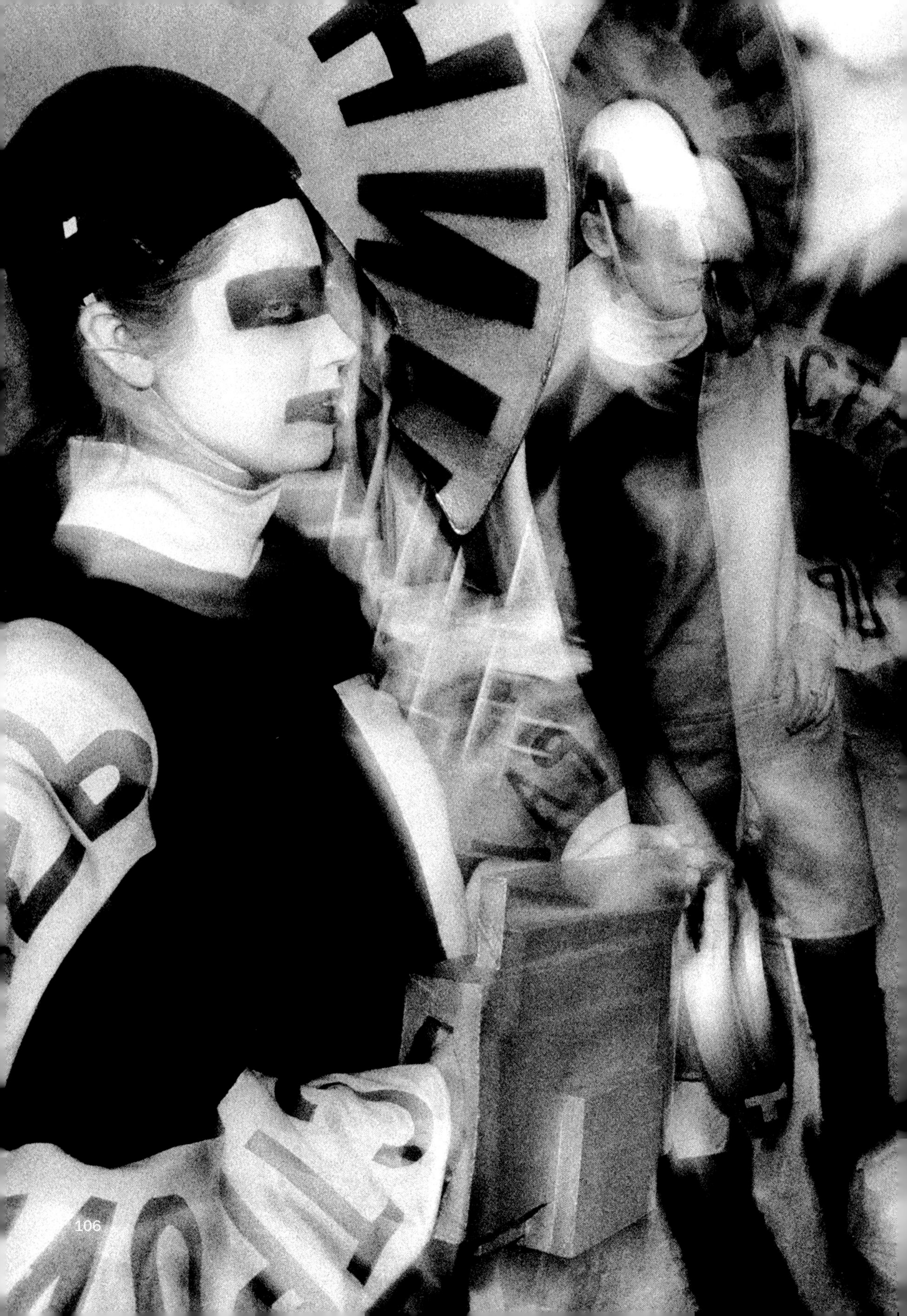

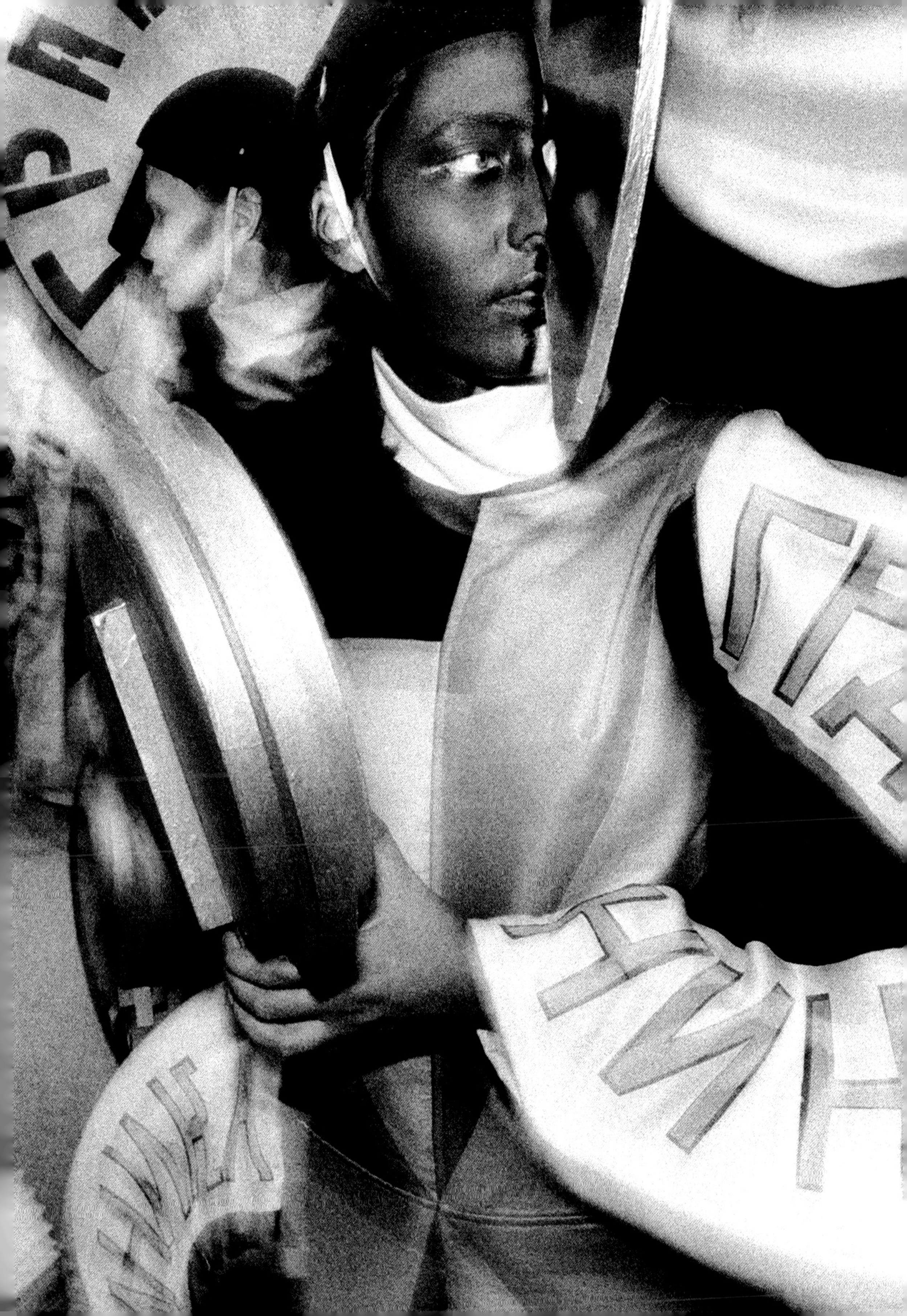

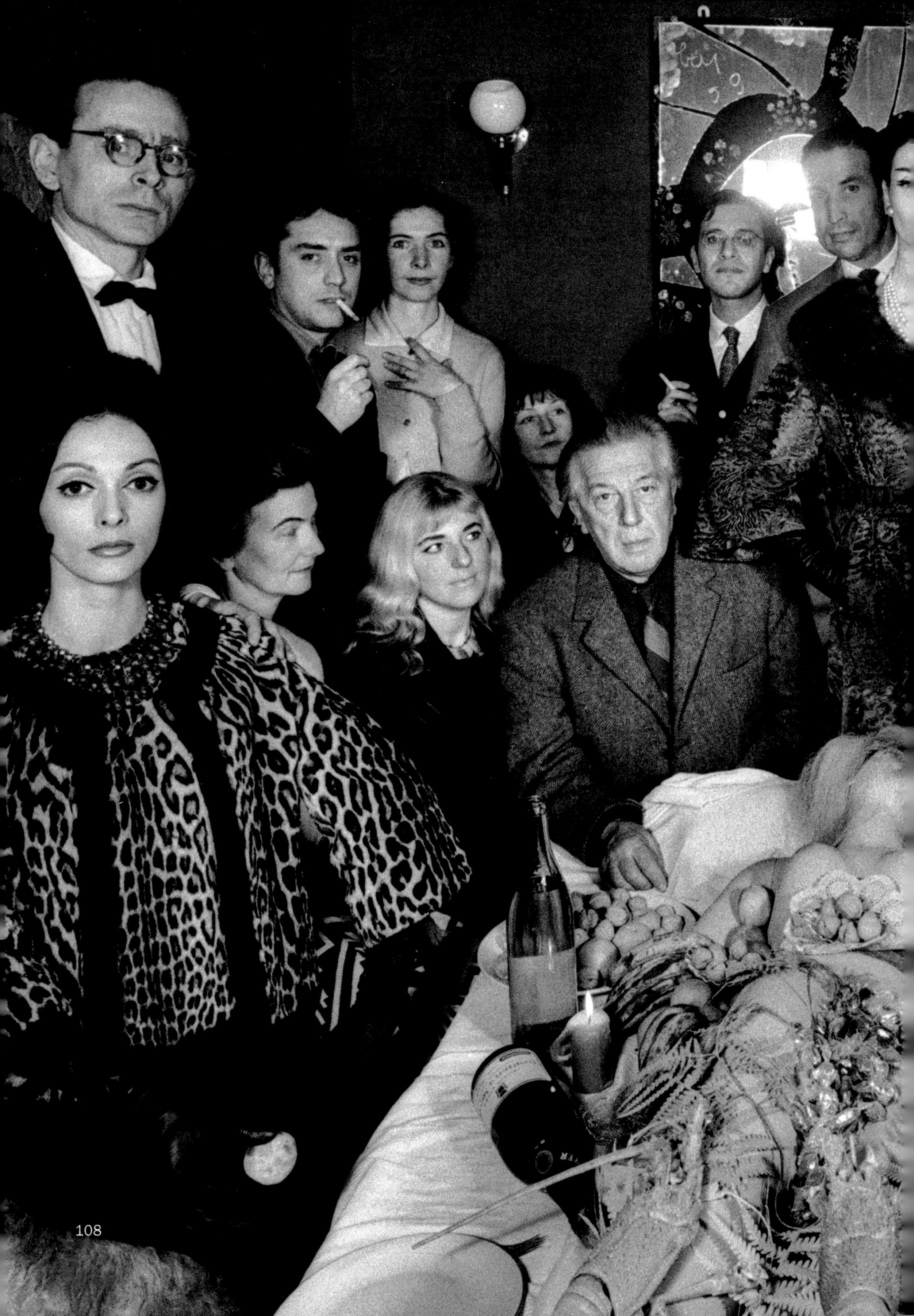

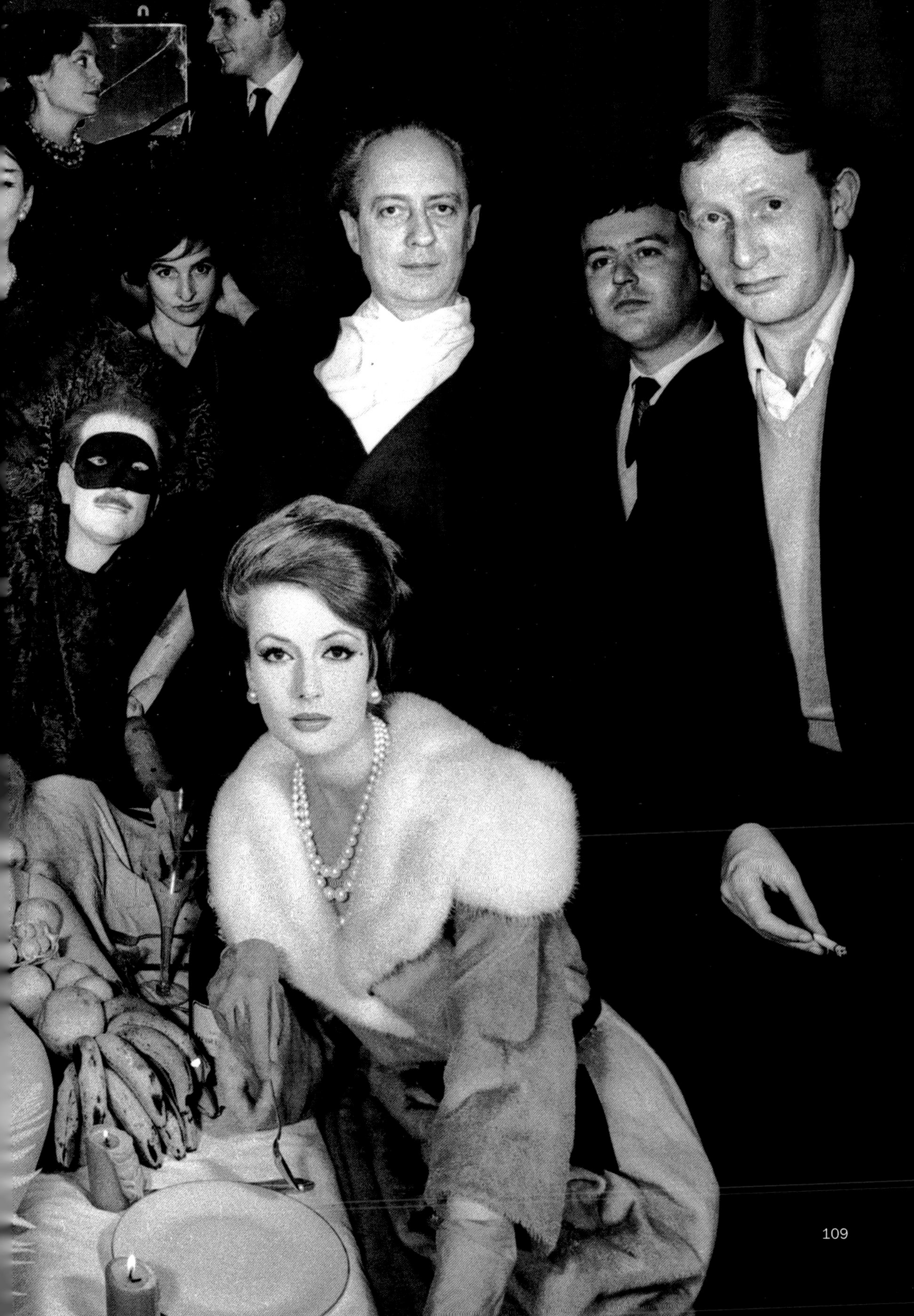

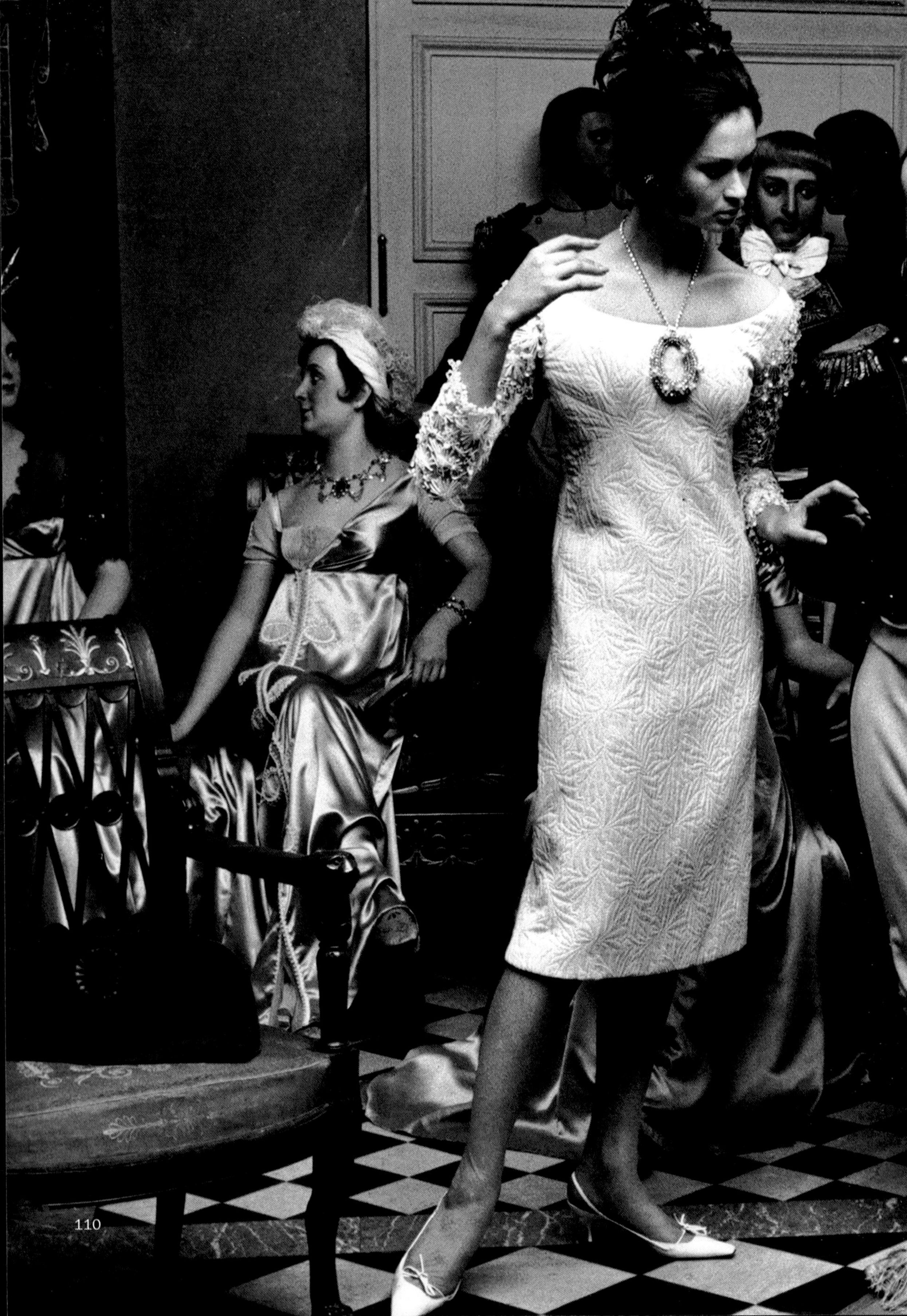

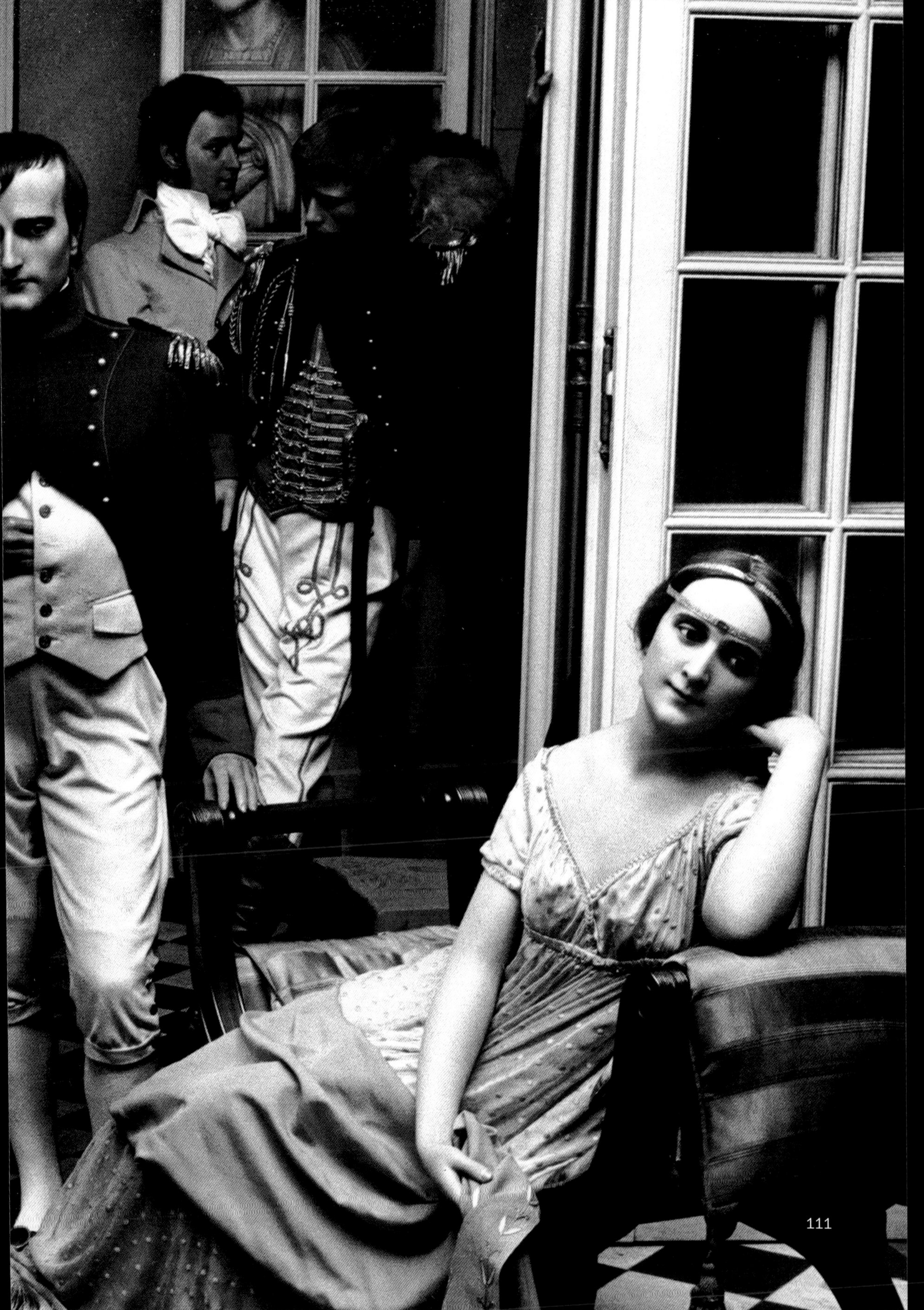

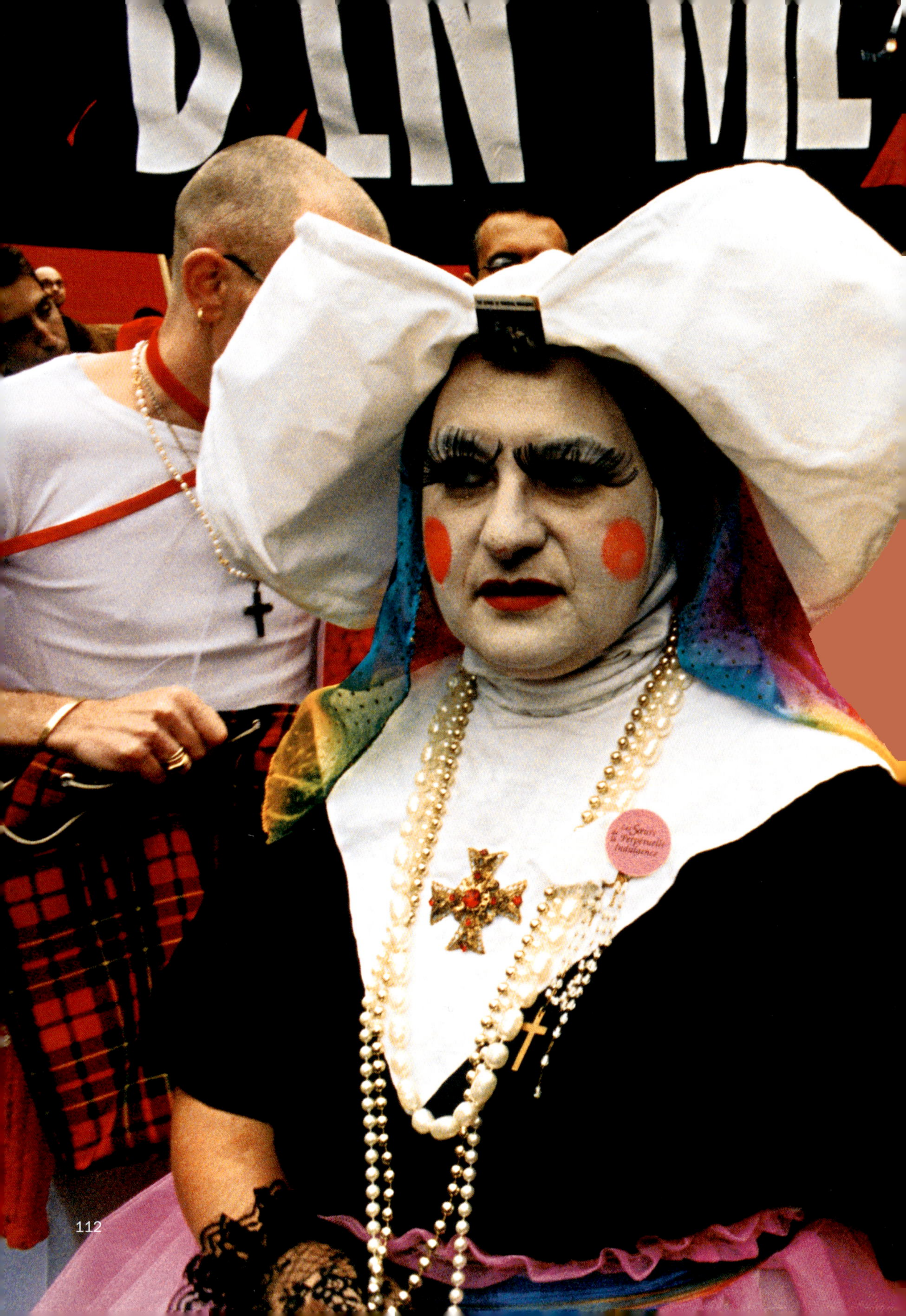
DAMN ME

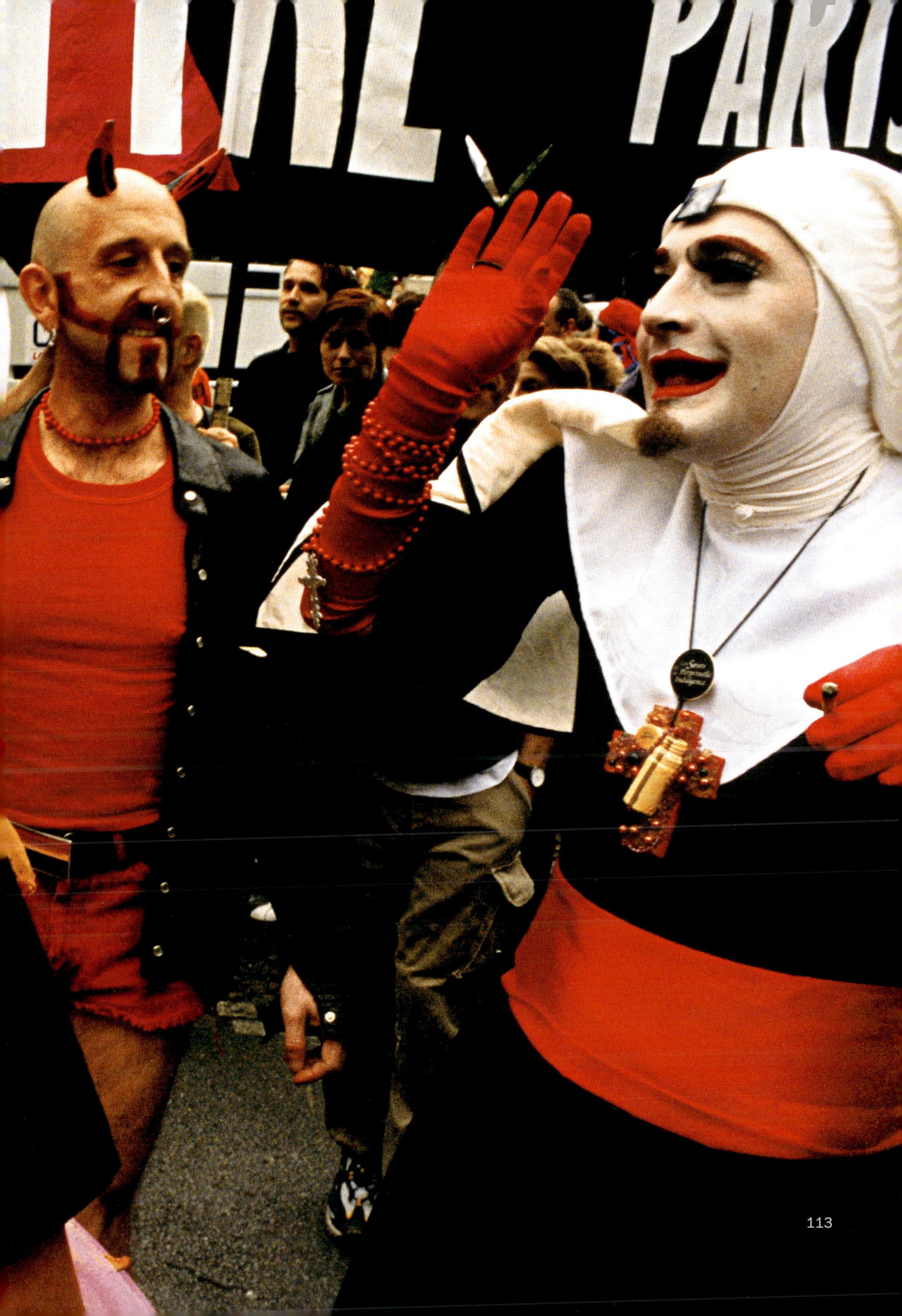
PARIS

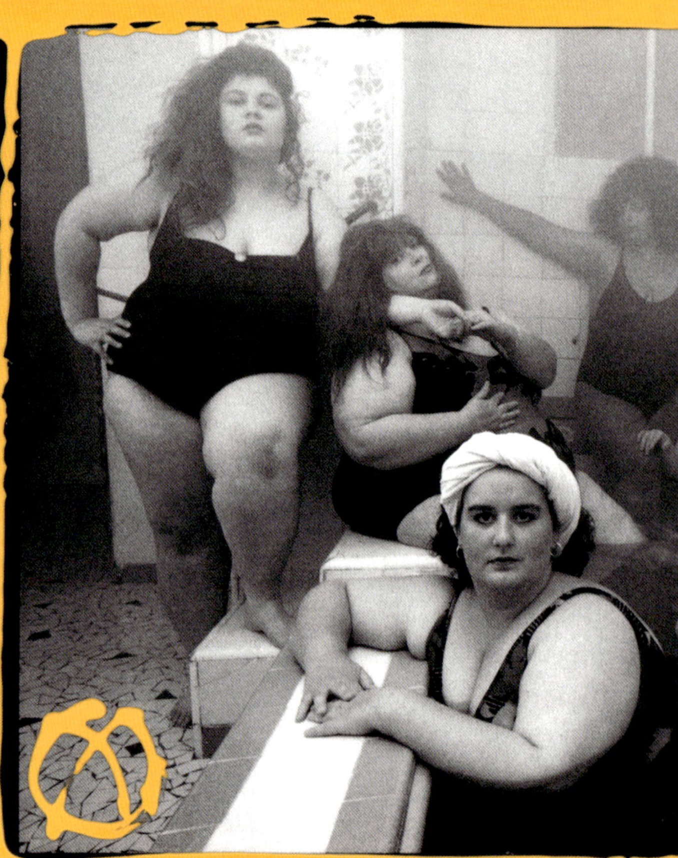

5053 TM
32
32

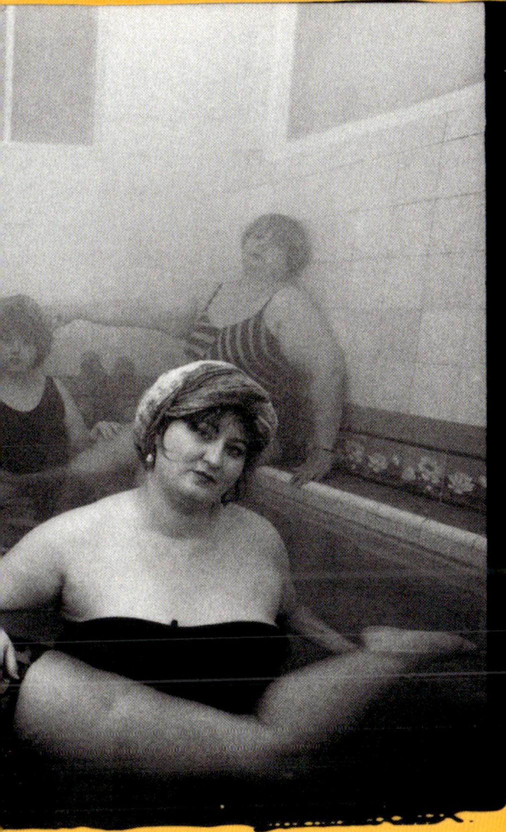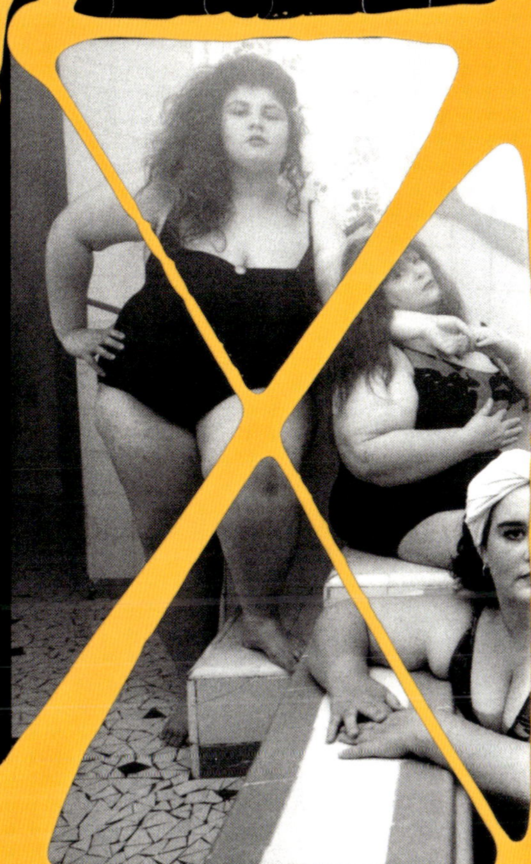

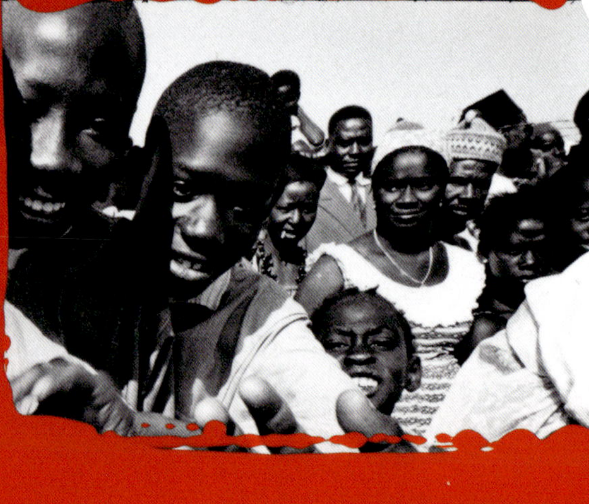
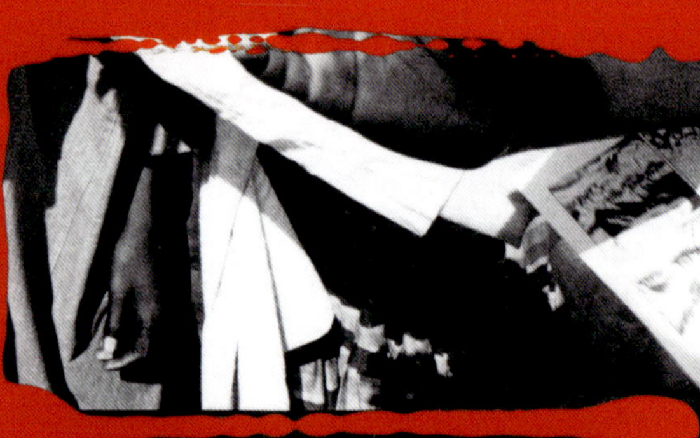
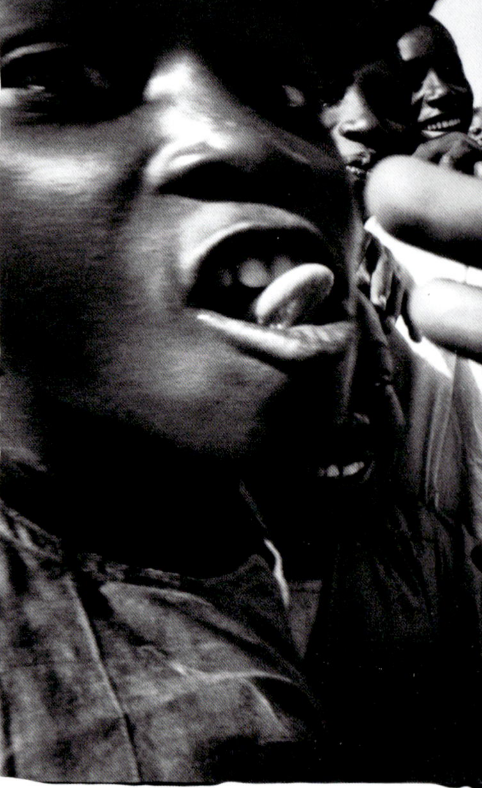
KODAK
34
34A

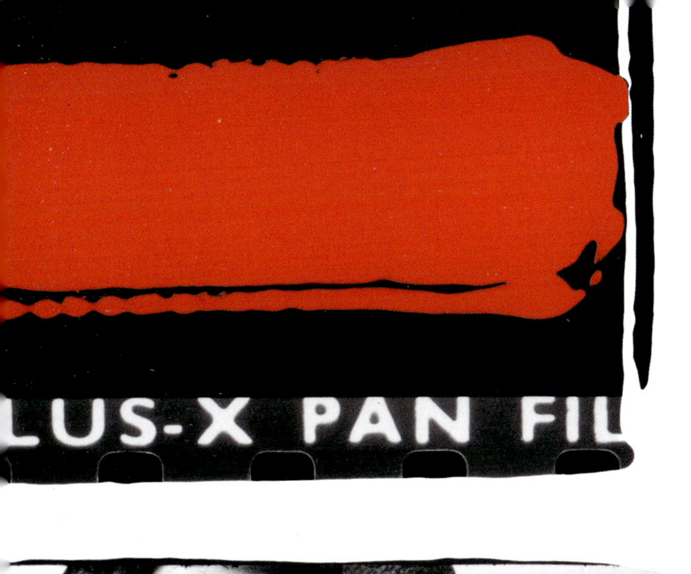
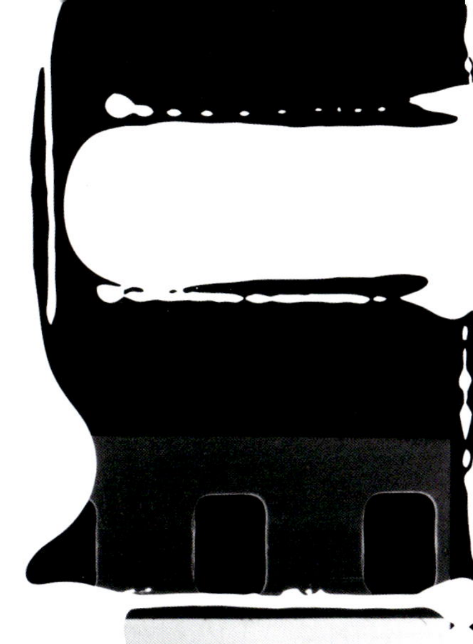

LUS-X PAN FIL

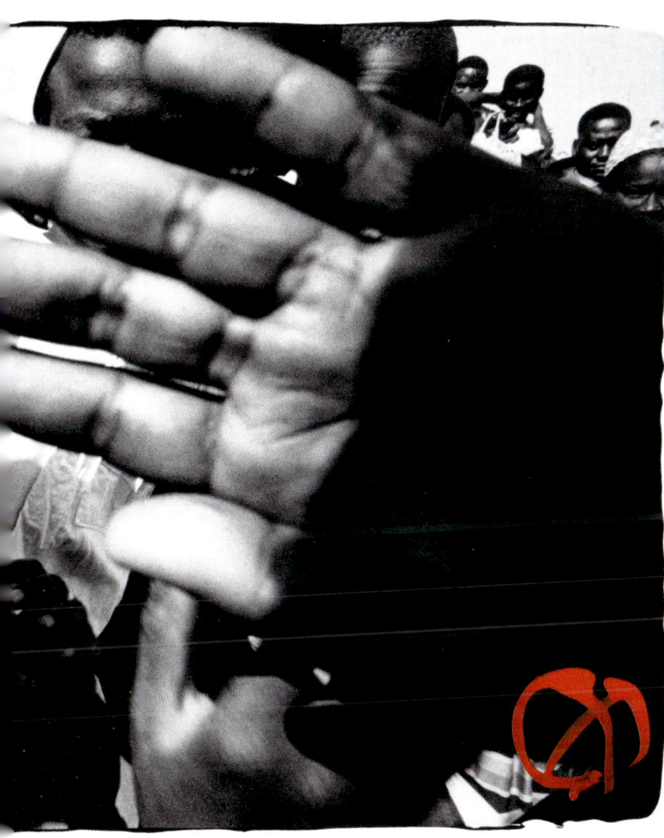
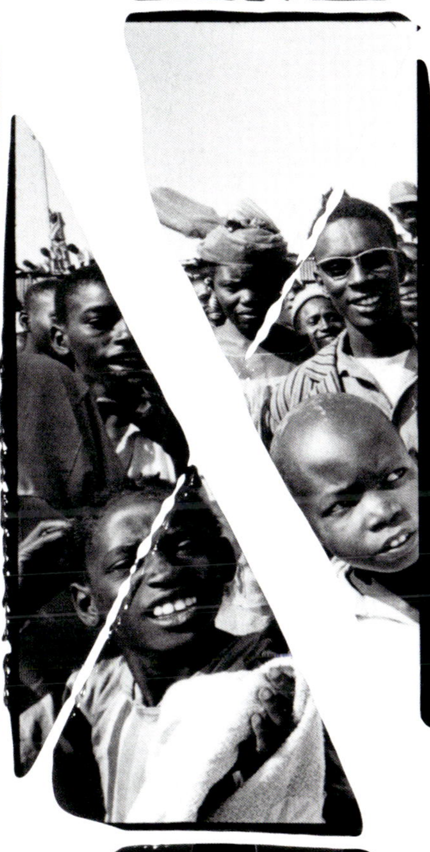
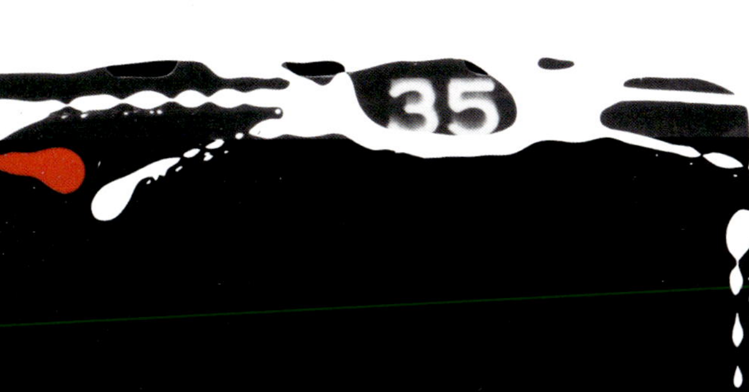

35

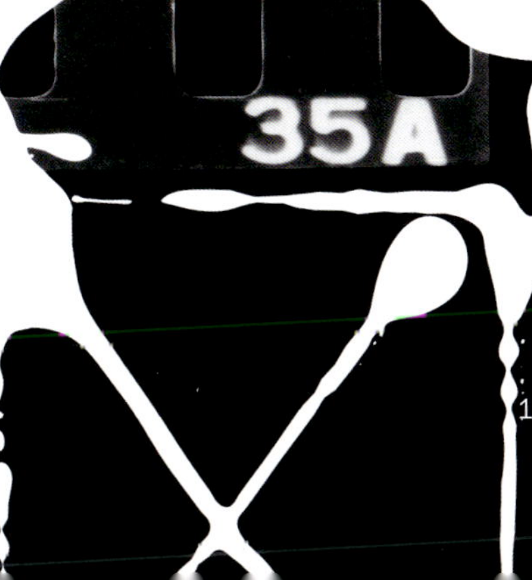

35A

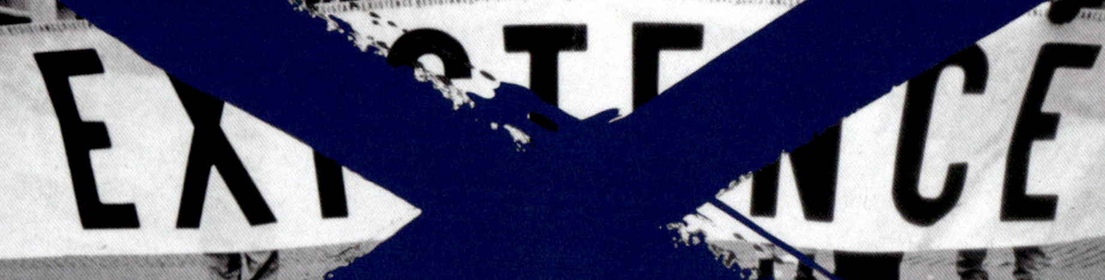

053 TMY
36
35A
36
EXISTENCE
CONTRE GÉNOCIDE SOCIAL

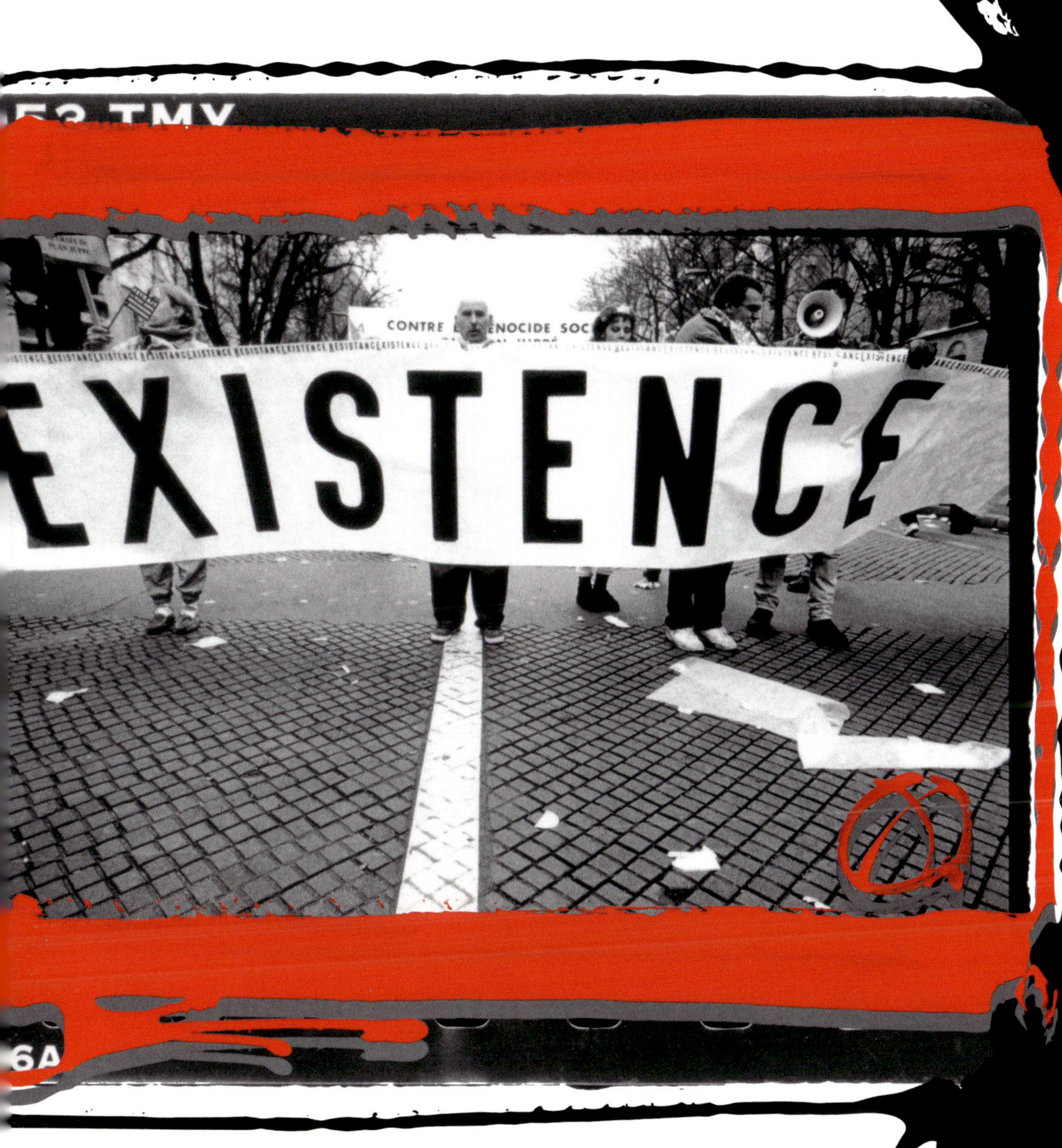

EXISTENCE
CONTRE LE GENOCIDE SOC

Madrid, 2019